Your Spirits Walk
Beside Us

D1332741

Your Spirits Walk Beside Us

The Politics of Black Religion

BARBARA DIANNE SAVAGE

The Belknap Press of
Harvard University Press
Cambridge, Massachusetts
London, England
2008

LONDON BOROUGH OF WANDSWORTH	
9030 00003 0287 1	
Askews & Holts	10-Jan-2013
277.3082	£13.95
	WWX0010327/0030

Copyright © 2008 by Barbara Dianne Savage
All rights reserved
Printed in the United States of America

Library of Congress Cataloging-in-Publication Data

Savage, Barbara Dianne.
Your spirits walk beside us : the politics of Black religion / Barbara Dianne Savage.
p.   cm.
Includes bibliographical references and index.
ISBN 978-0-674-03177-7 (alk. paper)
1. African American churches—Political activity.   2. African American clergy—
Political activity.   3. African Americans—Politics and government—20th century.
4. Civil rights movements—United States—History—20th century.
5. Christianity and politics—United States—History—20th century.   I. Title.

BR563.N4S37 2008
277.3′08208996073—dc22   2008027228

Contents

Your Spirits Walk
Beside Us

Introduction

MY EARLIEST ideas about African American religion and political struggle come from my first public memories as a child of the South of the late 1950s and 1960s. The civil rights movement entered our home through the televised images of black churches opening their doors for political rallies and the funerals of martyrs. Those pictures were accompanied either by the spirited call-and-response of black religious music or by the mournfulness of its dirges. I saw Southern black people speaking and singing a language of prophecy and praise that I had come to know in the sacred space of a country church in Virginia. There was something both familiar and unsettling in this. The people I saw were without a doubt "church people," but they were doing and saying things in public that I had never known black people, especially black church people, ever to dare to do.

I was born too late to be part of the movement, but my immersion from afar in its unfolding drama and denouement left in me gratitude and a drive to achieve when its legacy of affirmative action opened the doors of educational opportunity for my generation of black working-class children. The history I was later taught about that movement, and was later to teach, reinforced the religious sounds and images of my childhood memory, preserved in forms aural and visual. For those then and now, here and around the world, who had never set foot in a Southern black church, these images became theirs too. And so for many of them and for me, African American religion and political struggle seemed poignantly and inextricably intertwined.

The power in those images rested in part on the way they conveyed the surprising political potency of African American religion in the South. I say "surprising" because throughout the twentieth century there were spirited debates among varied groups of African Americans about whether religious doctrines, religious people, and religious organizations were a blessing or a curse in the struggle for black freedom and racial progress. Although churches were continually called upon to be savior institutions, historically they were most often criticized for failing in that mission.

In the first half of the twentieth century, the dominant political narratives treated African American religion with despair and disdain. The emergence in the late 1950s of a Southern civil rights movement with churches, church people, and church culture at its center was a powerful and startling departure from that story, rather than a natural progression. In many ways, the movement is best thought of not as an inevitable triumph or a moment of religious revival, but simply as a miracle. It was brief, bold, and breathtaking, difficult to replicate or sustain, and experienced firsthand by only a small remnant of true believers.

Many since have misread the successes of that period and applied them retrospectively over the entire span of African American political history, seeing the past through the haze of a post–civil rights consciousness. It was the movement itself that changed our notions and expectations about the relationship between African American religion and politics. Our failure to understand this has obscured the important history of the decades of complaints and controversies on the question of how or whether African American churches could be a progressive political force. Debates on the issue preceded and raged within the movement, and figured in its demise as well. This book retrieves the history of these important debates for the decades preceding, during, and after the civil rights movement, marshaling evidence from a wide variety of public lives and venues.

Why is the history of these debates important? Because they are evidence of an intraracial struggle for control of the spiritual resources of black people across the country and for control of the churches and religious networks they had built. These debates capture the overlapping challenges of creating a basis for black collective political activism, building independent black institutions, and determining the place of women and men in racial leadership. The fact that religious belief, religious institutions, and religious people came to be seen as so essential to this process remains the central paradox in African American political history.

THOSE TENSIONS were present even before the founding of black religious institutions. Black public protest against slavery and against racial injustices was cast, as was much of eighteenth-century discourse, in explicitly religious terms. As early as 1774, Africans in Massachusetts petitioned for release from their condition as "slaves for Life in a Christian land." In both the North and the South, Christian hypocrisy became a repeated refrain in the fight to abolish slavery—a line of argument made more urgent by the spread of evangelical Christianity during the late eighteenth century, which undercut social hierarchy and racial difference among its followers.

Yet by the turn of the nineteenth century, the power of Southern white Christians had forced a retreat. White Methodists and Baptists dampened their opposition to slavery, acting out racial discrimination within their own denominations and sanctuaries. Free blacks in the North established their own churches, beginning with two groups in Philadelphia in the 1790s. One left a white church to found an independent black Methodist tradition, the Bethel African Methodist Episcopal Church, while the other, the African Episcopal Church of St. Thomas, chose to remain within the larger Episcopal denomination. Those two decisions are an early indicator of the historical diversity among black churches, their ambivalent relationship to white American Christianity, and their political natures. Both Philadelphia churches supported the work of the Free African Society in Philadelphia, an organization dedicated to racial solidarity and the abolition of slavery.[1]

In the South, enslaved people held a variety of religious beliefs, often sharing segregated worship experiences under the surveillance of white Baptists and Methodists. Simultaneously, many of them forged a separate and largely invisible set of beliefs and practices, some Christian, some Islam-inflected, and some derived from African belief systems. Held in common, however, was the belief that slavery was a moral wrong and that retribution would ensue, an interpretation borne out with the coming of the Civil War and emancipation. Abolitionist claims, whether advanced by blacks or their white allies, were grounded in religious arguments.

During Reconstruction, black communities established their own churches, primarily Baptist, throughout the South. Many of those who emerged as black political leaders were ministers, empowered by their literacy and by their prominent role in building the black churches which served as the first forums for collective political organizing. Despite their best efforts, racial violence and the denial of black equality worsened after the federal occupation of the South was lifted and the brief period of black participation in electoral politics ended. It was no wonder then that as the nineteenth century drew to a close, questions had already emerged about the relationship between black religion and the prospects for black political advancement.[2]

When debates about that relationship emerged at the turn of the twentieth century, which is where this book begins, most African Americans were but a few generations removed from slavery. Oral histories and memoirs show that many of them had family memories and stories reaching back to their enslaved ancestors. Many rural black Southerners had forged a chain of memory to that history which they consecrated through song and ritual, continued to rely upon for daily inspiration, and passed on to their children. Ideas about the powerful and sometimes romanticized connection between religion, history, and memory remained in place decades later as illustrated in this poem published in 1944 by the then young black poet Robert Hayden:

> We have not forgotten the prayers you prayed,
> Black fathers, O black mothers, kneeling in
> The cabin-gloom, debased, yet in your hearts
> Bearing high springtime pageantries of faith.
> We have not forgotten your morning hope,
> More burning than the sun of cottonfields
> Upon dark, shackled limbs, nor songs your anguish
> Suckled.

Hayden linked the power of that faithfulness and hope during slavery to the continuing struggle to realize the possibilities of American democracy:

> And if we keep
> Our love for this American earth, black fathers,
> O black mothers, believing that its fields
> Will bear for us at length a harvesting

Of sun, it is because your spirits walk
Beside us as we plough, it is because
This land has grown from your great,
Deathless hearts.

Freedom had brought an end to slavery, but by the early twentieth century it had yet to yield an emancipation from gross inequalities, cruelties, and exploitation. The need for liberation continued as did the search for the material and spiritual tools with which to achieve it. Hayden's expression of indebtedness to the religious faith and struggle of enslaved people captures that key aspect of the debate among African Americans about religion and their struggle for greater freedom.[3]

In this period, public discussions about black religion were marked by a profound unease with the legacy of spiritual practices of enslaved people, a cultural heritage that many viewed as antiquated, primitive, tainted by the sins of slavery, and marked by pagan retentions from Africa. Some thought of black Christianity as a "slave religion" that had run its course and lost its political and spiritual potency to meet the new demands of a more modern struggle against racial oppression. Although most African Americans remained in the South, the many thousands who were steadily migrating to cities in the North and elsewhere brought with them a religious heritage that was quite distinct from that found in many established urban black communities, especially in Northern cities. Migration and rapid urbanization did little to relieve the persistent poverty that was made worse by economic depression, discrimination, segregation, and legal incapacity. The end of World War I brought a shattering of hope, a resurgence of racial violence, and virulent Jim Crow practices and not just in the South.[4]

All of this reminds us that public expressions of anxiety about the role of black religious institutions in alleviating these conditions were never mere academic or rhetorical exercises because far too much was at stake. These debates were part of a search for ways to reshape rural and urban communities into effective political collectives. Churches were seen as central to both projects because they were the only indigenous, black-controlled organizations with the potential for mass mobilization. Some people viewed this as a good thing and some as a bad thing, but most accepted that it was a reality.

The opening decades of the twentieth century also were marked by an intellectual clash between education and belief, modernity and religion, science and faith, the intellectual and the spiritual. Some of the conflict that emerged among African Americans about religious institutions reflected unanticipated tensions between the quest for religious freedom and the pursuit of education, two missions otherwise presumed to be closely allied in strategies for black uplift. Throughout the twentieth century, educated black elites were often at odds with the masses of black people they sought to speak for or to represent, including on important topics such as religion and politics. These controversies sometimes turned on differences between the religious beliefs and practices of the educated and those of the uneducated, manifested in attempts to control the religious freedom and religious choices of less privileged black people.

This, of course, was impossible. The first half of the century witnessed an ever-increasing African American religious diversification right alongside an exponential growth in the numbers of Baptist and Methodist churches, which served most black religious people. The practice of clearly identifiable African-derived religions persisted in the urban North and the rural South. Marcus Garvey's attack on white Christian hypocrisy, itself a persistent strand in black political thought, was coupled with his embrace of a black God and a black Jesus. At the same time, storefront churches established by Pentecostal and Holiness believers continued to reshape the religious landscape of black communities as did the emergence in the 1930s of smaller sects led by Father Divine, Daddy Grace, and, perhaps most significantly, Elijah Mohammed.[5]

These shifting demographic, social, and theological conditions made even more urgent the task of creating political unity among a racialized but religiously diverse minority. For all these reasons, the relationship between African American religion and political activism grew even more vexed and contentious—at once complementary and contradictory, full of promise but also damned by exalted expectations.

Three reinforcing paradoxes strain the nexus between black religion and black politics. First, the choices that individuals make about their religious lives—where and why they worship, whether and why they believe—are among our most privately informed and freely made decisions. The rich diversity of African American religious beliefs is itself evidence of this, as are the lives of the many who choose not to affiliate with or practice in any faith tradition. It is true, however, that in the twentieth century most religious African Americans remained Christians and that strands of black Christian thought were fueled by a liberationist legacy. Yet this did not make it easy or natural for "black religion" to provide the ideological cohesion needed for effective collective political mobilization. Ultimately, religious freedom also means the freedom to define not only one's religious beliefs, but also the balance between the personal and the political, between individual salvation and communal purpose. Black religious belief and black religious life, by their very nature, are resistant to external reach and control, including from those who seek to harness their powers for a collective political purpose on behalf of the race as a whole.

Second, black churches, like their other American Protestant counterparts, are among the most local, the most decentralized, and the most idiosyncratic of all social organizations. Despite common usage, there is no such thing as the "black church." It is an illusion and a metaphor that has taken on a life of its own, implying the existence of a powerful entity with organized power, but the promise of that also leaves it vulnerable to unrealistic expectations. The term is a political, intellectual, and theological construction that symbolizes unity and homogeneity while masking the enormous diversity and independence among African American religious institutions and believers. The concept imposes the notion of a unified command, a national entity, a papal-like authority that does not and has never existed. Yet the "black church" lives on precisely because it is political and cultural shorthand and an all-purpose stand-in for the dearth of other black institutions, especially in the twentieth century when large institutional responses to racial inequality were required. In reality, black churches elude schemes for national unification or uniformity in programmatic or political approaches, making them ill-suited for coordinated efforts, often even within particular local settings.[6]

In all this, both now and in the past, the underlying unresolved African American dilemma is that discrimination, segregation, and racial inequality culminate materially in a denial of access to jobs, education, and opportunity. An insufficiency of secular financial resources thwarted the evolution of a black business and philanthropic class and of independent political institutions. As a consequence, black churches, by default, were expected to assume the responsibility of addressing many urgent unmet community needs—something they were ill-equipped and financially unable to do. This is emblematic of the much larger problem of the dearth of indigenous black institutions, a quandary made even more complex in the age of desegregation.

Third and finally, to call black churches into public duty as a primary vehicle for empowering the race is to rely on an institution that was and remains largely male-led but female-dominated, not only in memberships but in fundraising and organizing activities. While the predominance of women is a feature of most religious systems, there are specific political consequences in this case precisely because of the centrality of religious institutions to black community and political life. Moreover, this reality aggravates persisting sensitivities about the strength and substantiality of black women and about black male authority and masculinity. Because the typical black church member was a working-class black woman, debates about the role that black religious institutions should or should not play in black politics were also implicitly, but rarely explicitly, arguments about the place of black women in American political life and about the unstated "problem" of their largely absent male counterparts.

The recurring social, political, and theological tensions which drove the debates recovered in this book remain as real and as pertinent today as they were a century ago. At a time when African American religion and politics are still viewed as inextricably linked, this book seeks to highlight rather than submerge the inherent and often incurable tensions that mark the connections between black religion and black political activism. It remains a delicate and daunting task to examine both the possibilities and the restraints that religion brought to the long struggle to end racial inequalities. If we ignore that duality, we will only perpetuate deep misunderstandings about the place of religion in African American political struggle—not just in the civil rights movement, but in the history of American social movements more broadly. And for those who remain committed to the idea that black churches remain central to the political prospects of black communities, bluntly acknowledging these difficulties may be the first step to overcoming them.

BEFORE THE author of the first history of African American people could proceed with his voluminous work, he had to devote an entire first chapter to disputing the notion that black people were the cursed biblical descendents of Ham. Published in 1883 by George Washington Williams, a Baptist minister, politician, and self-trained historian, that book, *History of the Negro Race in America*, symbolizes the way in which ideas about race, religion, politics, and history are entangled. More than that, it demonstrates that black scholars especially have been required to engage their work with contemporary debates and demands. In this case, Williams was forced to counter prevailing popular and scholarly notions that black people were not members of the human family before he could begin the task of tracing their history from ancient times to the end of the nineteenth century.[7]

By the early twentieth century, a very small but stellar first generation of formally trained African American scholars took up the work that Williams had begun by publishing what would become the foundational and canonical works in African American studies. The writings of three prominent academically trained African American public intellectuals of the twentieth century, W. E. B. Du Bois, Carter G. Woodson, and Benjamin Mays, form the underlying texts for an analysis of early ideas about black churches, black religious beliefs, and political progress. Throughout most of the twentieth century, as we will see, quite different African American scholars settled on a consensus intellectual critique of the "Negro church" as a failed institution that had plunged into political irrelevancy at the end of the Reconstruction period. By beginning at the beginning of black religious studies, we will see clearly that in the intellectual constructs they built, black religion and black churches figured first and foremost as innately a "problem" for the race.

Those early writings reiterate several persistent concerns, including unease about the political implications of charges that African American religion was primitive and marked by African retentions; claims that African Americans were "overchurched," the result of unbridled and potentially uncontrollable religious growth and diversity; and the need to build an educated male clerical class that could lead and control black religious and political life. Embedded but unacknowledged in these varied critiques, yet absolutely essential to them, were gendered and classbound notions of racial leadership and of the place of black men and women of all classes in the struggle for racial equality.

In the 1930s and 1940s, a new array of scholarly ideas about black religion rose to dominance when social scientists exerted their professional training to "prove" and bemoan the negative psychological influence of black religion both on youth and on the prospects for political activism. One finds this line of analysis in the works of the premier black sociologists Charles S. Johnson and E. Franklin Frazier, and in the way religion is discussed in two of the most enduring studies of African American life: St. Clair Drake and Horace Cayton's *Black Metropolis* and Gunnar Myrdal's *American Dilemma*, which draw on the same research data. These works examined religion and religious people with fresh methodological techniques including extensive interviews, attitudinal surveys, and questionnaires. Despite the fact that they documented the continued growth of religious institutions and the centrality of religion to black community life, these scholars persisted in concluding that religion's influence was waning and on a march toward extinction. On closer examination, however, these books actually demonstrate the enormous variety and flourishing of black religious practices in this period.

The black people who are the subjects of these social science projects were able to express their own ideas about their churches, about the problems they saw within them, and about the relationship between religion and politics. The underlying interview materials for these studies now provide vivid historical evidence of those ideas. In this way, the subjects "speak" back on the question of religion or, to put it differently, those written interviews contain within them a "hidden transcript." The people being studied astutely distinguish their resentment of failed ministerial leadership from their embrace of the nurturance and spiritual respite that churches offer; they applaud the churches' role in social and community service, but urge that more financial resources be directed to that effort and away from the clergy's personal enrichment and self-aggrandizement.

There was another group of scholars who were trained in social scientific methodologies but who worked on the margins of their scholarly disciplines, either by choice or as a consequence of racial or gender restrictions or both, and who also took on the study of black religion. Among these were Zora Neale Hurston, Hortense Powdermaker, and Arthur Fauset, all trained ethnographers who studied African American religious practices from a more open stance about the relationship between religion, politics, and lived experience. This disparate group produced pioneering works that bring us closer still to the practices, voices, and ideas of the people they were studying; but they also represented black people who explored less traditional forms of religious life, including new religions of the 1930s and 1940s and African-derived religions.

Taken together, these social scientific writings cover both the rural South and urban North, but generally neglect the urban South. This is a disadvantage that blinds them to the shifts in religious thought and activities in cities like Baton Rouge, Birmingham, and Montgomery which would eventually play prominent roles in the civil rights movement. For the most part, these studies also deny the possibility that religious belief and practice could be ecstatic in its expressiveness (seen as an unwelcome holdover from African, slave, or rural Southern cultures) and still produce political motivations for organized change; here, they followed scholarly notions about the incompatibility of charismatic forms of religion and activism. These scholars, especially Frazier who produced the standard synthesis on African American religion in this period, failed to anticipate that a minority of Southern black religious people would be able to play such a pivotal role in the civil rights movement, or that black religion would produce the leaders of that movement and engulf its culture. This short-sightedness speaks, I argue, to the inherent limitations of the tools of empiricism and intellectualism, especially in their encounter with religion.

The underlying concerns that drove these debates were recognized and reckoned with by many other prominent African American public figures, including women and men who had less formal education but who brought theoretical rigor and their own lived experience to these questions. In order to reach a broader spectrum of black intellectual and political life in the twentieth century, this book moves outside the exclusive realm of scholarly texts and turns toward the lives and popular writings of two extraordinary black women who confronted these questions over many decades: Mary McLeod Bethune and Nannie Helen Burroughs. Bethune was the most well-known and respected black woman of the first half of the century. Educator and founder of Bethune-Cookman College, political advisor to Franklin and Eleanor Roosevelt, and creator of the National Council of Negro Women, Bethune embodied a new kind of racial leadership bridged to the secular, white, masculine world of national politics. Taking a different path, Burroughs, from her position as a leader of the women's auxiliary to the largest black Baptist denomination, concentrated her life's work on black Baptist women, especially the masses of black working-class women who, like her, devoted their time, their talents, and their treasures to the churches they called home.

Each was critical of black Christianity and often had frustrating relationships with other Christians, both white and black, male and female. Members of the first generation that was born in freedom in the nineteenth-century South, they lived to see the Supreme Court's *Brown* decision in 1954 and, in Burroughs' case, the early racial struggles of the 1960s. They addressed the same questions that concerned scholars in the 1930s and 1940s, but carried those into the shifted contexts of the Great Depression, World War II, the Cold War, and the campaign for civil rights.

Bethune and Burroughs model two very different examples of political leadership in the decades preceding the civil rights movement. Bethune is often seen primarily as a political leader, and Burroughs is usually considered primarily a religious leader. That division is an inapt one, as both women occupied multiple sites of leadership. Bethune was as religiously oriented as Burroughs, but in a more unorthodox way; Burroughs was as adept a political operative as Bethune, in both religious and secular settings. By focusing on the last decades of their lives, which dovetail with the emergence of the civil rights movement, we can better appreciate their gifts not just as leaders, orators, and writers, but as intellectuals and political theorists wrestling with questions about racial leadership, about the place of black institutions in the age of desegregation, and about the relationship between religion and political struggle. Bethune died in 1955. Burroughs outlived her by almost a decade and, in that time, brought the young Martin Luther King Jr. into the protected fold of the Woman's Convention, a place where she and his mother had long labored together.

Like Bethune and Burroughs, Benjamin Mays and his wife Sadie grounded their public lives within black institutions. From that vantage point, they also struggled with complex questions about the place of black religious and educational institutions in an age of integration. Mays's scholarly publications in the 1930s established him as a founder of the field of African American religious studies, but he spent the next half-century as a prominent public figure at the helm of Morehouse College and as a public theologian. Unlike his female counterparts and his wife, Mays lived into the mid-1980s. In the later years of his life, he confronted both Black Power and the limitations and losses caused by integration in the public schools of Atlanta—a development he oversaw as elected head of the school board.

His complicated views, expressed in sermons, speeches, and popular writings, exemplify what I term "Southern black religious liberalism," arguably the prevailing political and religious ethos of the civil rights movement. Sadie Mays's activism focused more locally on Atlanta, but she, too, was an often independent participant in national and international religious and human rights networks. Her work helped to make her husband's political views on the place of women remarkably progressive for a man of his generation, including his outspokenness on the charged issues of race and sexual violence. Yet he was unable to shed a near-obsession with the need for male leadership; for him, black masculinity was defined by leadership. It was not so much that men led and women followed, but rather that if men did not have the capacity to lead, they were doomed to fail as "men."

Certain pivotal moments in African American political life have generated distinctive narrative forms, first the slave narrative, and then, in the twentieth century, the migration narrative. The civil rights era spawned yet another genre, one that I call the "movement memoir." These writings are lively accounts filled with revelations about the religious ideas and motivations (or lack of or aversion to them) of some of the young people in a movement that was immersed in Southern black religious culture. For some, that cultural milieu was a familiar comfort. For others, it was a new experience—sometimes alienating, sometimes seductive, and sometimes a political impediment. Yet all those who put their lives into the movement, whether believers or not, also experienced black religious culture as a salve for the trauma, loss, and violence that engulfed them.

Individual black Southern activists came to embody that culture and its resilience, but perhaps none more emphatically than Fannie Lou Hamer who lived out a faith in black religion and American democracy under the harshness of racial oppression in Mississippi. Beginning with Hamer, the sixth chapter explores religion and the civil rights movement from the inside out, from the perspective of a variety of male and female participants, including those who were neither religious, Christian, Southern, or black. Memoirs by Marian Wright Edelman, Mary King, John Lewis, and Stokely Carmichael give us insight into the religious and political theorizing of an entire generation of student activists, most of whom were young enough to look to Martin Luther King, who would die at thirty-nine, as an elder. In the end, I argue that the civil rights movement was itself a religious movement to those who lived and worked within it, including many who did not and do not consider themselves religious.

Finally, the civil rights movement spawned a series of intellectual, economic, and political changes in the decades following the 1960s that are charted in the concluding chapter of this book. The prominent place of religion in the movement and the advent of the Black Power movement required theologians, social scientists, and historians to grapple anew with questions about the nexus between religion and political resistance. The end of legalized segregation, especially in higher education and employment, opened new economic opportunities for African Americans, spawning an enlarged black middle class with the resources to build and support large megachurches. The lifting of voting prohibitions and other racial restrictions helped to create a new generation of black elected officials in both the South and the North. The confluence of all of these changes has generated new versions of old tensions between African American religion and politics, played out dramatically in the public controversy that erupted between Barack Obama and his pastor, the Reverend Jeremiah Wright.

THE LONG stretch of this book, covering much of the twentieth century and a wide array of ideas and people, challenges the oversimplification which characterizes much that has been written and said about black churches and black religious beliefs, including in the contemporary period. Ultimately, it argues that political negotiations must continue with the rich and varied world of black churches and black religion in all its mythic, metaphorical, and literal manifestations. One constant throughout these debates is people's faith in the emancipatory potential of spiritual belief, and their conviction that such belief is politically essential. Yet instead of a simple search for a Promised Land, there has been much talk of Pentecost, of a time when the peoples of the world will be able to gather together in peaceful coexistence, bridging differences of language and nationality, as well as those of religion, gender, and class.

The small rural Virginia church in which I was raised still sits on hallowed ground and is yet alive, although its membership rolls have been devastated by the passing of older generations and the migrations and wanderings of the younger ones. It was founded during Reconstruction in 1874 near a town then called Jerusalem, where four decades earlier Nat Turner had been hanged for enacting his vision for liberating the captives. Established in a different moment and witness to more than a century of births, deaths, weddings, funerals, and revivals, that church lives on through a caring community of believers for whom history, memory, and religion coincide. A remnant of ages past, they have lost neither hope nor faith. Inside, they hold steady to a sanctuary and an institution that, as the poet Hayden so aptly put it, nourishes "the roots of all our dreams of freedom's wide and legendary spring."[8]

1

The Reformation of the "Negro Church"

To speak now of the "Negro church" is to resurrect an anachronism. But in the first half of the twentieth century, this concept was at the center of debates among African Americans about the place of religion and religious institutions in the struggle for political progress. The first generation of African American scholars employed all the academic tools at hand to indict black churches, black ministers, and black congregants as a problem and a hindrance in the fight against racial inequality.

Their writings often portrayed as homogeneous the variegated spectrum of African American religious life and culture because religion itself was rarely the primary concern. Rather, these scholars, like the fields in which they were trained, treated black people's churches chiefly as social institutions and paid little attention to their religious missions. Still, they all conceded, though sometimes grudgingly, that churches were pivotal institutions in black communities, even as they also debated the key question of whether churches were an impediment or an implement for the political progress of the race. Embedded in their critique yet absolutely essential to it were gendered and classbound notions of racial leadership and of the place of black men and women of all classes in the struggle for racial equality.

The history of African American ideas about religion and political progress in the decades before the civil rights movement rests on the work of three of the most prominent African American public intellectuals of the twentieth century: W. E. B. Du Bois, Carter G. Woodson, and Benjamin Mays. Though the titles of their major works on churches and religion sound like variations on a theme, all of these scholars brought distinct intellectual approaches and arguments to their concerns. Coming from dissimilar political and religious orientations, they each sought to understand the nature of African American religious practices, the significance of retentions from African cultures, and the political implications of black church life.

These issues were pressing to them because all of them wanted black churches, their leaders, and their members to use their resources to uplift black communities and to fight against racial, economic, and political oppression. The repressive regime of Jim Crow already was firmly entrenched but the growing migration of rural African Americans fed new black urban communities not only in the South, but in the Midwest and the North as well. Each had already concluded that with few other institutional resources, local and national black political mobilization depended upon black churches.

Du Bois's book *The Negro Church*, published in 1903, combined historical and sociological methodologies to chart African retentions, denominational histories, and contemporary assessments. Yet the first comprehensive historical account of the evolution of black religious practices and institutions did not come until two decades later, in 1922, with the publication of Woodson's *History of the Negro Church*. In the 1930s, Mays's *The Negro's Church* became the earliest in-depth national sociological survey of the subject; his

The Negro's God still stands as an innovative history of African American ideas about God.[1]

All of these men were influential beyond narrow scholarly circles. Public prominence came to Du Bois early in his career and never left him; he was one of the most prominent American intellectuals of his time. His work at the NAACP as editor of *The Crisis*, among other venues, gave him access to a broad public, both black and white. Woodson is best known, and deservedly so, for being the father of black history as a discipline and as a subject for popular celebration. Mays's earlier scholarly work has been overshadowed by his later roles as dean of the school of religion at Howard University, as the president of Morehouse College, and as a theological mentor and eulogist of Martin Luther King Jr. These scholars occupied a public space that allowed them and their ideas to reach wider worlds. All of them wrote regularly for newspapers and popular magazines and traveled and spoke frequently in the United States and abroad. Their writings and ideas about religion were critical to the larger intellectual and political projects in which they were engaged and with which they were most commonly identified.

As a whole, their body of work forms the foundation for the study of African American churches and religion. It reflected and reinforced but rarely challenged prevailing popular conceptions of churches and public debates about their strengths and weaknesses. For all of their differences, Du Bois, Woodson, and Mays agreed that churches were indispensable to the well-being of African American communities and to the political fortunes of the race. They built a remarkably congruent critique of the shortcomings of African American religion and religious institutions while calling for a reformation of the "Negro church." Each, however, proposed a quite different institutional model for a more enlightened, more modern, and more politically engaged church. Their different approaches reflect differences in their political orientations, their assumptions about community organizations, and their ideas about local and national racial leadership.

The relationship between these black intellectuals and the black institutions they studied illuminates persistent tensions between twentieth-century black elites and the masses of black people they sought to speak for or to represent. At a time when the already limited ranks of African American scholars included very few women, the power to represent all black people in these realms resided almost exclusively with men. Black women, then as now, constituted the majority of black church members and were among the most devoted supporters of the churches, as is generally true in American Protestant churches. Yet in all of these writers' books, women and their work were rendered irrelevant to the larger intellectual and political questions at hand. Significantly, these scholars completely ignored a key problem: the fact that the majority of black men, unlike their female counterparts, remained outside the churches and the arc of their influence. How then were churches to accomplish their missions as communal, political, and "race" institutions when so many members of the race were not affiliated with or supportive of them?

Studying black churches became a proving ground for those who, like Du Bois, Woodson, and Mays, still saw the future of the race as dependent on reforming the one entity controlled by black people. Yet these studies silenced two large groups of unseen characters, the majority of church members, who were women, and the majority of men, who remained outside the churches. These three scholars offered a leadership model that depended on the creation of an educated black male clerical elite to lead the churches and, through them, to advance the race as a whole. Writing at a time when talk of secularization abounded, these scholars argued that black churches still mattered and that the control and leadership of those churches mattered even more.

DU BOIS was raised as a New England Episcopalian. Like many others born and educated in the nineteenth century, his writings never shed religious language and concepts, including for him the influence of the Book of Common Prayer. A product of his up-bringing, Du Bois came as an outsider to the African American religious cultures that he would later study and write about in Tennessee, Atlanta, and Philadelphia. His encounters with those communities revealed an unfamiliar world, but he was not immune to the spiritual experiences he witnessed. His early writings about black religion were not dismissive; he respected the religious commitment of his subjects and the power of their faith, even if he did not share their beliefs.[2]

At the same time, Du Bois persistently attacked the hypocrisy of white Christianity for its racism and its support of economic inequality. In this respect he is not at all singular; Christian hypocrisy is a charge frequently leveled by African Americans, extending at least as far back as David Walker's fiery appeals in the 1800s and stretching forward to ideas espoused by Marcus Garvey, the Nation of Islam, and leaders in the civil rights movement. He also recognized and accepted the centrality of churches to African American life and politics though he saw this not as an advantage but as something to be overcome or managed.[3]

Du Bois received his doctorate in history from Harvard in 1895 and by 1899 had published his pioneering ethnographic study *The Philadelphia Negro*, which included extensive interpretations of African American religion and churches. He characterized the organized church as "curious," linked it to African tribal life, and argued that it that blended both family and ritual functions. He portrayed churches as primarily social institutions and religious ones secondarily. Du Bois predicted that African American social and political movements would center in the churches because they were places where the "race problem" was under continuous discussion. He was more concerned, however, that churches were not providing sufficient moral leadership in black Philadelphia. His idealization of the two-parent household led him to argue for a more rigid separation between family and church and between private life and a communal public. He believed that the home should serve as the primary socializing and moral influence in black communities, especially since he believed that churches had already failed in that mission.[4]

Du Bois persisted in blaming sexual immorality for the high percentage of female-headed black households though available data showed that they were a result of the large number of widowed black women, which was hardly something within the churches' control. His vision here was clouded by fears that the many female-headed households would perpetuate a "submerged tenth" of black people who would remain mired in poverty and vice. This line of reasoning would later be expanded by E. Franklin Frazier who harshly portrayed black families and black churches as being plagued by the same weakness, namely the absence of assertive black male leadership and the domination of black women. Du Bois's reasoning here hints at a similar conclusion: if black men could reclaim family and moral leadership, this would be a far more effective way of uplifting black communities.[5]

These then were the conclusions Du Bois had already reached before he directed the study in his Atlanta University series that yielded *The Negro Church* in 1903. This small edited volume borrowed from several disciplines and authors; it made use of historical reviews, sociological surveys, and assessments of contemporary churches' effectiveness. Its historical sections not only provided denominational histories, but laid out in positive tones the relationship between African American religion and retentions of African religious practices found in expressive worship and music. He celebrated those practices as "the sole surviving social institution of the African fatherland" and credited them with black churches' "extraordinary growth and vitality." He argued that the churches themselves still needed to be cleansed and revived because the destiny of the race was linked to religion, "either as a solvent or as a salve." Du Bois explained the churches' prominence in political terms, arguing that they were forced to assume functions that normally would fall to black secular institutions which had been harshly suppressed and thwarted. What he did not say was the corollary: that the churches which were expected to fill that void had been enabled because they could operate privately under the protection of religious freedom.[6]

Here again, as in *The Philadelphia Negro*, Du Bois forged rhetorical links between black women, the churches, and racial progress but this time he did so in a different way. Women, he declared, were the truest believers. They formed the group on whom church reform would depend and to whom it would be of greatest benefit: "Upon the women of no race have the truths of the gospel taken a firmer and deeper hold than upon the colored women of the United States. For her protection and by her help a religious rebirth is needed." Du Bois credited black women for having laid the foundations of black churches, both figuratively and literally, estimating that poor and working-class women had raised three-fourths of the money used to acquire church property. He would return to this theme in later writings, for example in his 1919 essay "The Damnation of Women," again lauding black women for their sacrifices in building black churches. For this reason, he concluded that "despite the noisier and more spectacular advance of my brothers, I instinctively feel and know that it is the five million women of my race who really count."[7]

If young and intelligent people were to be attracted to the church, the Atlanta report concluded, the race's religion must first shed the "dross" of low moral and intellectual standards and the "curious custom of emotional fervor." Despite his poignant embrace of the power of black spirituals in his most well-known work, *The Souls of Black Folk*, Du Bois was never comfortable with the emotional displays he encountered in rural black worship. There, he described vividly his first experiences with what he called "the Frenzy or 'Shouting'":

> A sort of suppressed terror hung in the air and seemed to seize us,—a pythian madness, a demonic possession, that lent terrible reality to song and word. The black and massive form of the preacher swayed and quivered as the words crowded to his lips and flew at us in singular eloquence. The people moaned and fluttered, and then the gaunt-cheeked brown woman beside me suddenly leaped straight into the air and shrieked like a lost soul, while round about came wail and groan and outcry, and a scene of human passion such as I had never conceived before.[8]

Du Bois cast this kind of religious ecstasy as a remnant of Africa and slavery, without condemning what he witnessed or questioning the demonstrated power of the beliefs held. Instead, he questioned the passivity implicit in Christian doctrine, which he judged well-suited to slaves but not to the modern citizen's political and social needs. Those needs, in his view, were being ignored by the black Methodist and Baptist churches, which continued to emphasize religious feeling and spirit. Du Bois shared with his contemporaries an inability to imagine that churches stressing emotional fervor could also engage in uplifting or emancipating politics, but he called for a new religious leadership that would expand the churches' functions beyond worship and ritual practices. In editorials written for *The Crisis* in the decade that followed, Du Bois praised black churches and church people while criticizing their leaders for being "pretentious" as well as "dishonest and immoral," for failing to address the real economic needs of its members, and for driving away "colored men and women of education and energy" who did not subscribe to "unimportant dogmas and ancient and outworn creeds."[9]

These criticisms of black churches seem familiar because one can certainly still hear them today, but they are in fact a very long-standing assessment. Indeed, at the start of the twentieth century black churches were viewed by many as an aged, sleeping giant that squandered its potential to foster political activism and to serve the day-to-day needs of black communities. Most often, criticisms of the churches focused, as Du Bois did, on the black ministerial class and the need to improve it.

Writing in the same period, Kelly Miller, the Howard University sociologist, asserted that criticisms of black ministers masked a broader debate about racial leadership. In his 1914 essay "The Ministry," Miller argued boldly that the "talented tenth" of the race should simply take over the leadership of black churches; otherwise, "if the blind lead the blind, will not both fall into the ditch?" More explicitly, he painted the church as an institution where "the opportunity for the talented tenth is almost unlimited." Miller agreed that a better-educated ministry was the most effective way to uplift the race as a whole. Yet he was not advocating for improved training for the existing clergy as others had. Instead, he urged that the talented tenth of the race, those who were middle class and educated, ought simply to enter the ministry en masse and assume the leadership of black religious institutions. "When the talented tenth awakens to a realizing sense of the demands and opportunities of the situation," he wrote, "then will the tide turn toward the ministry as to an honest field ready for the reaper."[10]

Miller did not reject black churches or black Christian belief; he was convinced that African Americans were in fact the only true American Christians. Citing specifically the strong faith of black working-class women, Miller concluded that perhaps they would be able to "bring an apostate world back to God" and to "Righteousness." But he ventured no specifics on how women were to fulfill this messianic role, or, for that matter, even fit into his church takeover scheme, be they working class or elite. After all, his model rested on an idealized clerical class from which women were excluded, for the most part, by prohibitions on their ordination.[11]

Like Du Bois and Miller, many educated black women attributed their disappointment about black churches specifically to ministerial domination of church leadership. Ida B. Wells and Fannie Williams, for example, were among many black women activists who described black preachers as "corrupt" and "ignorant." Williams went so far as to claim that black advancement was hindered more by ministerial leadership "than by any other single cause." Wells had quit one church in disgust when a bishop failed to remove a minister who had been implicated in a morals scandal. On the basis of her experience organizing protest meetings and, later, sponsoring a settlement house for black men, Wells made a more pointed general criticism: black preachers were too timid politically. When she approached the larger Methodist denomination for financial support to expand her organizing work, she was refused because the bishop involved saw "no leading people" involved with her work. Wells reminded the bishop that "neither did Jesus Christ have any of the leading people with him in his day when he was trying to establish Christianity."[12]

Even as Wells aimed her criticisms directly at the political tim-
idity of male ministerial leadership, other black women shared Du
Bois's abhorrence for traditional black religious practices that were,
in their eyes, unrefined and too emotionally charged. Anna Julia
Cooper called that style of worship "ludicrous" and "semi-civi-
lized." For Mary Church Terrell and Alice Dunbar-Nelson, expressions of religious fervor by black women were especially distasteful
and frightful to some extent. Terrell said it was "discouraging and
shocking to see how some of the women shout, holler and dance
during services." Dunbar-Nelson chided those who participated for
reinforcing negative stereotypes of black women as primitive and,
though this was unstated, highly eroticized as well.[13]

Class and gender bias were implicit in this intraracial clash over
black worship practices, since the objects of scorn were almost always working-class women. Yet these particular criticisms were
much more than an attempt to impose a "politics of respectability"
on black women worshipers. The "backwardness" of the worship
style was linked to the absence of any meaningful uplift program
particularly in churches composed of members who were among
the most economically distressed. Those who attacked these practices saw them as largely symbolic of all that was wrong with black
churches of the masses, especially their failure to become a modern
political institution capable of responding to the day-to-day material needs of its members. Indeed, many black Baptist women who
objected to the emotionalism of black worship practices were not
rejecting the practices themselves, since some of them engaged in
similar expressions during their own worship services. Rather, they
were criticizing an excessive reliance on emotionalism in the absence of any meaningful social program or leadership.[14]

The women's criticisms of ministers were more nuanced than
those of Du Bois or Miller, in part because they allowed for the
possibility that emotional styles of worship could coexist with com-

munity engagement. They offered a different conceptualization of church leadership as well, believing that the church's most meaningful work depended on the congregants and not just the ministers. Women accused preachers of failing to provide moral and intellectual leadership, of being timid and conservative politically, and of offering their parishioners emotionalism alone. Nannie Burroughs, founder of the Woman's Convention within the National Baptist Convention, argued that "the church should not substitute shouting for service." She chastised the black clergy for preaching "too much Heaven and too little practical Christian living."[15]

Burroughs and other black Baptist women had in their minds a model of the black churches' public responsibilities that bore some similarity to the settlement house movement, social gospel tenets, and other progressive efforts of the late nineteenth and early twentieth centuries. In 1914 Burroughs wrote that "no church should be allowed to stay in a community that does not positively improve community life." This was the historical mission to which she believed black churches had been called. Much of the work of the Woman's Convention envisioned, on a smaller scale, exactly that kind of black church. These Baptist women wanted a service-oriented church, actively engaged in helping to meet the day-to-day needs of its community, providing literacy training, medical care, clothing, food, and recreational services. Yet the full realization of that model would require partnership with a politically progressive and better-educated ministry. Without such leadership, the best efforts of church women would be thwarted or remain too limited to meet the task of serving, spiritually and socially, growing urban black communities.[16]

THESE were the issues that were being debated when Carter G. Woodson began his scholarly career and his life's work creating and popularizing the discipline of black history. One of nine children born to freed slaves in Virginia, Woodson had labored throughout his childhood to help support his impoverished family. He was twenty years old when he started high school in 1895. After a circuitous and difficult journey as a laborer and a teacher, Woodson earned a bachelor's and a master's degree from the University of Chicago in 1908. Four years later, he earned a Ph.D. in history from Harvard, the first black American after Du Bois to achieve that distinction.[17]

The persistence and intellectual energy that drove Woodson's quest for education also marked his approach to his life's work. He created the Association for the Study of Negro Life and History (ASNLH) in 1915 when he was forty; he also founded the *Journal of Negro History* in 1917 and the *Negro History Bulletin* in 1937. Woodson was the originator and the force behind the establishment of annual week-long Negro History observations, which in the 1970s would become institutionalized as Black History Month. For Woodson, the study of black history was a weapon for combating stereotypes of racial inferiority that permeated the scholarly writing, politics, and popular culture of the early twentieth century. He maintained that it was critically important to bring that history directly to black people, not only through print media but also through the schools, colleges, clubs, fraternal groups, and churches that formed the communications infrastructure of black communities nationwide. In 1922, Woodson published a comprehensive textbook entitled *The Negro in Our History*, which went through nineteen editions and served as the standard black history textbook for more than a quarter of a century. He was one of the first historians to devote special attention to African history and culture as a source of historical roots and racial pride for American blacks.[18]

African American religion and church history were subjects that

Woodson engaged with at various times in his career, both in his scholarly work and in his writings for popular audiences. When he was a student at Harvard, he had wanted to write his master's thesis on the history of black churches; he may have been dissuaded in part by his advisors' view that there were too few primary sources. Woodson proved them wrong in 1921 when he published *The History of the Negro Church* which still stands as the only general historical treatment of the subject. The book traced the development of black churches from their origins in the eighteenth century to the period in which he wrote. It was not an attempt at standard religious history, but instead told the story as a social and political history.[19]

Woodson linked the churches' history in the eighteenth and nineteenth centuries inextricably with the development of black political leadership, with efforts to secure black educational opportunity, and with the short-lived political successes of the Reconstruction period. Du Bois, in *The Negro Church*, had neglected the period immediately after the Civil War and he would make little mention of religion or black religious leadership in his magisterial 1935 work *Black Reconstruction*. Woodson, however, reclaimed the history of Reconstruction-era church leaders in order to use them as a model for contemporary religious leadership. He relied largely and uncritically on the memoirs of black ministers and on official church histories which tended toward the laudatory and the celebratory.

Although Woodson cast his book as a work of history, he obviously was participating in the contemporary debate over who was to control the churches and what their mission should be. The progressive male minority that Woodson heralded had been represented in his own historical accounts as the founders of Northern independent black churches in the eighteenth century and as ministers who worked among the newly freed people in the South after the Civil War. Now, in the 1920s, Woodson saw a different set of challenges since the migration of rural black people into cities of the North and South had already begun. In this context, Woodson's analysis of the church's potential role assumed greater urgency, reflecting the worsening political and economic conditions in his own times and the need for a communal response from black people.

Woodson fashioned an interpretive critique in which Reconstruction-era black churches appeared, like the Reconstruction itself, as a "lost cause" shrouded in defeat. He portrayed the churches as institutions that had ceased to be engaged in political work on behalf of the race and that suffered from the fact that their educated ministerial leadership, which had emerged in that earlier period, had lost their influence. His declensionist model of black church history found its apex, or its version of a Puritan moment, in Reconstruction. Woodson characterized contemporary disagreements about black churches as an ideological fight over the political role of the church. He described a persistent battle over the true mission of churches, a battle involving two camps which he dubbed "the conservative" and "the progressive," the former being in majority control of the churches and the latter cast as the losing, challenging minority. When progressives, especially the "talented tenth" of the race and the educated, failed to persuade the majority, he argued, they simply abandoned the church to the conservatives. In Woodson's mind, this only served to weaken the churches and the prospects of the masses of black people in them.[20]

Woodson reflected the concerns of the 1920s, a period marked by clashes between education and belief, modernity and religion, science and faith, the intellectual and the spiritual. The contest that he described within black churches appeared on its face to be a conflict between the educated and the uneducated. Yet it also reflected unanticipated tensions between the quest for religion and the pursuit of education, two missions otherwise presumed to be in harmony in strategies for black uplift. All of this presented an intellectual and political challenge for men like Woodson who were searching for collective strategies to advance the race at a time when black churches remained the sole institutional base among African Americans. To dismiss the black church as irrelevant was not an easy option for these scholars. The divide between education and religion, or more to the point, between educated black people and black religious institutions, was decidedly more complex and difficult to reconcile.

Woodson's own efforts to popularize black history only reinforced his appreciation of the churches' importance. The work of his association, the success of its publishing house, and the institutionalization of Negro History Week all relied in large part on black church facilities, members, networks, and ministers. These efforts drew sustenance from black churches as they helped to spread the gospel of black history. Black churches were "begging for" written materials and other ways to better incorporate the teaching of black history into church youth programs. Yet many of the people Woodson hoped to educate about black history continued to embrace religious practices and a sense of the churches' mission that differed from his own strongly held beliefs.[21]

As critical as Woodson was, he rarely attacked lay people directly, reserving his verbal assaults for their leaders instead. He nonetheless positioned himself as a reformer who also often supported the churches. He defended them from what he called "a few radical members of the race" who saw them as a hindrance to blacks' advancement. Woodson characterized black churches as historical assets that now could have "tremendous results when properly exploited by honest leaders enjoying the confidence of the masses." To amplify this, Woodson offered specific examples of progressive churches that provided extrareligious activities and services. His models were the so-called institutional churches. These were large well-funded urban congregations led by prominent educated ministers who implemented social service programs such as daycare, kindergartens, and jobs services.[22]

Woodson's vision blended older, social gospel notions with an uplift ideology and was not unlike the vision that Burroughs and other religious women had endorsed. Yet, in all of his discussions, Woodson presented ministers as the lone embodiment of their churches and as being solely responsible for their future. There was no mention of church members, women, or any role for the laity. Woodson's model of the "Negro church" envisioned an educated male ministry leading churches on missions of direct service most often associated with the work of church women, but did not address the question of who would do the work or raise the money to support it.[23]

Woodson's overall conclusions emphasized the importance of the church to the success of other black political struggles and organizations. He pointed to its role in fighting against the Ku Klux Klan and in raising funds to fight segregation. "The National Association for the Advancement of Colored People," he wrote, "would be unable to carry out its program without the aid of the Negro church." At the same time, Woodson argued that electoral politics would be of limited utility to the advancement of black people and warned black ministers away from that arena. Most black preachers and most black leaders, he claimed, understood that "the hope of the blacks lies not in politics from without but in race uplift from within, in the form of social amelioration and economic development." Woodson saw the church as having a central role to play in that inward-looking nationalist strategy.[24]

In these ways, Woodson cast the churches' mission as that of politicized racial work rather than religious toil. He based his argument on the belief that white Christianity did not perform any re-

ligious function, but simply political work for the exclusive benefit
of white people. Black people, he teased, needed to learn "to imi-
tate the white people in substituting in their faith the doing of
the will of their race for that of doing the revealed will of God."
Woodson's idea of churches, white and black, as "race" institutions
was not offered entirely in jest since he came to see churches as the
route to unified national black political organizing. His idea that
black churches should be primarily "race" rather than religious institutions would soon take on bolder dimensions.[25]

Woodson reserved special criticism for the dwindling black rural
churches and the growing numbers of urban storefront churches,
which he called "really country churches moved to town." Once
again, his complaint was familiar: these churches were controlled
by fundamentalists and had no "tendencies toward modernism."
This new dichotomy—between "fundamentalism" and "modernism"—replaced his prior opposition between "conservatives" and
"progressives." These were theological terms taken from larger intellectual debates stemming from biblical criticism and other shifts
in approaches to literal interpretation of scripture and in understandings of religious authority. For this reason, Woodson explicitly excluded from his criticism those "congregations composed of
certain intelligent groups of Negroes who do not represent the
masses." In effect he created two distinct classes of black churches,
one for the small group of educated elite and the other for everyone else.[26]

Woodson noted once again the unique role of black churches as
a whole in the progress of the race, despite its domination by the
masses of black people who were not allied with the move toward
modernization. "The church is the greatest asset of the race," he
admitted, concluding "that the Negro would be practically helpless
today without the church." It was this dilemma that was the crux
of the problem of black churches: the dependency of other black

enterprises on the churches and the absence of any other black-controlled institution with a potential for national reach or resources.[27]

Du Bois seemed to ignore these arguments when he attacked Woodson in a scathing review of *The History of the Negro Church*. He accused Woodson of missing the point of the history he had chronicled. "Everything is there," Du Bois admonished, "except the church; except the inner spirit and motive of that marvelous faith and unreason which made a million black folk on the shores of exile dance and scream and shout the Sorrow Song; which raised from smoking entrails the witch-figure of that old black preacher, whose trembling hands built a spiritual State within a State, guarded and groomed it and made it spawn a new freedom for a world-old race, made it build and guide, shelter and teach, lead and train a people." This was true to the extent that Woodson's book was concerned with black churches as institutions and did not engage deeply with their religious practices.[28]

Du Bois believed that Woodson had understated the influence of black churches and he took it upon himself to elevate them to the pinnacle of black history: "The Negro church is the mighty central fact of American Negro History. It is independent, unique and Negro through and through, despite all imitation. It is a great astonishing, a contradictory social triumph with its feet in the African jungle and its head in Heaven." With this mixed geographic and theological metaphor, Du Bois developed his indictment of Woodson. That Du Bois had taken on the role of defender of the churches' place in history was perplexing in view of the criticisms that were leveled at his own earlier works. In the decade to follow, Du Bois's position would again shift. He would cease to defend black churches even on historical grounds while Woodson would continue to plead for their centrality and their reform.[29]

These debates over the political role of black religion and black churches were not limited to books by scholars like Du Bois and Woodson, but raged in popular newspapers and magazines of the 1920s and 1930s. The Great Depression brought a steady stream of black migration, a rise in urban black church membership, and an increasing variety of black religious sects. Marcus Garvey attacked white Christian hypocrisy even as his movement embraced black Christian percepts, rituals, and practices in its colorful mass meetings and other public displays. Along with his advocacy of a black God and a black Jesus, this approach was at the core of a movement that has been characterized as religious in nature and appealing strongly to masses of black people for this very reason.[30] At the same time, urban storefront churches established by Baptist, Pentecostal, and Holiness believers continued to reshape the religious landscape of cities that were absorbing large numbers of migrants from rural areas.

In this same period, a growing secular black press was expanding its coverage of religious issues which traditionally had been the domain of black denominational publishers. Prominent black newspapers reported widely on religion and on the activities of various churches and denominations. But they also devoted considerable attention to the unscrupulous practices, financial and sexual, of black preachers and denominational leaders, including several notorious and scintillating cases of alleged abuses. There was sensationalized reporting on the emergence of alternative black religious groups which were characterized as cults, including black Jews, for example, as well as followers of Father Divine, Elder Micheaux, Mother Catherine, and others. In these ways, the black press emerged as another independent black institution, which, ironically, created a new forum for considering the issue of the black churches' public role. All of these developments have been misinterpreted to mean that criticisms of churches and religion peaked during this period. As I have been arguing, the criticism was persistent and endures today. What changed was that the debate moved more dramatically into black public culture because of the increasing availability of print media.[31]

Black newspapers also provided a space in which black women could join and help shape the debates about black churches. Black women writers and activists were often enlisted as regular political columnists in black weeklies. Among these were the Baptist leader Nannie Burroughs who was a gifted writer and a powerful orator. Like most black women at the time, she never went to college and never had access to the academic training that was becoming available to a handful of gifted black men such as Du Bois, Woodson, and Mays. In the 1920s and 1930s, Burroughs wrote a syndicated column of political commentary for the Associated Negro Press. The themes in her speeches and writings were similar to those attracting the attention of other black intellectuals, activists, and scholars. They included discussions of racial leadership and partisan politics, critiques of black churches and Christian practices, and an area of special concern to her, accounts of the struggles of black women and the failings of black men. She brought powerful insights and a brilliant wit to those issues and the special perspective of a woman who spent her entire adult life working within black Baptist church networks.

The role of black churches in black communities was as heated a subject of debate within black religious circles as it was among observers outside the churches. Few were more incisive and direct in their criticisms of church leaders and church programs than Burroughs. She analyzed churches as local community institutions and as religious institutions in need of sound administrative and religious leadership. She focused on what churches and church leaders were doing to pool religious resources on behalf of the community as a whole, and not just for a few hours on Sundays. "Negroes have invested more money in churches than they have in any other enterprise in the world," she wrote. Yet the resources were spent on buildings that sat unused all week long because church leaders were "wasting time and money, fighting, masquerading, half preaching or preaching spurious doctrines, in the name of the Christian religion." As a result, most churchgoers were deriving little benefit spiritually or otherwise from their sacrifices.[32]

Burroughs laid the blame for this situation directly on what she called "lazy, standardless, visionless, selfish leaders." She excoriated "able-bodied men who claim that they are called of God" but who lacked vision and administrative skills. Her own notion of what black churches could offer was clear: "Churches under intelligent leadership can be run very much like a school and be made service stations. The Bible teachers would come to teach God's word, the doctors to teach health and to heal the people." If that were done, she predicted, "the masses would be lifted up and their investment in churches would pay in this world and in the world to come."[33]

Burroughs was most concerned about morally corrupt male religious leaders. "'Feed my sheep' has come to mean fleece my sheep," she wrote. Unlike Miller and Mays, who spoke so fervently about the need for an educated clerical class, Burroughs seemed more preoccupied with the need for men who were honest, sincere, and dedicated to the good of the churches and their congregations. "Character is the first qualification," she insisted. "Without that, the minister is a menace." Ministers, she argued, needed to be "cleaner in character, more unselfish in purpose, qualified in training, progressive in ideals, social-minded in spirit, devout in heart, and not lazy." They also needed to know how to get things done as administrators and leaders. She believed that education without character was troubling and potentially dangerous.[34]

Like others in this period, Burroughs was especially concerned because young black people, especially men, were falling away from the church. She tried to appeal to them by ascribing a virile masculinity to Christ, saying at one point that he was "no molly-coddle" but a real man who resorted to strong "cave-man tactics" when necessary, such as when he turned the moneychangers out of the Temple.[35] At the same time, she argued that black women carried more than their fair share of the race's political, familial, and economic burdens and that black men owed a debt of gratitude to black women. "The men ought to get down on their knees to Negro women," she wrote. The women "made possible all we have around us—church, home, school, business." She accused black men of lacking "manhood and energy" and urged them to "stop making slaves and servants of our women."[36]

Her own vision of Christianity's promises rejected the notion that the United States had any right to claim itself to be a Christian nation. "Would to God that it were," she wrote, "but it is the most lawless and desperately wicked nation on the globe."[37] About this, she and Du Bois were in agreement; but he refused to see organized Christianity as a force for progressive change. In an essay entitled "Will the Church Remove the Color Line?" published in 1931 in the liberal Protestant magazine *The Christian Century,* Du Bois maintained that the white Christian church would ignore the race problem as long as possible and then claim credit for any subsequent progress that did occur. For him, the Christian church was "consistently on the wrong side" of political issues, rejecting the despised, the lowly, and the unfortunate, and standing on "the side of wealth and power."[38]

What was new, however, was the way in which Du Bois reconciled his long-standing views on the weaknesses of black churches and white Christianity with his emerging belief in the virtues of segregated black institutions, a view that precipitated his resignation from the NAACP in 1934. He launched his opening salvo in the segregation debates when he argued, in *The Crisis,* that the emancipation of black people worldwide depended upon a racially conscious people cooperating in their own institutions and movements. He rejected the NAACP's long-standing position which equated discrimination and segregation, even as he argued that fighting against discrimination continued to be absolutely necessary. His broader call was for maintaining and strengthening all-black institutions, something he did not see as inconsistent with attacking discriminatory practices against black people. His was a search for institutional bases of power within black communities and for black people; and by 1934, Du Bois had come to see this as a surer route to black empowerment than waiting for enforced segregation to end.

The debate over segregation that was raging in *The Crisis* and among black leaders and thinkers necessarily touched on the sensitive and paradoxical question of the status of black churches. Some argued that they were segregated voluntarily; others saw racially separate churches as evidence of Christian hypocrisy. In a revealing exchange between Du Bois and Francis Grimke, the well-respected pastor of a politically prominent African American Presbyterian church in Washington, Grimke endorsed the NAACP's position. He agreed that discrimination and inferiority were implicit in segregation and that it was "contrary to the spirit of Jesus Christ and to the noble ideal of brotherhood." Du Bois was respectful in his dissent, yet he pushed his own view. "Why, then, in an argument on segregation, has Dr. Grimke said *nothing* of the 15th Street Presbyterian Church? This church is a result of segregation. It was founded because white Presbyterians could not listen to a pastor of Dr. Grimke's learning and character and would not sit in the same pews with the distinguished people who belonged to this church. There is no use trying to salve our logic by saying that this church represents 'voluntary' segregation."[39]

The particular success and prominence of Grimke's church fed Du Bois's argument that building strong black institutions not only

would benefit black communities, but would defeat the very doctrine of inferiority. He made this appeal to the NAACP board of
directors when it considered resolutions reiterating its opposition
to all forms of segregation: "Does it mean that it does not approve
of the Negro Church or believe in its segregated activities in the
20,000 edifices where most branches of the NAACP meet and
raise money to support it? Does it believe in 200 Negro newspapers
which spread NAACP news and propaganda? Does it believe in
Negro history, Negro literature and Negro art? Does it believe in
Negro spirituals? *And if it does believe in these things, is the Board of
Directors of the NAACP afraid to say so?*" In the end, of course, the
board could not answer Du Bois's questions as he wished; and for
this and other reasons, he severed his ties with the organization in
August 1934.[40]

The uproar over Du Bois's decision to leave the NAACP led
Burroughs to argue against the attractions of charismatic or messianic or one-person leadership, telling her readers that "the loss of
one man is as incidental as the loss of one grain of sand. Sorry!"
She called for the race to "close ranks," a jibe at the term Du Bois
himself had employed to marshal black support for World War I, a
position he later regretted. She also used this controversy to question the place of intellectuals in positions of political leadership,
concluding that "society admires the scholar but the world loves
the hero because it is the hero's consecrated blood that furnishes
the nation's working capital for tomorrow." Recounting Joshua's
fears when he assumed leadership after the death of Moses, she reminded the audience that God had said to him: "Moses, my ser-
vant, is dead. Therefore, arise and go over Jordan." She warned
that "there are no deliverers. They're all dead. We must arise and
go over Jordan. We can take the promised land."[41]

As a political theorist, Burroughs had a very strong and clear set
of views on how black people could improve their economic and

political position. She rejected the notion that individual achievement represented anything beyond itself, especially at a time when large institutions were accruing vast economic and political power. "We are a race of individualists, and weak ones at that, trying to function in a highly cooperative age," she wrote, concluding that black people would have to work together or they would fail to advance as a people. She called for blacks to invest their earnings in black-owned enterprises that could provide essential services to black communities. Economic strength alone would not be enough. Burroughs believed that securing the ballot was just as essential as the collective use of black dollars. "When the Negro has the ballot, he has the one thing that the white man fears," she advised, but "when he has the dollar, he has the only earthly thing that the white man worships."[42]

On this point, Burroughs and Du Bois concurred. By the 1930s, Du Bois had come to believe that the potential of black churches rested with their enormous economic potential as a cooperative enterprise, citing the valuable property holdings of black churches which were built with "the pennies of the poor." He called on churches to establish more systematic business activities, for example, purchasing homes for church members, getting them jobs, and organizing buying clubs and other cooperative activities. Black churches would then be in the business of helping and inspiring their members to live better and more economically secure lives. Writing at a time when the Depression was ravaging an already impoverished people, Du Bois turned to a socialist model but lodged it within the only black institutions likely to survive the severe economic conditions: black churches. No longer so protective of black worship practices, Du Bois argued for a shift toward a gospel of high ideals and good deeds, and chastised church leaders who did little more than entertain or scare church members.[43]

Whatever the differences that separated Du Bois and Burroughs, they both agreed that some mechanism for collective organization was needed to save black communities from further economic deterioration and to create the political strength needed for fighting racial inequality in jobs, housing, and education. This was the "New Negro Church" as Burroughs and Du Bois envisioned it; but Woodson offered an even more specific and dramatic model for converting black churches into a unified political institution. Woodson wrote a weekly column for the *New York Age* in which he freed himself from any pretense of scholarly objectivity. He commented on national racial politics, segregation, the failings of black leadership, and many other issues of the day. In 1931, black churches and black ministers became his special target when he devoted three full months' worth of his weekly writings to a relentless portrayal of their shortcomings and offered his own new approach.[44]

Part of the impetus for Woodson's columns was the resurgence of a debate between the two independent black Methodist denominations about merging their groups in order to strengthen, streamline, and expand their operations. Negotiations between the African Methodist Episcopal (AME) and the African Methodist Episcopal Zion (AME Zion) churches had failed to yield a union. Woodson found this especially frustrating since the groups shared doctrines, structures, and practices. At the same time, the mainline white Methodist denomination, which had split into Northern and Southern branches over the question of slavery, had likewise begun the process of reconciling, a move that would succeed and that would have consequences for the black Methodists whose congregations operated within the white conference. When the regionally split conferences united, black Methodist churches were relegated, some said "segregated," within a separate entity rather than integrated within their geographic regions. This arrangement was a concession to Southern white Methodists who had made it a condition for the Methodist reunification.[45]

In the midst of these developments, Woodson began to argue that black churches were a divisive rather than unifying community influence. They suffered from intense leadership rivalries both among and within denominations which created political fiefdoms, weakened the church's political potential, and squandered its resources. Underlying Woodson's critique was his strong distrust and resentment of black preachers in general, especially those he viewed as petty and ineffectual political brokers enmeshed in denominational and urban patronage politics. To his mind, the contemporary black church was "largely an institution exploited for the benefit of the individuals in charge."[46]

As a solution, Woodson proposed that all black churches dissolve their denominational differences and ties, and come together in a single national "United Negro Church." He urged the masses of black people to repudiate tainted, divided religious leadership and create one national religiously based institution dedicated to racial uplift and empowerment. In practical terms, Woodson called for a unified network of local institutional churches that would provide direct community services, as well as a base for political work and leverage, electoral and otherwise.[47]

Anticipating and deflecting objections that his views were simply those of a hostile nonbeliever, Woodson laid out his own religious beliefs and linked them to larger political commitments. A lifelong Baptist, he worshiped at Washington's Shiloh Baptist Church, which had a large, politically active, and progressive congregation. Black churches appealed to him because they provided a space for interclass alliances: "I go to church not because I believe that I have more religion than others who do not, but because I find there better people than I do on the outside fighting the institution, and I attend church, too, because I find my people there, and I cannot help them unless I remain among them. Wherever they go I want to go, and when they suffer and die let me share my part of the burden and go down to the end with them." Stressing that he was interested not in destroying the church but in reforming its leadership, he cautioned that "we should not be so foolish as to burn down the barn to get the rats."[48]

Woodson's proposal for a single unified church offered a theological and political model for a religiously based black nationalism, but one dependent on a common Christian heritage refashioned into an ethic of service and social justice, with an emphasis not on the world to come but on the challenges of the day-to-day. His proposal has obvious parallels with the kind of mass organization that Marcus Garvey envisioned and tried to build in the 1920s. The conceptual move from Garvey's "United Negro Improvement Association" to a "United Negro Church" would not have been difficult since Woodson himself was a strong Garvey supporter. Both men shared a belief in the unifying and politically redemptive power of black history and in the need for a black-directed self-help program with mass appeal. Woodson wrote a column for Garvey's *Negro World*, where his scholarly essays received favorable notice. When Garvey died, Woodson composed an essay for his *Journal of Negro History* commemorating Garvey's life and ideas.[49]

In Woodson's scheme for a united black church, the crucial question of who would rule was left unanswered. What was assured, however, was that the leadership of the United Negro Church, like that of Garvey's UNIA (United Negro Improvement Association), would not be white or interracial. Woodson's proposal rested on the idea that the masses of black Christians would overthrow their current ministerial leadership and replace it with a group of men who could build a racially cohesive interclass alliance. This seemed to be one of Woodson's driving aims, since he was suspicious of white-controlled labor unions and of the Communist party as avenues for black political and economic advancement. Woodson believed ultimately in organizing along "racial rather than class lines," having flirted briefly with socialism and lost faith in it.[50]

At the November 1931 annual meeting of the ASNLH held in New York City, Woodson set the tone and the stage for the ensuing debate about his proposed United Negro Church when he promised that the "so-called sacred veil will be thrown aside and disregarded." He pledged that "the most significant force in the life of the Negro will be analyzed just as a research man tests a mineral which he finds and does not quite understand."[51] The debate was open and pointed. Several prominent ministers participated. The Reverend H. H. Proctor, pastor of Nazarene Congregational Church in Brooklyn, defended the churches' achievements while the Reverend Vernon Johns, president of the Virginia Theological Seminary and later the pastor of Dexter Baptist in Birmingham, argued that unnecessary church hierarchies created "overlapping, duplication of effort, corruption, and the impoverishment of the people." The Reverend Adam Clayton Powell Sr. of Abyssinian Baptist Church in Harlem acknowledged some of the ministerial weaknesses that Woodson had decried, but did not concur in his broader solution since he believed that reform was already under way.[52]

Ironically, all of the association's conference sessions at its New York meeting were held in black churches. Once again, we see that Woodson was mounting an attack on churches despite the fact that his own work depended in large part on cooperation and support from religious institutions. Apparently, Woodson thought that black churches were of different classes or categories, some which he considered to be progressive and community oriented. Nonetheless, he criticized them all with a broad brush since it seemed to him that good churches were few and far between.[53]

Woodson's writing about the need for church reform kept its aim on male ministers and gave little attention to the black women in the pews. Even if we make allowances for the period's gendered and elitist notions of leadership, this is still a somewhat perplexing

omission for someone whose notions of black history included heroic black women figures. Black women, especially schoolteachers
and church organizers, constituted a large and loyal core group of
supporters for Woodson's many enterprises. In 1936, at his urging,
the prominent educator, politician, and women's advocate Mary
McLeod Bethune assumed the presidency of the ASNLH, a position she held until 1952, two years after his death and three years
before her own.[54]

Even as Woodson was writing his most scathing condemnations
of black church leadership, he was also lobbying for the inclusion
of black women in public life. "Certainly the women are more
faithful to our people," he wrote, "and they do more for the eleva-
tion of the unfortunate element than our men, who too often use
their ascendancy in leadership for the exploitation of the unenlightened." But he urged women to continue their efforts in the
"neglected spheres" rather than organize in the center of the political arena. Despite his view that women were more morally upright
leaders than men and that the advance of the race depended on
their work and progress, an expanded female leadership role in
the churches was not an option he explored. The place of black
women in his United Negro Church remained a mystery. In these
and other ways, Woodson and others who spoke about reforming
black churches largely erased black women from their discussions.
They also presented a simplified view of institutions that were idiosyncratic, complex, contingent, and already highly politicized, including along gender lines.[55]

THOUGH reluctant to embrace black women's leadership in
churches, Woodson remained deeply suspicious of black ministers,
even those as well educated as he was. In 1928, he had received a
grant from the Rockefeller-funded Institute of Social and Religious

Research to undertake a study of contemporary black urban and rural churches. Woodson hired his fellow historian and Howard University professor Charles Wesley, who also was an ordained AME minister, to direct the study. After Wesley had drafted a report based on extensive fieldwork, Woodson rejected it as "worthless" and fired Wesley, accusing him of being too generous in his assessments because of his own religious convictions. Woodson then pleaded with the sociologist E. Franklin Frazier to take over the project, and when Frazier refused, Woodson was forced to return the grant money.[56]

Although Woodson questioned whether a scholar who was also a minister could write with objectivity about black churches, the institute harbored no such reservations. In 1930 it awarded the grant to two scholars who were ordained ministers, Benjamin Mays and Joseph W. Nicholson. The project would launch Mays's scholarly career in the field of African American religion. Mays wrote that receiving the assignment was, "if not heaven-sent," then surely "heaven-bent." Their study was published in 1933 as *The Negro's Church*, a book that would become the standard interpretive demographic text on the subject.[57]

Like Woodson, Mays had traveled a long road to acquire an education and scholarly training. Born in South Carolina in 1894 to tenant farmer parents, his early schooling was marked by the long absences demanded by cotton farming. He left home at seventeen to attend high school and was eventually admitted to Bates College in Maine where he excelled as a student. After graduating in 1920, Mays taught at Morehouse College in Atlanta for three years while serving as minister at Atlanta's Shiloh Baptist Church, his only pastorate. Intending to pursue graduate training in religion, Mays entered the University of Chicago, where he earned a master's degree in 1925. But once again, he returned south. He taught for a while in South Carolina, went on to the Urban League in

Tampa, then moved back to Atlanta where he worked for the national YMCA. In 1930, he left to begin work on the institute's project. Mays's training in religion would influence his research on black churches and would distinguish his approach from that of the secularly oriented Woodson and Du Bois.[58]

The institute which commissioned this work was an outgrowth of John D. Rockefeller's interest in applying social scientific methods to the field of religion. When *The Negro's Church* was published, Mays expressed the hope that it would serve as a baseline for further studies of the church because it was the first comprehensive study of the subject. Mays and Nicholson spent nearly two years gathering detailed statistical information on 609 urban churches and 185 rural churches in both the North and the South. They also compiled surveys, interviews, and extensive firsthand observations.[59]

Mays depicted the formation of black churches not as a bold move by black people, but rather as a defensive retreat after whites expelled blacks from the Eden of a common religious polity. He reclaimed the work of George Washington Williams, in particular his 1883 *History of the Negro Race in America*, the first history of African Americans. Williams, a self-taught historian, a state legislator, and a Baptist minister, argued that in the Revolutionary era the "hateful and harmful spirit of caste and race prejudice" had led white Protestants to drive black people out of white churches. Mays used this explanation as a response to charges that black religious institutions were impelled toward racial separation, a sin he reserved for white Christianity. The persistence of a segregated religious polity became a driving theme throughout Mays's work which tethered the future of black churches to the emergence of a true interracial Christianity.[60]

The central problem of black religious life for Mays was that black people were "overchurched" because they had disproportionately more churches than white Americans. The term itself was most often applied to the large numbers of churches, whether black or white, that remained when farm families deserted rural areas for the cities. But in the case of African Americans, the concern had been present even at the very founding of Southern black churches. Indeed, in his 1883 narrative history of black Americans, the historian Williams had warned that "the danger of the hour" was that too many black churches were being organized. "We have the quantity," he wrote. "Let us have the *quality* now."[61]

With the proliferation of black churches came a larger and more enduring issue: the question of who was to have authority over the newly won religious freedom that Southern blacks had begun to exercise by establishing churches away from the chilling surveillance of whites, and often of other, disapproving blacks as well. Writing half a century later in the 1930s, Mays was struggling against another growth spurt in black churches, a burgeoning number of storefront churches in black urban communities which appealed to rural, less well-educated migrants. In this context, "overchurching" became a black urban vice which was rooted in class differences but which posed a threat to all African Americans. Mays explained that "the establishment of churches by a relatively illiterate mass has been unrestrained" and he emphasized that "the Baptists, the Spiritualists, and the Holiness groups, which are the most active in dotting the streets with churches irrespective of need, are doing nothing to prohibit this promiscuous crowding together of churches." His use of the word "promiscuous" effectively conveyed his fear of unregulated reproduction of institutions he saw as sabotaging a move to larger, more financially secure churches with more restrained styles of worship.[62]

The particular "problem" that Mays confronted was a result both of religious freedom and of black religious diversification. For the most part, there was no centralized authority that could limit or regulate church expansion, even among his own Baptist denomination. This is one mark of the unfettered independence of most American Protestant churches, and one that extended even to the churches of black people. In the period in which Mays was writing, the effects of the Great Migration on African American religious life were becoming apparent. This was a movement not only of rural masses, but of the rural ministers among them. The large influx threatened to overwhelm existing black urban communities, including their clergy. The problem of "overchurching," then, entailed not only the proliferation of city churches, but the growth in the number of uneducated, Southern rural ministers serving in urban Northern communities.[63]

Mays urged that many small black churches be merged into a smaller number of larger ones. These could promote a "healthier church life" because they would be more financially sound. Under the leadership of an educated clergy, they would anchor the formation of healthy black urban communities. At the same time, consolidation would result in greater control over black religious life by reducing the number of ministers, especially those of lesser education who were likely to be at the helm of smaller churches.[64] This was consistent with Woodson's and Du Bois's arguments for consolidation, although their interests were focused more narrowly on fostering religiously grounded political action and economic cooperatives.

Mays also believed that black churches needed to be led by a better-educated ministry, a position he shared with many others, though from a different motivation. He feared that unless a better-educated ministry emerged, racial leadership might not be dominated by a black clerical class. In his opinion, that would be a loss in and of itself. Given the increasing numbers of largely uneducated rural ministers, and the challenges to community leadership from black men who were not ministers, Mays feared that preachers would lose their special claim to racial leadership at a time when they were most needed to fill a broader role. "The Negro minister," Mays explained, "will be challenged to assume more and more the role of a true prophet—the one who interprets the will of God to men—in personal, social, economic and religious life."[65]

Yet Mays rejected the view that churches should dedicate themselves to meeting the social and economic needs of black communities. He acknowledged something that others had ignored: few black churches had the financial resources to assume this responsibility or to fulfill it. "The church is so limited by lack of funds, equipment and personnel that it could not adequately assume all of the responsibilities the public might place upon it." Mays was especially aware of the vast social welfare and social service needs of black communities because his wife Sadie was an activist social worker with considerable experience in Florida and Atlanta. Urging black churches to tend primarily to religious activities, Mays insisted that they leave to the state and to other social agencies the "nonreligious" functions. But he ignored the problem of inadequate state resources and the racially disparate distribution of those resources at all levels of government.[66]

Mays, like Woodson and Du Bois before him, believed that the black churches' potential for racial leadership depended solely on the pulpit and on male ministerial leadership. Although he insisted that black preachers speak out on the political issues of the day, his definition of the political and social obligation of black churches turned less on meeting the practical needs of its members than on adding a "black prophetic voice" that would be embodied by male ministerial leadership.

Mays was silent on the place of women and congregants in that prophetic mission. He did acknowledge the preponderance of female membership in churches in general and in black churches in particular. Personal observation led him to conclude that women accounted for two-thirds of church attendance, and that "women do more of the church work." The larger and mostly unacknowledged problem for Mays and for all those who believed black churches should become central to black community and political life was that fewer than half of black men identified themselves as church members, and actual participation levels tended to be even lower than membership rates. If black churches were to be effective religious and political institutions, they would need to start attracting more black men or else cast their lot with the women already assembled.[67]

But instead of focusing on the absence of males, Mays endorsed an analysis that characterized black women's higher commitment to churches as a problem. The U.S. Census Bureau had revealed that women far outnumbered men in most religious bodies, especially in Protestant churches where nearly two-thirds of the members were women. That proportion essentially held steady in 1916, 1926, and 1936. This presentation of the sex-ratio data for religious bodies overall was straightforward, with little interpretation or analysis. Yet the treatment of this same information for "colored organizations" was accompanied by a narrative that interpreted virtually the same sex ratios in African American churches with an emphasis on the absence of males. That critique evolved over the decades into even more pointed concerns about black women's "excess" participation rates. In 1926, the Census Bureau began referring to an entity called the "Negro Church" in which the "excess of females" was "very pronounced," a notion that became embedded in the methodology itself. The phrase "excess females" was reserved for black women despite the fact that women members continued to outnumber men in churches overall.[68]

The fact that women predominated in congregations—long known to be true even before the census made it "official"—had caused concern in many white denominations in the late nineteenth and early twentieth centuries. It was said that religion and pastoral leadership had become "feminized." Yet the census narrative did not characterize sex ratios as a problem to churches overall but reserved it exclusively for the "Negro church."[69]

Mays not only endorsed the Census Bureau's view but attributed religious emotionalism among black people to the overwhelming presence of black women. And in arguing that black churches needed to attract more members, Mays failed to acknowledge any special need to focus on the absence of black men. "Since only 46 percent of Negro male adults and 73 percent of Negro female adults are churched, wise evangelism must increase the number of Negroes in the church." But he does not emphasize that with nearly three-quarters of black women already attending church, any sizable increase in membership would have to come from men who remained on the outside.[70]

Mays's book highlighted many of the same aspects of black church life that earlier critics had noted: too many small churches, too few financial resources, an emphasis on otherworldly theology, and an uneducated ministry. Whereas Woodson had placed responsibility for these failings on black people themselves, especially on black preachers, Mays saw these shortcomings as the consequence of broader racial, political, and economic inequities, and as a result of "the failure of American Christianity in the realm of race-relations." He asserted, however, that black churches were permeated with a "thorough democratic spirit" which encouraged black people of all classes and occupations to mingle freely and happily without any class stratification. The implicit contrast was with white churches which Mays continued to cast as antidemocratic because of their racially discriminatory practices.[71]

The Negro's Church was reviewed in newspapers and religious publications as well as journals. It was treated as a "scientific study" of objectivity and fairness. The press emphasized two points:

that there were too many black churches and that black religious emotionalism was waning. The latter was a bit of public relations sleight-of-hand since the weight of the observational evidence in the book actually went in the opposite direction. But advancing the image that black churches were no longer emotional or primitive was in keeping with Mays's intellectual concerns. Indeed, his next project tried to refute the notion that all black people engaged in highly emotional religious practices aimed solely toward the otherworldly. He did this by setting out to explore a broad range of ideas about God held by black people.[72]

In 1934, Mays had assumed the position as dean of the School of Religion at Howard University, a post he held until 1940. He had completed his doctorate in religion at the University of Chicago and had published his dissertation *The Negro's God as Reflected in His Literature* in 1938. The book explored conceptions of God held by a wide range of African Americans, beginning in the eighteenth century.

In 1930, Marc Connelly's Pulitzer Prize–winning play *The Green Pastures* presented one of the most popular portrayals of black religion in that era. The play, which was later made into a film, greatly offended Mays and other African Americans with its buffoonish treatment of black religious life replete with giddy, childlike believers who were overly emotional. Mays aimed, in part, to contest the popular impression that all black people were guilty of religious primitivism, political passivity, and otherworldliness.[73]

Mays's work turned on a bifurcation of African American thought that distinguished the "Negro masses" from more literate and better-educated black people. As Mays put it, he wanted to see if the thinking of the black educated elite was in "harmony with or is a protest against the ideas of God as found among the masses." He was not so concerned about the accuracy of *The Green Pastures'* depiction of uneducated black religious thought; rather, he wanted to prove that it did not represent all blacks, in particular educated religious people like him. He used a rich variety of "classical" black literature—essays, memoirs, slave narratives, oratory, poems, novels, the work of social scientists—as primary evidence of the ideas of better-educated black people.[74]

To avoid becoming entrapped in the essentialist notion that black people were religiously different from other oppressed people or, more obviously, from white people, Mays emphasized shifting political conditions rather than racial difference as his key explanatory mechanism. For this reason, he concluded that the conceptions of God held by black people were driven not by any urge toward a separate racially specific theology or philosophy, but entirely by the shifting political and social restrictions under which they lived. He argued that their thoughts about God were not the result simply of their being of one race, but rather the consequence of the common conditions under which they suffered. Mays tried so hard to overcome assumptions of racially embedded characteristics among black people that he could concede no cultural differences between the races either. Instead, he tended to conflate race and culture, and did not allow for the existence of an identifiable black religious culture or racially specific theological distinctions.

Unlike Woodson, Mays acknowledged the presence of black women in early black church history but he did this in an unusual and telling way, by invoking a cautionary tale from the memoir of Daniel Payne, a very prominent AME bishop and educator. Black women in a local AME church objected to having a white woman join the congregation; when the woman was permitted to join over their objections, the women refused to pay their pastor's salary or contribute to Payne's salary as presiding bishop, unless they both supported their position. The pastor of the church acceded to the women's demand and "turned" the white woman out. Payne considered this an unchristian act and refused the pastor any other appointment in his conference, comparing him to "pro-slavery" ministers. Mays used this story to show how committed Payne was to the concept of nondiscrimination in worship, but the tale reveals the power of black women congregants while claiming they were somehow less truly Christian. Consequently, they needed an external check on their influence, here represented by the bishop's defiance of both the black women and their compliant minister.[75]

Mays's own concerns about the influence of black women were ultimately blended with his perception of the more urgent problem of the loss of Christian belief among his fellow African American intellectuals, especially those who were female. Woodson had warned of this loss of faith earlier and had blamed it on the absence of an educated ministerial leadership class. Mays blamed it on the political conditions of the day, but not directly on black clerical failings. Reacting to some of the dissenting religious views of prominent and popular black writers and activists, Mays appeared stunned and perplexed. He warned his readers that he was taking them into "new territory" where black writers "abandon the idea of God" altogether. He explained their "heretical" writings as the product of personal bitterness and disappointment with the unjust treatment of African Americans.

Mays's evidence on this issue came largely from the works of black women writers. Nella Larsen's *Quicksand* received his greatest attention. Mays called the novel the "most expressive" embodiment of a loss of faith. He seemed captivated by Helga Crane, the mixed-race protagonist, who attempts to reconnect with her own black folk heritage by marrying a Southern rural black preacher. Helga experiences a religious conversion that ultimately fails her. Deeply disillusioned by the political conditions and the suffering of black people, she rejects black religion altogether:

And this, Helga decided, was what ailed the whole Negro race in America, this fatuous belief in the white man's God, this childlike trust in full compensation for all woes and privations in "Kingdom Come." . . . How the white man's God must laugh at the great joke He had played on them! Bound them to slavery, then to poverty and insult, and made them bear it unresistingly, uncomplainingly almost, by sweet promises of mansions in the sky by and by.[76]

Helga seemed to embody for Mays what might happen if educated black people pulled away from religion because emotional and un-educated ministers espoused otherworldliness and ignored political realities.

Larsen's critique of Southern black rural religion simply hit too close to home for Mays and for the family he loved. The religion that Larsen rejected was the kind of faith that existed in the Southern rural world in which Mays had been born and reared, be-fore his move into the privileged worlds of Bates, Chicago, and Howard. Even though he no longer lived in that world, he re-mained loyal and respectful of it and this may have accounted for his visceral reaction against her analysis. "Long before I knew what it was all about, and since I learned to know, I heard the Pastor of the church of my youth plead with the members of his congrega-tion not to try to avenge the wrongs they suffered, but to take their burdens to the Lord in prayer," he recalled. His minister did this es-pecially "when the racial situation was tense or when Negroes went to him for advice concerning some wrong inflicted upon them by their oppressor." Mays believed that "this idea of God had telling effects upon the Negroes in my home community. It kept them submissive, humble, and obedient. It enabled them to keep on go-ing on." On this point, Larsen was consistent with Mays except she did little to concede any ameliorative benefit from religion.[77]

Mays had abandoned aspects of his own religious upbringing and had found ways to reconcile being black, educated, and religious, so that he could fight for political progress. Larsen's novel raised the specter of educated black women abandoning religion and the churches to the poor masses. Who, then, would be left to support the educated clergy Mays was calling to leadership? Certainly not the masses of black women and men already in churches but seen as immersed in otherworldliness. For him, Larsen's fictionalized move away from the realm of black religion threatened the future of the church he envisioned as being capable of advancing the social conditions of black people. His church would be led by an educated elite open to alliances within the wider world of interracial Christianity.

Larsen's own life and writings presented a model of modern black womanhood that challenged Mays's vision. Of mixed racial descent and rejected by her white mother's family, Larsen married into a prominent, religiously active, well-educated black family known to Mays. Being neither religious nor a mother, Larsen carved a path for herself that did not conform to traditional expectations. Openly dismissive of religion and of African American churches in particular, she managed to alienate religious African Americans like Mays and her educated in-laws, who had served in black churches for generations. Larsen also rejected the value of black colleges which were revered by many, including Mays who dedicated his life to black educational institutions.[78]

None of this would have endeared Larsen to many educated black readers, but her literary talent won her novel much attention and drew many admirers, including Du Bois. Praising Larsen for creating a female character who would not surrender to "hypocrisy and convention," he cast Helga Crane as "typical of the new, honest, young fighting woman—the one on whom 'race' sits negligibly and Life is always first and its wandering path is but darkened, not obliterated, by the shadow of the Veil." By this he meant that she was independent from the conventions of religion, gender, and politics that usually restrained many black women. He urged readers of *The Crisis* to buy the book and make Larsen "write many more novels."[79]

Du Bois had explored the question of black elite disillusionment with traditional black religion and the resulting political implications in his 1928 novel *Dark Princess*. This was a maudlin fantastical tale of an educated black male protagonist who rejects the corruption of black urban electoral politics embodied in the schemes of his ambitious black middle-class wife. Instead, he embraces a messianic vision in which political union with an East Asian princess produces a son destined to bring about worldwide revolutionary change. In *Dark Princess*, as in Larsen's and Mays's writings, a black woman occupies a central symbolic position. The black wife of the male protagonist stands in for and is rejected as the compromised believer in modern electoral politics. In Du Bois's revolutionary messianic vision, black women play no role at all, being denied even a cameo as the mother of the world's newest male savior. This role is granted instead to the brown princess from India.[80]

Set outside of orthodox politics and religions, the novel nonetheless engages directly the question of what kind of religion and politics are needed for true worldwide revolution on the question of race. For Du Bois, the struggle requires faith in the future and faith in the possibility of progress. Whether one believes in God or any god or no god matters less than faith and hope as necessary catalysts for political work, especially the most revolutionary kind.

The loss that most concerned Mays was the possibility that elite African Americans, including women, were abandoning faith and by implication denying any role for religion, religious institutions, and religious leaders in those struggles. Mays attributed such ideas in the writings of black intellectuals after 1914 to a general mood of disillusionment stemming from the massive destruction of World War I and the persistence of racial segregation. "The Negro's incredulity, frustrations, agnosticism, and atheism do not develop as the results of the findings of modern science nor from the observation that nature is cruel and indifferent; but primarily because in the social situation, he finds himself hampered and restricted." Mays allowed for the possibility of a shift back to a firm belief in God, provided there was an improvement in the contemporary social, economic, and political conditions facing black people in the late 1930s.[81]

While Mays's first book had generated much popular and scholarly attention, *The Negro's God* received less notice despite its innovations. It did attract Woodson's attention, however. Mays had treated Woodson's views on religion respectfully in his book; but Woodson did not return the favor and attacked him for the class assumptions he thought were embedded in the work. "We do not find in *The Negro's God* . . . the conception developed in the mind of the Negro backwoodsmen, sharecroppers, menials, mechanics and artisans who constitute the large majority of the Negro population." This, of course, was the same charge that Du Bois had made against Woodson's book. Even less generously, Woodson accused Mays of not crediting black people with any theological contributions of their own.[82]

Mays had searched for political and theological ground that could straddle the conceptual binary he had created between believers in the otherworldly and the politically engaged. At the end of his book, he identified himself with "that type of Negro modernists who took God out of the compensatory setting and used the idea in areas of social reconstruction. It was an effort to bring the conception of God up to date—to make God equal to the task required in social rehabilitation stimulated by the War."[83]

Inserting himself into his text, Mays credited faith in God with saving black men in particular from resorting to violent revolution to achieve their rights. "His faith in God has not only served as an opiate for the Negro," he explained, "but it has suggested and indicated that pacific and legal methods are to be used in achieving them." For Mays, religion was still the avenue through which black manliness and the rights of black manhood could be achieved peacefully. His ideas about progress for the race rested on gendered notions of black religious and political leadership—an ideal later embodied through his leadership of Morehouse College.[84]

Mays issued a warning and a call for a new kind of politically informed religious leadership that could work toward this end. "It is not too much to say that unless liberal prophetic religion moves more progressively to the left in the effort to achieve complete citizenship rights for the Negro, he will become more irreligious and he will become more militant and communistic in his efforts to attain full manhood in American life." This admonition seemed aimed at both black and white religious leadership, as Mays tethered his hopes for black religious reform and black male political leadership to the future of white Christianity. He envisioned an interracial and ecumenical enterprise that called for an end to segregated churches and, as a logical and theological corollary, included an end to separate black churches. Faith in the "Negro's God" as defined by Mays would challenge the very existence of the "Negro's church."[85]

Du Bois, Woodson, and Mays diverged on many points, but they believed in the centrality of churches to the institutional structure of African American communities and to the political fortunes of the race. For them, black churches were too emotional in worship style and too focused on heaven and not enough on earth. Churches were too small, too many, and too independent of any centralized authority, including any control over their growth and direction. The masses of poor black people were comfortable with emotional services and otherworldliness; middle-class and elite blacks were not, but had no way of acquiring influence over black religious life. As a result, black churches had been in steady decline since Reconstruction and were failing to meet the growing contemporary needs generated by war, migration, economic depression, and Jim Crow.

When reforms were suggested, they rested upon the development of a class of educated male ministers who would lead their churches to a larger political and social role in their communities. Most argued for a religiously based collective identity that would depend upon a consolidation of church resources perhaps best embodied by Woodson's proposed United Negro Church. This vision offered the tantalizing potential of uniting millions of black people not just by color but by religion, and organizing them for political purposes through a nationwide network of local churches. But Mays dissented and linked the future of black churches to his call for an interracial Christianity.

Each of these men blamed the weaknesses of the "Negro church" on the failings of its uneducated male ministers. The millions of black women who worshiped and worked in the churches empowered those ministers. When Woodson urged the masses of black people to rise up against corrupt ministerial leadership and transform their churches into the model he envisioned for them, the people in the best position to do this were mostly women. The scholars' resentment of church leadership rested on an implicit belief that the churches were controlled not only by the wrong men, but by the leaderless and misguided women who financed and supported them. Thus, the churches suffered from the failings of an uneducated and flaccid male leadership as well as from the persistent authority of the emotional women within them. The women within the church were seen not so much as passive in the pews, but rather as obstacles to progress.

In order for the true historical mission of the church to succeed,

Du Bois, Woodson, and Mays called for a new black male ministerial leadership that could control and harness the power of the overwhelmingly female membership. The fulfillment of this vision depended on a nonexistent cadre of educated men called to ministry in sufficient numbers to lead the churches, the most local and numerous of all institutions. And in order to fulfill their mission as these thinkers envisioned it, the churches would need considerable financial resources.

These two requirements—a sufficient number of educated progressive ministers and churches with ample financial resources—were a demographic impossibility for Jim Crow and Depression-era black America. Du Bois, Mays, and Woodson knew this. So beneath all of their complaints about the churches and their hopes for reconfiguration lay the sad reality that these small local institutions could not bear the enormous political responsibilities being laid upon them. The search for an institutional base for black political and social advancement seemed to run into a dead end at the church door. That, in the end, was not so much just the problem of the "Negro church," but the more fundamental issue of the dearth of black political and economic institutions and of the financial resources to support them.

2

Illusions of Black Religion

THE first generation of African Americans who studied black churches had questioned whether those churches could be reformed to function effectively as "race institutions" that could provide political leadership. In the late 1930s and 1940s, a new group of social scientists shifted attention to the nature of African American religious belief. Under an aura of social scientific rigor, these scholars became increasingly influential and recognized voices of public authority on the place of religion in African American political life.

Their works were part of an explosion of social science interest in American life and culture in the early twentieth century. There emerged new techniques to explore the lives of immigrants, rural Americans, young people, and city dwellers caught in the vast structural, economic, and social shifts of early twentieth-century America. Questions about urbanization, poverty, race, discrimination, and ethnic tension received special notice in the wake of increased population density, economic depression, dramatic global developments, and a world war based on fascist claims. Deteriorating economic conditions were relieved only by the industrial buildup of World War II, which in turn generated even greater waves of black migrants.

African American internal migration in the 1940s had truly reached "great" proportions as black people streamed out of the rural South into Northern, Southern, and Western cities that offered new jobs and opportunities created by wartime demand. In cities, blacks formed larger communities with greater political potential than those in rural areas. Their claims for an end to segregation and for equal access to jobs, education, and housing took on even greater fervor. These demands helped fuel political organizing, mobilizing, and debating on race relations and poverty. The problem of race could no longer be seen as unique to the South, although the majority of black people remained in that region.

A nascent field of "race relations" stimulated a boom in philanthropic funding for research on ethnic and racial groups. The worlds in which African Americans lived and worked became laboratories in which social scientists sought answers to the problem of daunting racial inequities. These shifts also created a new set of opportunities for that small cohort of black men who had received doctorates in social science from major white institutions. Among the most prominent were those trained in sociology under Robert Park at the University of Chicago—in particular, Charles S. Johnson and E. Franklin Frazier. In addition to their work, two of the century's most important works of social science—*Black Metropolis*, by St. Clair Drake and Horace Cayton, and the collaborative study *An American Dilemma*, led by Gunnar Myrdal—also took on African Americans and race relations as their topic of inquiry. Religious life, beliefs, and practices received special scrutiny from these researchers, since churches remained undeniably the most ubiquitous, influential, and stable institutions in black communities.

In contrast to Du Bois, Woodson, and Mays, these social scientists employed more sophisticated techniques such as questionnaires, surveys, interviews, attitude tests, and opinion surveys. With those tools, they shifted focus away from African American churches and looked more closely at individual and collective religious beliefs through psychological and personality analyses. In some cases, the data were collected in such a way as to allow the voices of the people in the community to filter through and tell us what they believed their own religious practices meant and what they thought about black churches and black preachers.

At a time when the world of formally trained scholars was almost entirely closed to black women, it was these men who constructed social scientific knowledge about black religious belief and institutions. In doing so, they occupied overlapping roles as trespassers, as intermediaries, as experts, and, ultimately, as creators of narratives they told about respectability and deviance in black communities. They viewed their task as one of charting the race's march toward a modern civilized present. They believed themselves empowered to judge the degree to which African Americans were adjusting to the larger white culture, a world in which they considered themselves the best representatives of black manhood and the race as a whole.

Despite their training and dedication, however, these men were intellectually and emotionally unprepared for their confrontation with the dominance and power that religious beliefs, practices, and institutions held in black community life, especially among the masses of working-class, rural, and Southern people, including those who migrated to cities. Attempts by scholars to rationalize religious belief were made more difficult by their engagement in other ongoing debates about black religious primitivism and African spiritual legacies. All of these men were publicly engaged intellectuals called upon to represent and to speak for the black community in multiple venues. They were expected to do the work of documenting and describing black religious belief and religious institutions as well as offer prescriptions for reform. Their influence continues to this day because, along with Du Bois, Woodson, and Mays, they established the paradigms for studying black religion. Yet their work rested on the untested assumptions of those who preceded them and they often advanced old arguments without questioning them or listening to the ideas of their human subjects.

A few scholars on the margins of the social scientific enterprise did challenge the received wisdom of the professions in which they were trained. For different reasons their work and their approaches did not enjoy acceptance or wield influence until well after their deaths when larger political and intellectual shifts brought them renewed attention. Among these were Zora Neale Hurston, Hortense Powdermaker, and Arthur Fauset, all of whom were anthropologists and ethnographers who studied African American religious cultures and practices. They were more attuned to hearing the practices, voices, and ideas of the people they were studying and took a more flexible view of the relationship between religion, politics, and lived experience.

CHARLES Johnson enrolled in the Sociology Department at the University of Chicago because he wanted to train in a school that had a strong religious affiliation like Virginia Union University, the black Baptist institution where his father, a minister, had sent him for his preparatory and college training. At Chicago, Johnson studied with sociologist Robert Park, whose courses on race and African Americans covered subjects that at the time received little attention at white institutions. Park's work veered from the virulent racism that characterized much American scholarship on the subject. At the same time, his belief in "scientific objectivity" meant that he did not see racial reform as part his mission, though he believed that sociological knowledge could help in this process. By the time Franklin Frazier arrived at Chicago in 1927, Park's commitment to studying race relations and African Americans was well established as was his interest in training black scholars.[1]

Johnson and Frazier, with their doctorates in sociology, belonged to the second generation of black scholars in that field. Although they were nearly the same age, they earned their degrees more than a decade apart—Johnson in 1918 and Frazier in 1931. Their careers eventually mirrored each other, as both came to spend most of their scholarly lives at two of the most influential black universities of their day, Fisk and Howard. In 1928, after serving for seven years as director of research and editor of *Opportunity* magazine for the National Urban League, Johnson assumed the chair of the newly established Department of Social Sciences at Fisk. He held that post until 1946 when he became Fisk's first black president. Frazier worked with Johnson at Fisk from 1929 to 1934. He then returned to Howard where he had studied as an undergraduate. In 1934, he became chair of Howard's sociology department, a post he held until his death in 1962.[2]

Frazier and Johnson were among the first professionally trained black sociologists with access to the funds and institutional resources needed for large-scale research projects. In the late 1930s, they directed a series of extensive case studies of black communities and institutions in the rural South and the urban North. In the course of that work, they confronted some of the questions about black churches and black religion that Du Bois, Woodson, and Mays had raised. One of Johnson's earliest works, the 1934 book *Shadow of the Plantation*, a study of rural black life in Macon County, Alabama, described emotional black church services and funerals, where congregants sang "lustily."[3] Johnson argued, like Woodson, that the emotionalism of black worship was not a survival from Africa, but had been borrowed from Southern whites during slavery. It was "now discarded by whites, and discarded by many Negroes as well, as they advance from one level of culture to another." He interpreted the continuation of these religious practices in 1930s Alabama as a sign of cultural lag—but one due to economic rather than racial hindrances.[4]

The powerfully resistant presence of black religious belief in this community and in the lives of the people in Macon County was undeniable. Of the 612 families studied, all but 17 belonged to a church and attended regularly. The services Johnson observed were filled with enthusiastic people who used body and voice to express spiritual power and ecstasy. "Nowhere," he conceded, did he observe "anything approaching religious skepticism." Rather, "the dominant attitude was one of unquestioning belief in and reliance upon God as a protection against everything that was feared, and an answer to everything that could not be understood."[5]

Johnson's findings echoed some of the ideas that Du Bois, Woodson, and Mays had expressed about black churches, especially those in the rural South. While they had viewed black churches as problems, Johnson was more ambivalent. He was unable to dismiss the power of the faith and the religious commitments of the people he had observed and documented. Indeed, he seemed resigned to accepting the God-centered world he encountered in Macon County. Johnson's own religious upbringing may well have had some residual influence on him.

In 1938 the American Council on Education created an American Youth Commission which invited a number of social scientists to undertake research on the impact of the economic depression on young people. An important group of reports on black youth were included in the research agenda and four classic texts were produced in this series: Allison Davis and John Dollard's *Children of Bondage*, which focused on black youth in the Deep South; W. Lloyd Warner's *Color and Human Nature*, about black Chicago youth; Johnson's *Growing Up in the Black Belt,* which was based on studies of black communities in states surrounding Tennessee; and Frazier's *Negro Youth at the Crossways,* which studied young black people in the border cities of Louisville and Washington.[6]

All the researchers were instructed to produce studies that would explore this question: "What are the effects upon the personality development of Negro youth of their membership in a minority racial group?" Implicit in the query was the expectation that the studies would document the deleterious impact of racial prejudice and discrimination on young black people. In some ways, this research was designed to provide ammunition for ongoing debates about the impact of political, social, and cultural factors on black achievement, as well as to provide evidence for the need for institutional reform and supports. Both Johnson and Frazier sought to answer the question in part by inquiring whether black churches and black Christian beliefs were demonstrably hindering the psychological and political development of black youth.

Johnson and his researchers administered six questionnaires to more than 2,200 young black men and women in Tennessee, Mississippi, and Georgia. In addition, each respondent was contacted for an interview, as were the parents in more than 900 families. The result was a series of "personality profiles" followed by chapters devoted to particular aspects of the young people's lives, such as their social worlds, schools, and recreations. Other sections concentrated on their attitudes toward their current status, toward their job and economic prospects, and toward whites and blacks.[7]

Johnson acknowledged that religious attitudes were an important part of the cultural and psychological heritage of young black people and devoted a chapter to this topic. As in his earlier book, he presented several case studies of emotion-laden black worship services based on firsthand observations.[8] For the specific discussions of the views of young black people toward ministers, religion, and the church, he depended on personality and attitudinal tests as well as on extended follow-up interviews with them and, in many cases, with their parents. In one of those tests, composed of questions with true-or-false answers, the only statements about religion which a majority of respondents thought true were these: "The preacher tells us to do a lot of things that he doesn't do himself" and "All ministers want to do is to get as much money out of people as they can." When it came to the remaining questions which imputed negative traits to the church or to religion, more than two-thirds of the participants disagreed.[9]

From this and interview data, Johnson confirmed that young black people had a profound disrespect for black ministers because they viewed them as morally hypocritical and poorly educated. Yet this distrust of black ministers did not translate into a general criticism of the church itself. Many young people, for example, expressed enthusiasm for their church Sunday schools which were often run by schoolteachers. And overall, Johnson found that young blacks were not antagonistic to religion or opposed to the church; only a small percentage were at all skeptical about the value of religion in their lives. Indeed, many of those interviewed related stories of their own religious conversions, even as Johnson cast doubt on the depth of their convictions.[10] There was a stark contrast then between the harsh attitudes they expressed toward preachers and the strong endorsement they gave to the church and to religion in general.

The embrace of religion's traditional functions by these young people seemed hard to differentiate from that of their parents or that of the adults in Johnson's earlier study. Despite their expressed desire for a more moral and better-educated ministerial leadership, they still embraced the church and the power of religion. If Johnson was looking for evidence of a generational rebellion from the churches and their teachings or evidence of the churches' ill effects on the development of young people, his research methods had failed to yield it.

Johnson's overall conclusions downplayed the degree to which his subjects allied themselves with religious beliefs. He simply accused the rural church of preserving anachronistic cultural values that might otherwise have been altered to better suit modern urban life. "Its greatest present value," he wrote, "appears to be that of providing emotional relief for the fixed problems of a hard life." Young people required this less than their parents because they were "more mobile and less docile" and more literate and better educated, but he presented no evidence to support this conjecture. He concluded that black churches needed to develop specific programs for young people in order to remain a "vital social and spiritual force in their lives."[11]

When Frazier began the research for his study in 1938, he was an accomplished sociologist who had already completed his seminal work on the black family, *The Negro Family in the United States*, for which he had conducted thousands of extended interviews with black men and women. Blending those with an account of the evolution of the black family in slavery and beyond, Frazier had written a bold and controversial history. In his work on young black people, *Negro Youth at the Crossways*, Frazier relied on similar qualitative techniques but drew on a far smaller sample. More comfortably than Johnson, he applied psychological and sometimes psychiatric explanations to the attitudes of the young people he interviewed. His chapter on black churches treats them and the family as the two most crucial institutions affecting personality development. Yet his findings about the relationship between the church, religion, and young people presented a very different picture from Johnson's, because he had approached his work with a different set of questions in mind.[12]

On the basis of extended interviews with more than 250 young people in Louisville and Washington, D.C., most in their late teens and early twenties, Frazier drew several critical conclusions about the role of churches in the development of black youth.[13] First, and most assertively, he declared that although the churches were run by black people, there was nothing about the churches' "ideology" that helped young people develop greater self-respect. "The majority of black youth of all classes believe that God is white . . . that He resembles a kindly, paternalistic, upper-class white man. They believe that because of His goodness and justice, colored people will not suffer discrimination in the other world." Second, the church paid no attention to the problem of the low status of blacks in this world, offering merely the release of ecstatic worship and the comfort of heavenly rewards. Third, young black people were extremely critical of the way churches avoided the daily problems of survival in a prejudiced world.[14]

Frazier's final and most intriguing conclusion was that most young black people were deeply harmed by their belief that God was white. He sought evidence to reinforce the certitude of his belief. "Some of them accept literally the pictures of God and Christ given in Sunday school lessons," he wrote. "Although many are perplexed about whether to picture the Deity as black or white, their responses imply that the idea of white dominance is extended to include even God."[15] He presented his verdict as having been proved conclusively by his research, but excerpts from the interviews work to diminish the certainty of his claims.

What is clear from the answers given is that his subjects struggled politely to answer questions many seemed to find absurd. Asked if Christ was a white man or a "Negro," they answered matter-of-factly that Christ was definitely not a "Negro," that he was either white or a Jew, or both. "Jesus was white," said one. "At least he ought to be if he isn't. His parents were white. The Bible says his mother and father, Joseph and Mary, were Jews; so he must have been too." Another explained, "As a Jew, He might have been dark, but Jews are supposed to be white, so I guess that makes Him white too."[16]

As they tried to make distinctions between depictions of Christ and the historical Christ, these young people were keenly aware that the power to represent Christ has rested with white people, with consequences that they noted with touches of irony and humor.

> White men paint all of the pictures of Him. So, black or white in life, He is made white in reproductions of His likeness.

> Negro or white, by the time white people got through [with depicting him], they made him white too.

> He was a white man. If by any chance He was anything else, the white people would have taken great pains to make him a white man throughout those many, many years.

> Pictures I've seen of Him are all white, so I just took for granted He was a white man. Had He been a Negro, I'd sure heard about it and these Negro preachers would be constantly reminding white people of that fact.[17]

Frazier's central claim that most of the young people in his study thought of God as a great white father presiding over a racially egalitarian heaven may have been linked to his own political position on religion as much as to the interviews themselves. His conclusion that his subjects had suffered psychological damage seems driven in part by his own political beliefs which had been embedded in the interview questions. At some point in his own adolescence, Frazier had grown deeply contemptuous of organized religion and had become an outspoken atheist, a position he held throughout his life. Writing in his diary later in 1950, Frazier cast his own general frustration with Christian doctrine as a simple conflict between intellect and belief: "What intelligent and intellectually honest person believes in the immortality of the soul or that we shall be punished after death for our sins?"[18]

The conclusions he drew may reflect his own disappointment that the bright and articulate young people he interviewed brought with them so much evidence of the churches' presence in their lives and in the communities in which they lived. For Frazier, the perpetuation of a Christian belief system generation after generation impeded black political development, and by that measure these young people were yet another lost generation. His assertions about the psychological and political implications of their embrace of Christianity and its white icons were consistent with other radical critiques of his day such as Garveyism and the Nation of Islam. And so he rested his case after presenting evidence that young black people were still being brought up worshiping a Jesus depicted as white and believing in a racially egalitarian heaven.

What is most remarkable in these interviews for us today—as it must have been for Frazier—was the degree to which the church and religion were integrated into these young people's lives. When asked about their religion rather than about the color of Jesus or the color of people in heaven, many of those interviewed related their own religious experiences. One of them said, "I was reared in the church. My mother is church organist. I think I had religion six years before I was baptized. I was very bashful. I was ashamed to get up in front of people and tell them I had religion. This worried me a great deal. Finally, during one revival I got up enough nerve to admit I had religion. I felt very happy and cried a great deal."[19] Another interview went this way:

Q. Why do you shout?
A. I shout because I just feel the spirit coming on me.

Q. How does it feel?

A. When the spirit comes on you it feels just like a bucket of water has been poured on me.

Q. What is the spirit?

A. The spirit is the grace of God. When the preacher starts to telling the things you know is true and have experienced, it makes you feel so good you feel like shouting.[20]

Frazier concluded that black youth resented the emotionalism of the church although the transcripts reveal very few complaints along those lines. In fact, preacher hypocrisy seems to have been the more common source of disaffection—a criticism focused on the individual minister, not on the churches or on religion itself. Several of those interviewed strongly condemned impropriety among preachers, primarily on the grounds of sexual misconduct:

It's a shame the way most of the Baptist preachers flirt with the women in their church. I remember when I used to go to Rev. C's church, he was the fastest man I've ever heard of.

Rev. J sure has got a bad reputation. You just can't talk to him without somebody saying you are flirting or Rev. J is running after you.

Old S. is an old-time colored preacher. He believes in all this Hallelujah come to Jesus. He believes in coming to see the sisters, too. . . . He likes to make easy money too.[21]

In this respect, young people in Louisville and Washington expressed views consistent with those that Johnson had found in his study of their Southern rural counterparts. They were not being driven away from the churches in droves as had been claimed. They seemed to hold fast to religious belief even though they were critical of black ministers but not because of their emotionalism and otherworldly theology; rather they judged them to be morally and sexually corrupt and financially irresponsible, often preying on the women in the pews of their own churches. It was moral hypocrisy rather than lack of education that was the primary cause of their disrespect and dismissal of black ministerial leadership.

Frazier remained focused on ministers and not on the internal logic of black religious people in the rural South. This was partly due to the limits of the sociological methods and interpretive frameworks on which he and Johnson had relied. They would have needed to use the tools of ethnography to conduct more sustained community research, but there were only a handful of people interested in African American religious culture who employed those techniques in the 1930s. Among them was the brilliant black writer, folklorist, and intellectual Zora Neale Hurston who studied anthropology with Franz Boas and Melville Herskovits while an undergraduate at Barnard and a Ph.D. student at Columbia. Although she abandoned work on the doctorate, she used her methodological training in her years of extended excursions documenting rural folk cultures in the American South, and eventually in Jamaica, the Bahamas, and Haiti. By the 1930s, she was the most respected expert on the folklore of black people in the United States and the Caribbean, even though she chose writing over teaching anthropology as her life's work. She incorporated material from her fieldwork into the novels for which she is best known and reported on other aspects of that work in scholarly articles and in her important collections of folklore. The daughter of a preacher and a Sunday school teacher, she gave her novels titles that attest to their religious themes, including *Their Eyes Were Watching God*, *Jonah's Gourd Vine*, and *Moses, Man of the Mountain*.[22]

An interest in a wide variety of religious beliefs and practices also was at the heart of Hurston's anthropological investigations and writings. In Nancy Cunard's 1934 anthology *The Negro*, Hurston published several essays, including one on conversions and visions and one on spirituals. In the latter, she chastised Du Bois (although not by name) for calling spirituals "sorrow songs" despite the fact that they were filled with life, joy, and vitality and continued to be created well after slavery. On the basis of her fieldwork, Hurston emphasized that conversions and visions were not simple hysterical eruptions but were produced only after long periods of praying, fasting, and seeking. She characterized the vitality of black religious services as a "conscious work of art," marked by a seeming informality but governed by a set of definite forms, especially in its prayers. "The beautiful prayer receives the accolade as well as the beautiful song. It is merely a form of expression which people generally are not accustomed to think of as art. Nothing outside the Old Testament is as rich in figure as a Negro prayer."[23]

In one way, however, Hurston differed sharply from Frazier. She allied herself with her teacher Herskovits and argued that shouting was undoubtedly a survival of the African belief in spirit-possession which she had observed in Haiti. "The implication is the same," she wrote. "It is a sign of special favor from the spirit that it chooses to drive out individual consciousness temporarily and use the body for its expression." She linked that back to Africa. "The Saints, or the Sanctified Church is a revitalizing element in Negro music and religion. It is putting back into Negro religion those elements which were brought over from Africa onto Christianity as soon as the Negro came in contact with it, but which are being rooted out as the American Negro approaches white concepts." According to Hurston, black sanctified churches were restoring primitive altars but were doing this under the new name of Christ. More emphatically, Hurston characterized the proliferation of urban sanctified churches, which was of much concern to Mays and Woodson, as a form of active protest against the religious practices of black Christians who had more education and money. Members of sanctified churches ridiculed the idea of the educated black preacher. "They say of that type of preacher, 'Why he don't preach at all. He just lectures.' And the way they say the word 'lecture' make it sound like horse-stealing. 'Why, he sound like a white man preaching.'"[24]

The bulk of Hurston's work on religion was focused on voodoo, obeah, and other practices whose origins she traced back to Africa. Studying voodoo in New Orleans and Haiti, and similar practices in Georgia, Jamaica, Florida, and South Carolina, Hurston eagerly embraced these diverse incarnations of African-derived religions. In contrast to many of her contemporaries, she treated these practices not as primitive magic but with the respect usually reserved for the major world religions. She saw these smaller religions as secret and potent, but entirely legitimate and spiritually legible. Of voodoo in Haiti, she wrote: "It is as formal as the Catholic Church anywhere." Like most systems of religion, she argued, its symbols were taken by outsiders too literally and were misunderstood and caricatured. Hurston took her role as participant-observer to include undergoing rites of initiation in voodoo in both the United States and Haiti, although she protected many of the most important secrets of those rituals in her accounts. While others were trying to disavow connections to Africa, Hurston insisted that African American religions could best be understood within a diasporic framework that looked not just to Africa, but to the other places in the hemispheres of black enslavement.[25]

In her work on religion, whether in fiction or in her essays, Hurston refused to rely on sociological archetypes and was incensed when her portrayal of a particular black preacher was referred to as an emblematic account of "the Negro preacher," precisely the sort of generalization she was trying to avoid. She wanted to write about black people, even preachers, as individuals and not racial representatives, as fully rounded characters with flaws, but who were not necessarily backward, broken down, or dispirited. In an era when other social scientists were busy charting the deleterious effects of racial oppression, Hurston cast her gaze elsewhere. "We talk about the race problem a great deal but go on living and laughing and striving like everybody else." The reaction to racism that she was most interested in was the "creative response" by which black people experienced joy and beauty in a variety of cultural settings, including especially religion and its prayers, dances, songs, rituals, and music. Moving beyond notions of acculturation, she argued that everything black people touched was reinterpreted for their own use, especially in their religions.[26]

Hurston showed great fidelity to the religions she studied and the meanings they held for the people who practiced them. She resisted the urging of those contemporary critics of her work, such as the philosopher Alain Locke and the writer Richard Wright, who chided her for not exploring the despair they believed racism wrought. Hurston emphasized that to evoke the image of "fourteen million frustrated Negroes" was insincere, a conviction based on her work and on her experience living among black people who had the fewest economic resources. "Racial bitterness," she argued, belonged in sociology, not in folklore or literature or religion where she found "black joy" in ample supply, despite the persistence of virulent racism.[27]

Some of Hurston's work on religion was not published until the 1980s after Alice Walker and a new generation of scholars rediscovered her and began to retrieve and collect her vast body of writings. Had her opportunities and her personal choices been different, perhaps she would have been able to produce an extended study of black religious practices among people in the Americas and Africa, as she had hoped to do. But this task was left to others

who were better positioned in the world of social scientific produc-
tion and who chose to follow that path.

One of those who had the training, the inclination, and the opportunity to pursue this work was the pioneering anthropologist
Hortense Powdermaker, who undertook an extended study of black
rural life in Mississippi in the early 1930s. Johnson and Frazier supported her efforts, but felt that prevailing racial conditions might
well work against her. Powdermaker was a white woman from Baltimore and a former labor organizer. She had received her Ph.D.
in anthropology in 1928 from the London School of Economics,
where she studied under Bronislaw Malinowski. Trained as a cultural anthropologist but with a keen interest in psychoanalysis, she
began her scholarly career with a close ethnographic study of a
Pacific island community which became the topic of her first book.
She returned to the United States and took a position as a research
associate at Yale's Institute of Human Relations. There, she pursued her interest in applying ethnographic methods to African
American communities.[28]

With funding from the Social Science Research Council,
Powdermaker spent a year in 1932 and 1933 living in the small
Mississippi delta town of Indianola studying both white and black
communities. In preparation, she had spent time residing at Fisk
and working for Johnson. Both Frazier and Johnson advised her to
hide the fact that she was Jewish, fearing that her religion, when
combined with her race and her sex, would create further obstacles
to her work. During the time she was in the South, she followed
their advice and passed as a Methodist. She occasionally was mis-
taken to be black, because of her dark hair, dark eyes, and olive
complexion and her association with black people. This fed rumors
among some blacks that she really was black but was passing for
white so she could have access to whites and gain their support for
her study. As a consequence of the racial and gender conventions

of the time, the primary informants for her study were black women, mostly schoolteachers, who paved the way for her repeated visits to black churches and religious meetings. Every week she attended many religious services and church-related functions with both blacks and whites and across a range of denominations.[29]

The book that resulted, *After Freedom: A Cultural Study in the Deep South*, provides thick descriptions that take us deep inside the worlds of Southern religious life. Powdermaker focuses on the pews rather than the pulpit and on the eloquence of the prayers and songs offered by the laity. Her writing captures the fluidity and formality of black liturgical practices, and the very real spiritual powers that were unleashed in emotional religious services where black church audiences were "actors" more essential than the preacher himself. Powdermaker portrayed black religious life as being rich and lively. The small churches that Mays had criticized for holding services only once or twice a month left their members free to visit other churches in nearby communities, worshiping easily across denominational lines. She concluded that there was less difference between Baptist and Methodist churches than between town and country churches, but she did notice the distinctiveness of the Church of God in Christ, a Holiness church. She also recognized that churches were important sources of communal entertainment and leisure activities. Going to church was taken seriously, but it also was fun and a place for socializing, humor, great music, and good food.[30]

Powdermaker concluded that shouting and getting religion were not spontaneous expressions, but were induced religious experiences that came only after long periods of prayer and fasting which culminated in feelings of being "as light as a feather" or in flight. These experiences were the work of devotion, sometimes over months and years of seeking. In this way, the people she studied defined religion not as simply a set of beliefs or creeds, but rather as a set of experiences that linked them to God. "Getting religion" meant just that. Religion was something to be achieved, to be earned through work, sacrifice, and personal devotion. The relationships that her primary informants, black women, had with their God were personal and profound, less concerned with the hereafter, and focused mainly on finding the strength for the struggles of daily life.[31]

Powdermaker attended both black and white churches and saw stark theological differences between the two religious communities. While white ministers preached "dread and doom," their black counterparts pictured "with equal vividness the joys that await the godly." For blacks, "benevolent mercy rather than stern justice" was the chief mission of their God. "The accent has shifted from hell to heaven, from retribution to forgiveness, from fear to hope." The Christian duty to love one's neighbors actually had been taken to heart by black believers.[32]

Much of the work of religious training was done in Sunday schools which were often taught by black public-school teachers, a fact mentioned in Johnson's work as well. In one Sunday school, a discussion ensued around the question of whether it was possible not to hate whites. Someone answered, to much laughter, "Yes, it is possible, but hard." The teacher expressed pity for the hatefulness of white people and warned that they would have to answer to God for their misdeeds. "'If we hate them,' she says, 'we poison ourselves. Christ loved His enemies and asked for their forgiveness; we should have Christ in us.'" In the discussion that followed, the older men present made the point that they feared whites more than they hated them, and they did not want to associate any more closely with them. They just wanted more economic opportunities and to be left alone to live in peace.[33]

The discussion shifted to racial politics. The Sunday school teacher spoke of Mahatma Gandhi and all that he had been able to achieve through sincerity of purpose and love. "'He has Christ in him' she declares, and adds: 'Christ suffered and so we must suffer. Christ even died for the world. It is through love we will conquer.'" The teacher, speaking in Mississippi in the 1930s, was making an argument that would be associated with the Southern civil rights movement decades later.[34]

The reference to Gandhi is not as surprising as it may seem. Readers of black newspapers like the *Chicago Defender* and the *Pittsburgh Courier*, which had national reach, or regional papers like the *Norfolk Journal and Guide*, the Atlanta *Daily World*, and the Baltimore *Afro-American*, or the journals of the NAACP, the AME Church, and the United Negro Improvement Association, would have been very familiar with Gandhi's campaigns in South Africa and India. All of those publications and many other black newspapers had embraced an internationalist vision that included extensive coverage of India's struggle for independence when Gandhi returned to the country in 1915. In particular, Du Bois enthusiastically championed Gandhi as an anticolonialist and used *The Crisis* as a forum for heated debates among African Americans about whether Gandhi's techniques could prevail against racial inequality in the United States. A number of prominent African American religious and political figures traveled to India in the 1930s to meet with Gandhi. Their travels were well-publicized in black newspapers as were visits to African American communities by Indian political figures. Gandhi himself addressed black Americans through the press, linking himself to Jesus and to their struggles against racism in the United States. One strand of American social scientific analysis had turned to India's Hindu caste system as an analytic tool for understanding American racial and economic stratifications.[35]

These early debates about the applicability of Gandhian techniques to the American example included Frazier, who vehemently opposed the idea that love and faith could overcome oppression. He advocated a "violent defense" because he saw the strategy of nonviolence as impractical and dangerous. "But suppose there should arise a Gandhi to lead Negroes without hate in their hearts to stop tilling the fields of the South under the peonage system; to cease paying taxes to States that keep their children in ignorance; and to ignore the iniquitous disfranchisement and Jim Crow laws. I fear we would witness an unprecedented massacre of defenseless black men and women in the name of Law and Order, and there would scarcely be enough Christian Sentiment in America to stay the flood of blood."[36]

Frazier's was a minority voice, however, as black newspapers in the 1920s, 1930s, and 1940s repeatedly carried pleas from journalists and activists for a black American Gandhi who would lead civil disobedience campaigns against segregation. Editorials with titles like "If We Had a Gandhi" and "Will a Gandhi Arise?" carried predictions that were far more optimistic than Frazier's. "We believe that some empty Jim Crow cars will some day worry our street car magnates in Southern cities when we get around to walking rather than suffer insult and injury to our wives and children." As prescient as this was, the "we" here referred to black men acting on behalf of black women and children. Few anticipated that the women would do some of that walking for themselves.[37]

Although Powdermaker made no comment on the reference to Gandhi in that Mississippi Sunday School, the willingness among religious African Americans to consider the idea that an Indian Hindu was another Christ deserves attention. It illustrates that African American Christianity was not a closed book, but that it was open to other prophets as they emerged, and remained alive to the possibility of the new so long as this resonated with its underlying theological and political principles. Black religious beliefs were not static in the 1920s and 1930s but were ever evolving and shifting. For this reason, they were elusive, and difficult to capture and categorize. Evidence of this characteristic was plentiful, though declensionist secularization narratives dominated in those years.

Even as astute and sympathetic an observer as Powdermaker struggled to fit her observations about black religion into narrow academic theoretical constructs. In a volatile combination, she borrowed the matriarchy thesis from Johnson and Frazier, but linked it to Freud's idea that religion was a substitute in adulthood for the loss of familial comfort and protection, especially from the father. She argued that it was the matriarchal nature of the black family that had led to the theological differences between blacks and whites reported in her research. Among blacks, the traditional model of God as a distant, stern father could not serve as a proto-type, since such a father figure did not exist among blacks. "It is in line with this theory, then, to find that, although like the White, the Negroes continue to call upon the Lord as Father, He seems rather to be conceived in the image of the mother," therefore exhibiting more maternal and loving characteristics. The "Negro's God," in her scheme, was a black woman and not a father at all.[38]

Powdermaker snared herself in another contradiction when she tried to explain the predominance of women in black churches, a feature of white churches as well. She endorsed the theory that women in general embraced religion more than men because churches provided sites for sublimated sexual expression. But this analysis hardly worked for the matriarchal theological inversion she attributed to black churches. With Jesus and God cast as feminine figures, by her logic it should have been the men who predominated rather than the women.

Here again, Powdermaker reached for a psychoanalytic explanation. She confirmed that black ministers were "notorious violators of the seventh commandment" even as they preached against adultery. She theorized that the erotic behaviors of black ministers toward their women congregants enabled women to reconcile their worship of a feminized God with their own need for sexual expressiveness in worship. At the same time, she conceded that her analysis offered no explanation for why black male preachers were so much more physically dramatic in their preaching than their white counterparts. "There is much to be said for the theory that the repressions caused by the inter-racial situation find relief in unrestrained religious behavior. Such an explanation is partial, however. Other factors, unrevealed by this study, are still to be sought."[39]

Although Powdermaker concluded her research in 1934, her book did not make its way into print until 1939. By that time, John Dollard, her better-known colleague at Yale, had already published a sociological study of Indianola which received considerable notice even though it was based on only five months of study, relied on leads and informants suggested by Powdermaker, and applied a rigid caste analysis to race relations in the town. His conclusions about religion were preoccupied with the intense communal experience of black religious services, something he attributed to a need to abandon the "controlling self of everyday life." More than that, Dollard's account revealed that he was deeply envious of the oratorical, intellectual, and physical prowess of black ministers whom he likened to "confident panthers."[40]

When Powdermaker's book was released, it received favorable reviews from social scientists who rarely agreed on anything, including key figures such as Johnson, Woodson, Park, and Du Bois. They all praised Powdermaker for revealing the existence of a black middle class in a small Southern town and for discovering a generational shift in attitudes among young blacks who were, in Du Bois's words, "keen and outspoken" in their opposition to notions of white racial superiority. The Southern black middle class she profiled included the schoolteachers who taught Sunday schools and who served as her primary informants. At the same time, Du Bois chided her for spending entirely too much time on the subject of religion, while he ignored the depth and distinctiveness of her material and analyses. His critique illustrates that his intellectual and political interest in religion had waned by the end of the 1930s. Melville Herskovits reviewed Powdermaker's book and pointedly criticized her rejection of the idea of African retentions in the religious practices she witnessed in Mississippi and those that followed Southern migrants as they moved north.[41]

ONE of those Southern migrants from Mississippi was Richard Wright, the author whose canonical works in the 1940s, *Native Son, Black Boy,* and *12 Million Black Voices,* captured aspects of a migrant experience which he knew firsthand and depicted the effects of racial oppression with gritty social realism. Interestingly, he credited the "scientific facts" of social scientists at the University of Chicago for giving inspiration and meaning to his work. Wright lived in Chicago and admired the work of Robert Park and his associates. This is how Wright came to write the introduction to one of the most influential and enduring social scientific works on African Americans, St. Clair Drake and Horace Cayton's *Black Metropolis.* Writing precisely from the stance that Hurston had rejected, Wright argued that the book assumed that "the Negro's conduct, his personality, his culture, his entire life flow naturally and inevitably out of the conditions imposed upon him by white America." His treatment of religion also followed a reactive analysis. "And, too, perhaps for the first time, we can see how the Negro has had to take Protestant religion and make it into something for his own special needs, needs born of an imposed Black Belt existence. To what extent has racial religion replaced Christian religion in thousands of Black Belt Churches?" Whatever the answer, he cast the blame on white Christianity. "And what is wrong with religion in America that it has turned its back on the Negro and his problem? And to what degree is religion in America officially and ideologically identified with the policy of White Supremacy? Is this the salvation which Christian missionaries have brought to the 'heathen from Africa'?"[42]

Black Metropolis, which devoted ample coverage to black churches, was based on data collected in the late 1930s under a research project funded by the Works Progress Administration and written up jointly by Drake and Cayton. Both had trained at Chicago, Drake as a social anthropologist and Cayton as a sociologist who later turned to journalism. Drake was the son of a Baptist minister from Barbados and a Virginia schoolteacher; trained at Hampton Institute, by the time he came to Chicago he had already done research in Mississippi for Alison Davis' book *Deep South*. Cayton, the grandson of former U.S. senator Hiram Revels, had been raised in Seattle and had spent time teaching at Fisk before going to Chicago.[43]

Both men brought considerable interviewing and ethnological skills to their work with residents of Chicago's black communities. "The most striking thing about these comments," Drake and Cayton wrote, "was the prevalence of grumbling against preachers and the church—a habit found among members and non-members alike." They categorized those complaints as follows: "Church is a 'racket,' (2) Too many churches, (3) Churches are too emotional, (4) There's no real religion among the members, (5) Churches are a waste of time and money, (6) Ministers don't practice what they preach, (7) Ministers don't preach against 'sin,' (8) Church places too much emphasis on money, (9) Negroes are too religious."[44] The direct and vivid language of the people interviewed made the largely subjective nature of these beliefs much more explicit than in earlier studies which essentially said the same thing.

At the same time, however, Drake and Cayton noted a continued increase in black churches throughout black neighborhoods in Chicago that was not wholly a result of the influx of black Southerners. For the two scholars, "this plethora of churches" was "no less baffling than the bewildering variety and the colorful extravagance of the names": "Nowhere else in Midwest Metropolis could one find, within a stone's throw of one another, a Hebrew Baptist Church, a Baptized Believers' Holiness church, a Universal Union Independent, a Church of Love and Faith, Spiritual, a Holt Mt. Zion Methodist Episcopal Independent, and a united Pentecostal Holiness Church. Or a cluster such as St. John's Christian Spiritual, Park Mission African Methodist Episcopal, Philadelphia Baptist, Little Rock Baptist, and the Aryan Full Gospel Mission, Spiritualist."[45]

The vibrancy and diversity of African American religious life forced Drake and Cayton to raise an obvious question: "'Why,' it may be asked, 'in the face of widespread criticisms and such apparent dissatisfaction, does the church still flourish?'" Their attempts to answer this question served instead to document the ways in which a variety of religions and faiths functioned as a basis for community cohesion. While Woodson had argued that denominational divisions served to divide African Americans politically, Drake and Cayton found instead, like Powdermaker, that there was a "mutually shared core of religious custom that cuts across denominational lines." Moreover, they discovered, "people 'feel at home' in any of the major Protestant denominations, and interdenominational visiting and shifts in church membership are widespread." As a cultural and religious force, mainline churches seemed to be holding their own among all the increasing diversity. In general, churches remained "centers of entertainment as well as places of worship" with "collective ceremonies" that "lend a certain rhythm to existence." These observations are consistent with earlier conclusions about the place of rural churches in black community life in Alabama, Georgia, Mississippi, Tennessee, and elsewhere. Their centrality was not limited to those areas, but extended to urban Northern migrant communities as well.[46]

Black Metropolis offered contradictory findings about the political role that churches played. The authors asserted that the church was the most influential black institution in the period between the end of the Civil War and the start of the Great Migration. But, they argued, it was no longer the center of community life even though they admitted that it remained just that for many people. That Drake and Cayton imposed a declensionist narrative in the face of all the evidence of religious growth may have had more to do with their own expectations than to do with the evidence itself. Like many of the people they studied, they expected the churches, in addition to serving a religious function, to be a political and economic force in the life of their communities. Those who defended the churches most vehemently did so on the grounds that they were politically essential. "Churches are a necessity," said one respondent, "for I believe that it is through them that our people first got the idea that we must co-operate with one another." Drake and Cayton found that "both members and non-members expect the church to play a prominent role in 'advancing the Race,' and they often judge the institution from this angle alone." For many, churches failed to meet the expectation that they needed to serve as sites of collective political identity and activism. Churches were criticized less on religious grounds than because they functioned poorly as "race institutions."[47]

Most community members believed that preachers had great political independence since they were "answerable to no one except their congregations." As a result, they were expected to be "real race Men." And that expectation, Drake and Cayton argued, accounted for the constant barrage of criticism that was directed at ministers. Preachers were criticized not for a failure to exert religious leadership, but for their reluctance to help their communities through "political action, protest against discrimination, advice on securing jobs and legal aid, and the encouragement of Negro business enterprises." That was the crux of the matter.[48]

Like others who preceded them, Drake and Cayton turned to class as the analytical tool to help understand community attitudes toward religion and churches. They asserted that churches provided a source of stability for members of the black lower class through the prayers and music of collective religious ritual. Still, they believed, even among the most religiously devout of the poor, a shift in thinking had emerged under the stress of Depression-era economic conditions. Members of Chicago's black community had come to expect churches and religion to help in the "here and now" as well as in the "sweet by-and-by." For this reason attacks on preachers continued, but they did not translate into sentiments against the churches themselves or against the importance of religious belief.[49]

In the religious life of the black middle class, Drake and Cayton found, worship practices were "very this-worldly" and the church was seen primarily as a "Race institution" engaged in supporting black political work and secular institutions like the NAACP. The newer black middle class, the "New Negro," attended churches not so much for theological reasons, they argued, but rather because doing so furthered "racial advancement." Unlike the elites, this new middle class had not abandoned the churches, as Woodson and Mays feared, but had transformed them into social or political organizations with less emphasis on religion and more on political progress.[50]

In contrast to earlier scholars, Drake and Cayton wrote more bluntly about the tensions between men and women in churches. "The church world is a women's world, for less than a third of the lower-class church members are men." Referring to the ministry as a "male monopoly," they reported that "the preachers guard the pulpit against female infiltration, but they must depend upon women for the bulk of their regular attendance, financial support, and church work." They related the story of one Baptist minister who had been accused of encouraging women to preach and was called to explain his actions to his district convention. "He tried to mollify his fellow preachers without alienating the women in the audience: 'I know somebody said I had the women down at my church preaching. If doing their Christian duty and talking about Christ is preaching, then I hope every woman in my church starts soon. But there is enough work for the women to do without them swinging around up here [i.e., in the pulpit]. You can do all of your preaching right down there [on the floor], but not up here.'"[51]

According to Drake and Cayton, the fact that women were excluded from Baptist and Methodist pulpits accounted for much of the appeal of Holiness, Pentecostal, and Spiritualist churches where women could more freely "rise to the top" as religious leaders. These were the same churches that Mays had characterized as "promiscuous" in their growth. Still, they concluded, the majority of black church women "do not challenge or resent male dominance in the pulpit" and "accept their place in a church pattern where the shepherds of the sheep are men."[52]

Black Metropolis still presented the churches and religion as essential to black community life, even in the face of secular competitions and what the writers called the "acids of modernity." Ministers, on the other hand, continued to be uniformly criticized for a lack of political leadership; they were blamed for failing to meet the expectation that churches would also serve political and economic purposes. Those criticisms took "the form of a protest against the alleged cupidity and hypocrisy of church functionaries and devotees. The preachers bear the brunt of the attacks, and comments on ministers are sometimes violent." In these ways, the opinions of the people interviewed were consistent with the views expressed by Woodson and Mays, those held by the young people interviewed by Johnson and Frazier, and those observed by Powdermaker.[53]

Black Metropolis was one of two encyclopedic works that provided extensive data and a new interpretive framework on World War II–era black urban life, including its religious institutions and practices. The other was the collaborative research project that yielded Gunnar Myrdal's book *An American Dilemma.* The two books drew on some of the same research and data. In particular, material on black churches that was gathered by Drake for *Black Metropolis* also formed much of the basis for Myrdal's analysis, although the two men treated this material differently and arrived at quite different interpretations and conclusions.[54]

The same disposition to class analysis, denigration of charismatic ministers, and criticism of preachers for failing to lead congregants out of poverty and oppression underlies the interpretation of black religion and black churches in *An American Dilemma.* Myrdal came to this part of the project deeply suspicious of religious emotion. One of his earliest encounters with black religion had come when he was taken to a highly emotional Father Divine service in Harlem. With this experience in mind, Myrdal suggested that the methods best suited to the study of black religion were those of abnormal psychology.[55]

Consistent with his general indifference to cultural aspects of African American life, Myrdal placed no particular emphasis on religion. Just as importantly, he brought a different set of analytic questions to the exploration of black religion. He used his analysis of the "Negro church" to reinforce his overarching argument that black Americans were essentially "exaggerated" Americans. In this case, he worked hard to demonstrate how much African American religion conformed to American religious patterns. As among whites, more women than men attended church, older people attended more than the young, the uneducated went more than the educated, and the lower and middle classes attended more than elites.

Many of the attributes identified with black religious life were, Myrdal argued, quintessentially American religious traits, only taken to an extreme. For example, he explained the proliferation of storefront black churches, which he called "miniature congregations," as just an extension of what he saw as a peculiar American tendency toward small congregations. He did acknowledge, however, that "the spirituals are different from anything that can be found in the white churches." Still, he continued to argue for class rather than race as the key to understanding religious life. Apart from their "emotionalism," black churches were no different from "any lower-class white Protestant church."[56]

Conceding that black churches were powerful community institutions that provided "ideological cohesion," Myrdal recognized that they had the potential to advance a political program because they already had "the Negro masses organized." But he also judged the churches to be weak instruments of "collective action" because as Christian churches focused on heavenly salvation, they were theologically doomed to fail. For Myrdal, Christianity itself and Christian churches in general were passive by nature, designed only as refuges for providing "escape and consolation" from a difficult existence and not as "spearheads of reform."[57]

Here, Myrdal, like Johnson and Frazier, diverged from Du Bois, Woodson, and Mays who, despite their criticisms of Christianity, looked favorably on religion as providing support for social-justice work. Citing a few exceptions where black churches had taken on political issues, Myrdal nonetheless concluded that "on the whole even the Northern Negro church has remained a conservative tradition" in the sense that it did not pursue social or political justice.

Compounding these tendencies were the people in the churches, whom Myrdal viewed as "the subordinate caste of American Negroes" and as the "downtrodden common Negroes who craved religious escape from poverty and other tribulations." Like others, he tended to see religion as an opiate that soothed the people with an otherworldly outlook and emotionalism. Myrdal predicted that only when church members demanded more would the churches change. He cast the church as a follower rather than a leader.[58]

Despite his own conclusions about the churches' failings, Myrdal admitted that "the solidarity behind the abstract church institution in the Negro community is simply amazing." Black intellectuals were far more willing to cooperate with churches than were their white counterparts. Myrdal, like Johnson and Frazier, found that widespread criticism was aimed at preachers, but not at religion or the churches in general. In the end, Myrdal's assessment of the churches' potential for political engagement was pessimistic even as he resigned himself to their continued centrality in black communities. "Nevertheless, the Negro church means more to the Negro community than the white church means to the white community—in its function as a giver of hope, as an emotional cathartic, as a center of community activity, as a source of leadership, and as a provider of respectability."[59]

Myrdal was decidedly more optimistic and more certain about the continued ascent of the black press as being crucial to the political prospects of black people. Seen both historically and in the contemporary period as "an organ for the Negro protest," black newspapers and journals were held up as "a fighting press," "a special pleader," and "an advocate of human rights." Myrdal portrayed black newspapers and journals as a nationally unified race institution with a consistent political critique of racial injustice, even across differences in region and locale. The "race cause" was implicit in all aspects of newspaper coverage, from hard news to sports to entertainment. But Myrdal also saw the press as the principle means by which the producers of newspapers, the black upper class, exerted political influence over the opinions held by the black lower classes. "The importance of the Negro press for the formation of Negro opinion, for the functioning of all other Negro institutions, for Negro leadership and concerted action generally," Myrdal wrote, "is enormous."[60]

Myrdal concluded that the press was far more powerful than either the churches or the schools. This influence could be expected to grow "as the educational level of the Negro masses rises, . . . as race consciousness and race solidarity are intensified, as the Negro protest is strengthened, and disseminated even among the lower classes—as all these closely related processes are proceeding, partly under the influence of the Negro press itself, the Negro press will continue to grow." In contrast to most analyses of black churches, Myrdal's study predicted that rising educational levels would add to the strength and potential of the black press. "Whether or not this forecast of an increasing circulation for Negro papers comes true, the Negro press is of tremendous importance. It has rightly been characterized as 'the greatest single power in the Negro race.'"[61]

This strong assessment of the potency and importance of the black press stands in contrast to Myrdal's bleak analysis of black churches. *Black Metropolis* also had positioned the black press as a vital force in the formation of black public opinion and, in this respect, as "a victorious competitor" with the churches. Crediting the events surrounding World War II as pivotal, Drake and Cayton had contended that the press had "emerged as one of the most powerful forces among Negroes in America" due to its ardent support of black wartime activism against segregation in war-related enterprises, public and private. Still, they had not made predictions about the press's continued importance in race politics, nor had they sought to elevate it above all other black institutions in

terms of community and civic influence as had Myrdal. While acknowledging the power of black weeklies, Drake and Cayton had
still ceded to black churches their traditional place as the primary
institutional power. This may have been done through compromise or grudgingly, since their discussion of the press was entitled "The Face of the Press," while the section on the churches
was called "The Grip of the Negro Church."[62] Yet the plethora of
churches in Drake and Cayton's study undermined the notion that
there was such a thing as a singular "Negro church." Other works
from the same period would challenge the idea that black people
were even worshiping the same God.

WHEN the Philadelphia Anthropological Society sponsored the
publication of Arthur Huff Fauset's *Black Gods of the Metropolis* in
1944, his fellow members at the society considered him uniquely
qualified to conduct a study of black religious cults in Philadelphia.
"Himself partly of Negro origin," the society's Publication Committee wrote in a foreword to the book, Fauset "was endowed for
this study with a background, a point of view, and an entrée to the
field which could never have been possessed by one of exclusively
European tradition and descent."[63] Citing only his racial creden-
tials without commenting on his other qualifications, the foreword
vividly illustrated the position of black social scientists in that era.

Fauset's fellow Philadelphia anthropologists had judged him especially well suited to study African American religion because
of his racial heritage but they ignored its complexity. Born in New
Jersey in 1899, Fauset was the son of Redmon Fauset, a prominent black AME minister, and of Bella White, a Jewish convert to
Christianity. Fauset spent most of his life in Philadelphia where he
graduated from the University of Pennsylvania with an A.B. degree in 1921. He began a career as a teacher and was soon pro-

moted to principal in the Philadelphia public school system, a position he held from the 1920s to the late 1940s.

During the 1920s, Fauset also pioneered the study of black folk culture, and like his much better-known older half-sister Jessie Redmon Fauset, engaged in literary pursuits as well. In addition to his love of writing, Fauset developed an interest in black folklore and he received a master's degree in anthropology from the University of Pennsylvania in 1924. Fauset published articles and books based on his work collecting folktales from black people living in Nova Scotia, in the South, and in Philadelphia. Some of his literary writing in that period reflected the influence of his study of folklore, including his three entries in Alain Locke's influential anthology *The New Negro* in 1925. Fauset developed a commitment to political activism that came to full expression in the 1930s and 1940s. Increasingly critical of national racial politics, he served for several years as vice-president of the National Negro Congress, working alongside labor leader A. Philip Randolph. His wife, Crystal Bird Fauset, also was politically active and in 1938 became the first black woman to be elected to a state legislature.[64]

This is the life that Arthur Huff Fauset lived before he became the fourth black person to earn a Ph.D. in anthropology, a degree he received from the University of Pennsylvania in 1942. His dissertation became his fourth book, *Black Gods of the Metropolis*. Half of its text was devoted to case studies of five black religious sects in Philadelphia; the other half built an interpretive frame for understanding the rise of cults, their appeal, and their implications for broader debates about African American religious practices. The case studies were a compelling example of urban ethnographic work. Drawing on two years of repeated visits to worship services and extended interviews with leaders and lay people, Fauset presented the case studies in a dispassionate, respectful, nonjudgmental tone. The fluidity and grace of the writing reflected his broader abilities and experience in both narrative fiction and journalism, especially in its attention to telling descriptive detail.[65]

Fauset profiled five different sects: Mt. Sinai Holy Church of America, Inc., a Christian Holiness church founded by Bishop Ida Robinson; United House of Prayer for All People, a Bible-based sect led by Daddy Grace who emphasized a prosperity doctrine; Church of God, a group of so-called "black Jews" who taught that all "white Jews" were imposters and that Jesus was a black man; the Moorish Science Temple of America, founded by Noble Drew Ali who wrote his own Holy Koran and drew from the teachings of many prophets, including Jesus, Mohammed, Buddha, and Confucius; and, perhaps the most well known, the Father Divine Peace Mission Movement, an eclectic racially egalitarian and communitarian sect.

By choosing to focus on these sects, Fauset did not follow the lead of other scholars at the time who designated most Holiness, Pentecostal, and storefront churches as "cults." Instead, he distinguished those institutions by referring to them more aptly as "orthodox evangelical churches." He justified his inclusion of Mt. Sinai because of its charismatic founding bishop and its marriage restrictions which limited members to in-sect partners.[66]

Whether Fauset intended this or not, his selections for study made it difficult for him and his readers to easily draw comparisons or generalizations. His case studies clearly reveal the idiosyncratic nature of each group. Yet his examples did offer a glimpse of the adventuresome range of religious ideas and practices that appealed to disparate groups of African Americans in the 1930s and 1940s. For each sect, Fauset detailed its historical origins, organization, membership requirements, financial structure, sacred text, theological beliefs, and the rituals of a typical service.

This methodology yielded an insider's view that was rare even in studies of more traditional religious groups. Indeed, few others had approached religious studies in this way, by applying the tools of cultural anthropology to urban religious institutions. Because Fauset also relied so heavily on oral interviews and personal testimony from group members, the book preserves the words of ordinary black men and women explaining why they made the religious choices they did.

When Fauset asked "why the cult attracts," his subjects told him that their driving motivation for joining their chosen sect was a "desire to get closer to some supernatural power." Most of the biographical accounts Fauset relied on included explanations of why members of these sects found that more orthodox religious organizations no longer met their needs. The reasons given mirrored those of the churches' critics: the hypocrisy of preachers, excess emotionalism or insufficient spiritual presence, and specific theological disagreements. Many but not all of those who joined the sects did so after a conversion or healing experience of some kind.[67]

In other words, people joined primarily to meet their own deeply personal religious and spiritual needs. This exegesis, as plain and as obvious as their own words, was often given short shrift in the psychoanalytic, political, and functional explications of religious motivation that other scholars imposed from their studies of religious practices and institutions. Fauset did not abandon those constructs in his own analysis, but, to his credit, he deferred to the findings of his own research, taking as final arbiter the testimony of his subjects.

The ongoing debate over the presence of African retentions in African American religious practices and the related notion that black people were by nature overly and primitively religious framed Fauset's book. Much was at stake in these disagreements since they carried deep and subtle implications not only about the essentials of race and the transmission of culture, but about the prospects of political progress for African Americans. What many most objected to in Herskovits' formulation was his conclusion that black people's orientation toward spiritual practices "causes them, in contrast to other underprivileged groups elsewhere in the world, to turn to religion rather than to political action or other outlets for their frustration." Frazier and others found especially disturbing Herskovits' implication that African American religiosity and the primitivism and political passivity associated with it were somehow an innate and immutable racial characteristic. Allying himself with his mentor Park, Frazier had offered instead a functional and historical explanation for the appeal of religion and Christianity to black people. Though an ambivalence about the relationship of black Americans to Africa and Africans was at play in various objections to Herskovits' work, so too were class-driven concerns that the religiosity of the masses of black working-class people, with its cultural and political implications, was being imputed to well-educated blacks.[68]

Fauset advised "considerable caution" in accepting the claims of African retentions in black religious practices. He grudgingly acknowledged that although there might be a "modicum of such influence," it had been "overwhelmingly outweighed by American cultural influences." Fauset used his own research on black religious cults to argue that the nationalistic tendencies in some of the sects demonstrated a blend of religious and political activity. But he was unable to escape the conundrum that the most political of the sects often looked back to African-based or Moorish inspiration for their origins.[69]

Fauset's main problem was that his research, for all that it revealed about the practices of these five fascinating religious groups, was too limited to counter the weight of Herskovits' sweeping claims which though spelled out in anthropological terms would also have required historically grounded disputation. Cults attracted sensationalized press and scholarly attention in the early decades of the twentieth century, but the numbers of black people involved with these sects were always extremely small. The overwhelming majority of religiously oriented black people remained then, as they do now, in Baptist and Methodist churches. One needed to be cautious in making broad generalizations about black religious practices based solely on the study of small cults and sects, except as evidence of the varieties of African American experiences.[70]

The limited parameters of Fauset's study did not diminish contemporary assessments of the strengths, overall quality, and importance of the work. Reviewers praised *Black Gods* for its "vivid reporting" and for its accounts of "the testimonies of the faithful." The book's engagement with the Herskovits debate also was noted, with one reviewer observing that Fauset found "little use for the alleged factor of 'racial temperament' and is inclined to deny the importance of African cultural survivals." Though all of the reviewers were complimentary, most classified the book as sociological, failing to recognize Fauset's innovative application of an ethnographic methodology to an urban setting. "The complete objectivity of the author, his thoroughness, his impartiality, and a fine sense of fitness involving the 'feelings' of the cults discussed," one scholar wrote, "make this work a scholarly and valuable contribution to the field of sociology and comparative religion."[71]

Of the studies on black religion in this period, Fauset's is the one that embraces and documents the vitality of urban black religious cultures, an area that most others avoided or ignored out of fears they would be accused of racial essentialism or out of adherence to disciplinary focus on institutions or leaders and not on practices. Had Fauset been an anthropology professor rather than a high school principal, or if he had focused like Powdermaker and Hurston on rural rather than urban folk, perhaps the anthropological nature of his work would have been noticed. Fauset's non-

judgmental reporting of his findings was both remarkable and re-
freshing coming as it did at a time when "black cults and sects"
garnered an inordinate amount of bad press. Often held up as the
province of charlatans and easily duped followers, these religious
groups were subject to dismissive ridicule and outright attack.

Black Gods hints at Fauset's own views on the debate over
the political potential and obligation of orthodox black churches.
Fauset predicted that "the American Negro church is likely to witness a transformation from its purely religious function to functions
which will accommodate the urgent social needs of the Negro
masses" and concluded that "the original revolutionary potential of
the American Negro church may again be in evidence in these
phenomena." As his example and model for this potential, in a re-
velatory move, Fauset directed his readers not to any of Philadelphia's traditional black denominations but to one of his case studies: the one on Father Divine.[72]

In his political writing for the weekly *Philadelphia Tribune*, Fauset
displayed none of the reticence he exercised in his book. In a 1939
column, he had accused black ministers of "crying sour grapes"
over Father Divine's success at attracting followers. For Fauset, this
response was evidence that Divine's efforts were "the most significant and potentially important movement among Negroes today." "As for me," he wrote, "I greet the Father Divine movement,
and its emphasis on social usefulness, cooperation, sobriety, dignity
and honesty, with something like the feeling of one who comes out
of a stuffy smoked-filled room into the clear country air." To those
who criticized Divine's followers for calling him "God," Fauset had
an eloquent reply. "I know many a hungry Negro who would call
me God if I could discover a way to keep his mind occupied, his
stomach contented, and his spirits soaring. If I could accomplish
this miracle, I might even come to believe that I was God." Fauset
vowed to match Divine's sincerity and his devoutness "against any-

thing the National Baptist Convention or the AME Conference has to offer."[73] This was high praise from someone who was the son of a prominent AME minister.

This respect for Divine's possibilities as a political potentate was printed at a time when few scholars held him in high esteem, or knew what to make of him or could even acknowledge the power of his ideas and his following. The black sociologist Oliver Cox, who published a pathbreaking caste analysis of American race relations in 1948, invoked Divine to answer the recurring Gandhian-inspired question of whether black people could use "soul force" to win the fight against inequality.

> Leaders are in large measure produced by their followers; therefore the question may be put thus: "Will American Negroes arise solidly in revolt behind a Negro holy man starving to death, say, for the purpose of having the modern black codes abrogated in the South? Or will they be aroused in a body to take action against American whites because a Negro offers himself to be shot in the interest in the race?" By putting the query in this way, the answer becomes obvious. Surely the Negroes might make Father Divine a universal symbol if such a prospect would not make their cause seem ridiculous.[74]

In the end, Fauset, like Du Bois and Woodson, warned against the emergence of black "preacher-politicians." "Yes, we need our preachers in politics," he explained, "but the politics they need to be pursuing are those of teaching our people in churches the simple principles of organization, cooperation, thrift, what civic virtues to demand, and Christian militancy." He advised black ministers to "lead the people in their demand for good housing, jobs, better working conditions, food for the masses, etc., and let them raise money and men to fight for these things against the political bosses instead of being political yes-men in order to have jobs for themselves."[75]

Despite his criticism of black religious leadership, Fauset did not hesitate to offer praise when he found reason for it, something few others did. He commended AME church leaders for their strong support in 1941 of an attack against discriminatory practices of the Philadelphia Housing Authority. This action heartened him so much that he proclaimed that "the day of 'take all the world and give me Jesus' is over" as he described religious leaders who were becoming "increasingly militant." He predicted that "as the church continues to lend impetus to the struggle of our people on the important fronts which affect their daily lives, we can expect it to grow, not only in influence but in numbers as well, and with regard to its real meaning as a progressive force in the struggle for the liberation of the Negro people."[76]

IT IS surprising that the classic book on the subject of African American religion was written by Frazier, whose research on religion was as limited as his interpretations were caustic. It is more a credit to his prominence as a sociologist than to any expertise in religion. In 1948, he was elected president of American Sociological Association. In 1957, he published his controversial critique of the black middle class, *Black Bourgeoisie*. While serving with UNESCO in Paris at that time, Frazier was invited to give a series of lectures at the University of Liverpool on the broad problem of the relation of religion to social structure or, more specifically, "the role of religion in the social organization of Negro life in the United States." Those lectures were published posthumously in 1964 with little revision as *The Negro Church in America*. The book went on to become the standard interpretation of the history of black religion and black churches and has been reprinted more than nine times.[77]

Frazier's work on the topic did not rest on any new or primary research in part because the book was prepared as lectures and written while he was living abroad. He simply borrowed heavily from published sources, including those by Du Bois, Woodson, Mays, and Fauset, and offered a synthetic account of the historical evolution of African American religion. He brought together many strands of his own earlier sociological studies, especially his critiques of the black family, women, and notions of matriarchal power, but in *The Negro Church* he brought them to bear on black churches.[78]

Beginning with the religion of enslaved people, Frazier saw no evidence of any African influences in black religious culture. Rather, the adoption of Christianity provided the basis for black social cohesion. In the post-emancipation period, Frazier argued, an organized religious life was the key to the formation of a structured social life among the masses of black people. Although he relied on Woodson's account of a heroic post-Reconstruction black church, Frazier emphasized that the churches offered a political arena to black men "who had never been able to assert themselves and assume the dominant male role, even in family relations, as defined by American culture." This exercise of black masculinity was at the center of the churches' function.[79]

The founding of black independent churches in the eighteenth and nineteenth centuries had been cast by some as proof of the race's capacity for community self-governance, not simply as vindication of black male leadership prowess. Frazier charted a flawed evolution in black religion that merged the "slave religion" of the masses with the "manly" religion of free blacks in the North. He credited the churches and their male leaders with providing moral support for the institutionalization of a patriarchal family, with the father in a position of authority. He saw this as an essential escape from the slavery tradition of strong black women, absent fathers, and weak men. At the same time, he feared that a "pattern of autocratic leadership" and anti-intellectualism might enable preachers to dominate all forms of black political life and "cast a shadow over the intellectual outlook of Negroes."[80]

Frazier went on to argue that churches serving the elites were dominated by secular interests, that is, they had begun to show concern for the pressing social conditions facing black people. He saw these developments as further evidence of class stratification within black communities. The majority of black people, who were not members of elite churches, were lumped together and cast aside by Frazier as members of storefront churches, cults, and sects, for him the modern-day remnants of "slave religion." Even spirituals, which some saw as expressions of political resistance, were dismissed by Frazier. "In recent years there have been some efforts on the part of Negro intellectuals, encouraged sometimes by white radicals, to invest most of the Spirituals with a revolutionary meaning or to claim that they represented disguised plans for escape from slavery. It is our position that the sacred folk songs or Spirituals were essentially religious in sentiment and, as we shall see, otherworldly in outlook."[81]

Frazier's broader point was that black churches represented the "most important institutional barrier to integration and the assimilation of Negroes." This is a quite different analysis from that of Du Bois, Woodson, and Mays who attacked the racial hypocrisy of white Christianity and white churches as the obstruction to political progress and as a threat to the continued viability of Christianity among black people. Frazier instead cast black churches themselves as the greater impediment, not white Christian failings.[82]

The only hope, Frazier concluded, was that the church's place as the dominant institution "crumbles as the 'walls of segregation come tumbling down.'" He argued for an end to the dominant cultural and intellectual position that black churches held in their communities. With their removal or demise or replacement, Frazier envisioned an easier route to black assimilation into mainstream American life. This was the concluding analysis of the leading black sociologist and the standard synthetic account of black religious history. It was written in the 1950s but published in 1964 at the height of the civil rights era, and was acclaimed then and for decades to follow as the definitive treatment of the subject.[83]

Frazier's thinking about African American religion and politics remained unchallenged by the emergence of the Montgomery bus boycott. But an eighty-nine-year-old W. E. B. Du Bois noted that the boycott was an uprising of "black workers" led by "young, educated ministers." In 1929, it was Du Bois who had invited Gandhi to publish a message to American blacks in *The Crisis* because of his admiration of Gandhi's nonviolent campaigns in South Africa. Writing in 1957, Du Bois observed: "Only in the last year have American Negroes begun to see the possibility of this program being applied to the Negro problems in the United States." He credited the Montgomery success not to the fact that King knew of Gandhi's philosophy but rather to the underlying fundamental truths recognized by Gandhi and those black workers. Yet the boycott merely amplified Du Bois's belief that ending racial discrimination would be extremely difficult despite recent changes in the law. He predicted that the enforcement of those laws and the realization of human equality would come to the United States only "under the leadership of another

Gandhi." Two years later, in 1959, the quixotic Du Bois mixed his admiration of King's leadership in Montgomery with criticism that King had no positive program other than a refusal to submit to evil.[84]

IT WOULD take the civil rights movement itself to restore African American religion to academic relevancy. As part of the resulting boom in black studies, many of the social science works of the 1930s and 1940s were brought back to life. In the late 1960s, Johnson's *Growing Up in the Black Belt* and Frazier's *Negro Youth at the Crossways* were both reprinted with new introductions by St. Clair Drake. In the essay he wrote for Johnson's book, Drake argued for the study's continued relevancy by linking the young people Johnson had written about in the 1940s with those engaged in the Southern struggle for black freedom in the 1960s. Johnson had concluded that the young people he studied suffered from growing up under the influence of churches that preserved "dated cultural values" and provided only "emotional relief for the fixed problems of a hard life." But in Drake's reappraisal a different assessment emerges. "Thousands of Southern Negroes eventually did find a way to 'fix things' in the Black Belt—marching behind a new type of preacher and singing 'We Shall Overcome'; or going to jail alongside young people from the North. . . . Reading *Growing Up in the Black Belt* deepens our understanding of black marchers trudging the road from Selma to Montgomery, or registering to vote under the glare of hostile white officials in some Black Belt county."[85]

In his introduction for Frazier's book on black youth in the border states, Drake made special note of Frazier's "striking finding that 'the majority of the Negro youth of all classes believe that God is white'" endorsing the view that "the low esteem implicit in such a belief profoundly affected the personality of these young people." Drake made no attempt to reconcile that starkly different assessment of the political legacy of black religion in the 1940s with the courage of those black men and women who twenty years later were staging protests to the strains of black spirituals and whose actions he had extolled in the introduction to Johnson's book.[86]

In her 1966 memoir, Hortense Powdermaker admitted that her work in 1930s Mississippi did not lead her to foresee that black Southerners would demand full civil rights decades later. She credited the development of the modern civil rights movement to the churches she had described in her book, places where black people trained themselves in organization, administration, leadership, and cooperation. Of Martin Luther King Jr., she said that although he was well educated, he still possessed the charisma and mystique of the Southern black preachers of the past, including his "militant maternal grandfather and father." She drew links between King's philosophy of love and nonviolence and the black Christian theology of love and sacrifice she had found in the Mississippi Delta. "The faith in God's and man's love which enabled the Negroes in Indianola to maintain their self-respect and to channel their aggression in acting the meek role demanded by whites now sparks forthright demands for full equality."[87]

Powdermaker then made an observation that few other scholars would make until many decades later. She emphasized without surprise that black women played a prominent role in the movement, citing the examples of Rosa Parks in the Montgomery bus boycott, Autherine Lucy, who integrated the University of Alabama, and Daisy Bates, who organized to protect the Little Rock Nine. Her immersion in the world of Southern black women in the 1930s had left her deeply impressed with their leadership and organizational abilities. What she did consider remarkable, and a divergence from the findings of her own female-centered research, was that black men seemed to have taken "their rightful place in the leadership of the revolution." But even this she associated, in a convoluted psychoanalytic nexus between sex and power, to the resistance that black women were newly able to make to the sexual advances of white men, crediting "the open defiance of Negro men to white men who refuse to grant them civil rights" to those shifting sexual mores.[88]

When Myrdal later looked back at *An American Dilemma* after the intervening decades of the civil rights movement, his 1940s assessment that black churches were in political decline seemed to haunt him. Writing in 1972, Myrdal claimed that his work had predicted what he called the "Negro rebellion" in the South in the 1950s and 1960s. He was forced to temper this assertion, however, with the admission that he had had no idea that black churches would play any role in challenging the racial status quo. "What I did not, and could not, foresee was the arrival on the scene of dynamic church leaders—in the first place, Martin Luther King Jr., who almost transformed the Negro church into an effective fighting organization with considerable discipline, a program, and a tactic." Even while Myrdal credited King's leadership, he hedged in his assessment of any longer-term institutional transformation, conceding only that the church was "almost" transformed.[89]

Drake and Cayton oversaw a 1962 reissue of *Black Metropolis* but their brief, new afterword was preoccupied with the implications of the dramatic demographic changes that had ensued in Chicago since 1945. The black population had doubled to 800,000, and only 60,000 of that increase was due to migration. At the same time, white flight to the suburbs, where blacks were unwelcome, was progressing at full throttle. The increasing hypersegregation that characterized Chicago and other urban areas seemed to rob their observations of any optimism.

The two men were especially critical of their former academic home, the University of Chicago, for its creation and expansion of Hyde Park as an enclave closed to the poor, including most blacks. They searched for signs of hope among the city's few integrated apartment buildings and the even smaller number of interracial churches. They made no other mention of black religious life, which had received such close attention in the book. They noted, without enthusiasm, the emergence of "the ritualization of equality at civic banquets and 'brotherhood' ceremonies" which had become routine. Whatever hopes they had held for the future of the black metropolis had been lost. They cast their political sympathies with sit-ins led by "middle-class Negro women" demanding better schools for their children and with students protesting the university's creation of Hyde Park. The triumphs of the Southern civil rights movement with which the other authors had been quick to associate had no place in their afterword because Chicago, like other Northern cities, had come to represent not a promised land but a desolate and worsening place for the hopes of the migrants of the 1940s.[90]

In an author's note to the 1971 paperback reissue of *Black Gods*, Fauset also had the benefit of thirty years of hindsight. "A full decade before Rosa Parks' tired feet focused a world spotlight on Montgomery, Alabama, and the Reverend Martin Luther King," Fauset wrote, "this University of Pennsylvania study indicated the likely direction that future black religious leadership would take." While it is certainly true that in the 1940s Fauset urged black churches to become more politically engaged, he did not base that call on his own research which had a compelling but altogether different focus. The quandary for him, once again, was that his study had focused on five small sects in the urban North, none of which bore a direct role in the civil rights struggle as it came to be embodied by Parks and King. Fauset recognized this himself, as he spent the remainder of his author's note straining to forge fragile links between Father Divine and the worldwide "love not hate" movement of the 1960s and 1970s, and between the Moorish Science Temple and the Nation of Islam, Malcolm X, and the Black Panthers.[91]

It was left to the anthropologist John Szwed, in his introduction to the 1971 edition of Fauset's book, to better establish its enduring significance. He credited Fauset for writing "one of the first books of urban American ethnography." Szwed also placed the book's religious focus in the broader context of African American intellectual history, designating the work as a powerful articulation of the "distinctiveness and power of Afro-American culture." He explained how Fauset had produced "a singularly important book" whose subject matter, African American religion, still suffered from a need for more basic study.[92]

This need still persists. The construction of knowledge about African American religion has been framed and weakened by the repetition of untested assumptions. The most glaring is the insistence on black religious uniformity in the face of overwhelming evidence of just the opposite—the enormous diversity of African American religious beliefs and practices both within and outside of Christianity. So urgent was the need to use religion as a basis for racial unity that to acknowledge its internal differences was to deny its usefulness. Yet this diversity has been preserved for us in Du Bois's early accounts of Philadelphia and rural Tennessee, in Johnson's studies of rural Georgia, Alabama, and Tennessee, in Frazier's accounts of the border communities in Louisville and Washington, in Powdermaker's reports from the Mississippi Delta and in Hurston's testimony from the rural South and Harlem, as well as in the studies conducted by Drake, Cayton, and Fauset in 1940s Chicago and Philadelphia.

HURSTON may have said it best when she observed that black religious life was composed of practices that were at once communal and absolutely individualistic. The same can be said of black churches as institutions. Yet the illusions of the "black church" and "black religion" remain as vivid as ever. Both of these narrow intellectual constructs have been alloyed with other restrictive rational explanations and analytic frames, including those invented by Freud and Marx, Frazier and Du Bois, Park and Powdermaker, Durkheim and Weber.[93]

Instead, the materials preserved in these studies capture the fluidity, vitality, and expansiveness of African American religious beliefs. These beliefs were open not only to African and Eastern religions, but to other prophets and Jesus figures and other gods. Some of these divergences fit under the rubric of Christianity, but some of them could not. This also was the period in which the Nation of Islam was created although its rise to notoriety would take two more decades. Such were the many varieties of African American religious experiences in the early twentieth century.[94]

At the same time, talk of Gandhi in rural Mississippi and the persistence of the ethos of love over hate, hope over fear, justice over inequality remind us that those strands of thought were already firmly in place before Martin Luther King Jr. was born. King embraced the performative arts and language of African American religions and made them resonate for his audiences who became the believing minority that would bring him and the civil rights movement to public consciousness.

In this way, as we will see, King and his generation and younger followers built on the work of an earlier group of Southern black religious intellectuals—represented by Mary McLeod Bethune, Nannie Helen Burroughs, and Benjamin Mays—who combined a missionary impulse with a public ministry founded on sacrifice and service, in education and in politics, both within and outside black religious institutions. For them, these were lived tensions which they struggled to reconcile in practice and not merely as an academic enterprise.

3

In Pursuit of Pentecost

WHEN Mary McLeod Bethune died in 1955 just months shy of her eightieth birthday, newspapers reported that she had sensed her impending death, planned her own funeral, and written the epitaph for her gravestone. It reads: "She has given her best so that others may live a more abundant life." Of course, Jesus had already said the same thing about himself. It is a measure of Bethune's supreme confidence, both in her faith and in the meaning of her own life of service, that her last words would so unabashedly place her in such company.[1]

Bethune was the most prominent black woman public figure of the first half of the twentieth century. Her many and varied roles included founder and president of Bethune-Cookman College, political advisor and confidante to Franklin and Eleanor Roosevelt, and creator and longtime leader of the National Council of Negro Women (NCNW). Her public presence took on iconic proportions even during her lifetime. She came to embody a new kind of racial leadership that was lodged in black educational and women's organizations but that bridged the secular, largely white male world of national politics. Bethune's many successes depended on interracial alliances and, less obviously, on her embrace of religious ecumenism. She rejected the limitations of what she called the "orthodox Negro church" at the same time that she opposed the hypocrisy and exclusivity of western Christianity. Toward the end of her life, she embraced a controversial new international religious and political movement called "Moral Re-Armament" because she believed it to be the best hope of the world for unifying and empowering the many diverse peoples of a modern world drawn together by the threat of atomic annihilation.

Her vision of effective racial leadership did not concern itself with the male ministry or with black churches. Her own institutional base was an educational institution dedicated to providing black students with the moral and spiritual undergirding needed in the broader world of economic institutions, secular politics, and interracial coalitions. Religion was for her a deeply private matter, but she believed that spiritual strength, a moral foundation, and faith in humanity's capacity for change were all necessary for effective leaders. Her life's work was motivated by her faith in religion, in education, in electoral politics, and in an egalitarian national state. Along the way, she challenged prevailing ideas about the role of men and women in racial leadership, about the relationship between African American religion and politics, and about the false divide between the sacred and the secular. Hers was the first generation born into freedom but her adult life was spent fighting modern racism in new venues.

BETHUNE was born Mary Jane McLeod in South Carolina in 1875 as the fifteenth of seventeen children of parents who had been "married" while they were still enslaved. The family's history in slavery was etched in Bethune's memory through the stories her maternal grandmother, Sophie, told her and her siblings. She had heard her family's story of slavery so often that "she had felt the story, in effect, she had lived the story."[2]

Her grandmother's descriptions of slavery did not spare her young listeners the gruesome details of forced labor and physical and sexual abuse; her own body still bore the scars of whippings she had received when she refused the sexual advances of her master. She taught her grandchildren that their mother, Patsy, had been fathered by a proud descendent of a West African ruling family. Like her own mother, Patsy had refused to submit to sexual abuse at the hands of her owner, and still carried the punishing marks of a scalding on her breast. These stories of resistance inspired Bethune to think of her family, and especially its women, as strong-willed and independent, traits she emulated in her own life. Her family's narrative allowed her to lay claim to being "proudly black" and of "African heritage" with no visible evidence of any racial "admixture" because all of Patsy's children had the same black father.[3]

Born from that lineage into the first free generation of Southern blacks, Bethune inherited high family hopes that freedom would permit her to excel in life. Because she was the first of the family's children to be born free, Patsy said to her husband: "She is a child of prayer, Samuel. I asked the Master to send us a child who would show us the way out. Of course, I expected He would bless us with a boy. But His will be done." Religious belief and observance were central to her family's life which was structured by morning and evening prayers and Sunday services.[4]

Bethune was born into the expectation that she would be a leader. When her parents spared her from farmwork so she could attend a local missionary school, they did so on the condition that she share what she learned with the other children in her family and neighborhood. Bethune so impressed Emma Wilson, the young black missionary teacher at the school, that Wilson nominated her for a scholarship to the Presbyterian-run Scotia

Seminary in Concord, North Carolina. Staffed by both black and white teachers, the school had a deep influence on Bethune's ideas about the potentialities of religious and interracial enterprises. At Scotia she was exposed to whites who were invested in her success and encouraged her ambitions, a stance that in the 1890s contrasted with the South's virulent racism. Her experience there led her to decide at an early age that she wanted to be a missionary like Wilson and engage in Christian social service.[5]

After completing the program at Scotia in 1893, Bethune received another scholarship, this time to the Chicago Evangelization Society (later renamed the Moody Bible Institute). The nondenominational school, which had been established by white evangelists working with Dwight Moody, trained ministers and lay people for missionary and religious work. At the age of eighteen and a very long way from the rural South, Bethune became the school's first black student. She was the only one during her tenure there, but in her later recollections of that time she made little mention of any disparate treatment or alienation. Indeed, she credited Dwight Moody with providing the sanctification experience that undergirded her life's work. She had vivid memories of what she had felt during a special service he led. "I realized a quickening and awakening that I had not words to express from that day to the present."[6]

Bethune's proud ties to Africa had awakened her desire to serve as a Christian missionary there, an ironic instinct for black Christians of her generation who viewed Africa with affection but still primarily as a place in need of the "civilizing" influence of Christianity. A year before she enrolled at the Moody Institute, she had a revelation that she was to become a Presbyterian missionary to Africa. She was deeply disappointed, however, when her request to serve there was turned down by Presbyterian church officials because she was not white, another racial irony. When her dreams of service to Africa were dashed, Bethune returned to her native South Carolina and became an assistant at the school where her own education had started. After a year's service there, Bethune requested and received a transfer to work under Lucy Laney at Haines Industrial and Normal Institute in Georgia. Bethune was inspired by Laney's example as a religiously motivated educator and institution builder who was committed to nurturing black women leaders.[7]

Following Laney's model, Bethune wanted to build her own school and dedicate it to educating a generation of religiously motivated black women as "community workers." She taught at other missionary schools in the South, including South Carolina, Georgia, and eventually Florida. During that period, Bethune met and married Albertus Bethune and had a son, but it proved difficult to reconcile her husband's expectations of a traditional marriage with her own bold professional aims and ambitions. In 1908, after a decade of marriage, she and her husband separated; he moved away to live with a sister and died of tuberculosis in 1918. After he left, Bethune sent her son, an only child, to boarding school at Laney's Haines Institute. She never remarried. Like many other black female public figures of her generation, Bethune turned from the obligations of domestic life and devoted her considerable energies to working in the public sphere.[8]

Bethune attributed her strength for a long life of public service to a "consecration" she received from the black Holiness evangelist Amanda Berry Smith. In a chance encounter between the two women, Smith declared, "Mary McLeod Bethune, I have been to Africa three times; I have traveled around the world; I have been looking for someone upon whom to throw my mantle. As I talk with you, Mary Bethune, I believe you are the one to wear my mantle. Get down here, child, and let us pray." As they dropped to their knees together, Bethune received what she believed to be a consecration for Christian service and discipleship, but one that she chose to live out in civic worlds rather than the sanctified one of Holiness churches. Bethune's move away from the world of black evangelization, despite the hand of Smith's powerful consecration, was an early sign of her religious independence. Perhaps it also indicated that Bethune was uncomfortable with the Holiness tradition's focus on an interior world of devout personal religious practice to the exclusion of engagement in more worldly affairs.[9]

Bethune's dream of her own school was realized in 1904 in Florida where she founded the Daytona Educational and Industrial School for Negro Girls. Many factors drew her to Daytona, including its well-established, resourceful, and supportive black community and a racial climate that was relatively peaceful, tempered by its wealthy white winter residents and the service economy they spawned. By the end of its second year of operation, the school had provided 250 female students with a basic education. A decade later, the school had nine teachers, a classical liberal arts curriculum, and a mission to provide higher education devoted to the formation of "strong, useful Christian women." The school's mission rested on Bethune's belief that the future of the race rested primarily on the type of education available to black women. "Very early in my life, I saw the vision of what our women might contribute to the growth and development of the race,—if they were given a certain type of intellectual training. I longed to see women,—Negro women, hold in their hands diplomas which bespoke achievement; I longed to see them trained to be inspirational wives and mothers; I longed to see their accomplishments recognized side by side with women anywhere."[10]

Bethune proved to be an excellent fundraiser, attracting the support of prominent white male philanthropists Marshall Field and John D. Rockefeller. After a decade of expansion, she was growing increasingly exhausted by the endless search for funds. Yet she resisted offers of state support or takeover because she wanted the school to remain private, immune to the whims of legislative control. With this in mind, she went in search of a religious denomination that would provide some stable financial footing for the school, but the black denominations that supported many institutions in the South were themselves struggling with limited resources.

Forced to turn to predominantly white denominations with a history of supporting black education, Bethune approached them all with little regard for their theological differences. The Presbyterians, who had trained her and with whom she affiliated, claimed to have insufficient funds; the Catholic Church had money to spare but insisted on complete control, which she refused. The Episcopalians were slow to decide, but the white Methodist denomination offered its support if Bethune would consolidate her school with the all-male Cookman Institute in Jacksonville which they had already funded.[11]

Ever the pragmatist, and with no other real choice, Bethune accepted this offer even though it meant that her chosen mission of serving black women students would have to expand to include men. When the merger was completed in 1923, the newly named Bethune-Cookman College in Daytona went on to become the first accredited black college in Florida. The Methodist church's support provided a more stable though still inadequate source of permanent funding for the school, without removing Bethune's control of it. She was able to preserve the school's nondenominational status. The school did not have compulsory chapel services at a time when many similar institutions did. Students were free to worship or not as they chose; if they wished, they could attend one of the three local black congregations, Methodist, Baptist, or Catholic.[12]

Bethune's persistent and creative fundraising efforts over the years brought in enough money to ensure the survival of the school, which by the early 1920s had a thirty-two-acre campus and four hundred students. Bethune held the position of president for another twenty years, until 1942, but even then, like other founder-presidents, she had great difficulty relinquishing authority over the institution she had sacrificed so much to build. She kept her hand in the governance for many years to come, and today Bethune-Cookman University is flourishing, having graduated more than twelve thousand students. The institution's founding and growth represented a formidable achievement for Bethune, who never knew the joy of receiving a college diploma herself.[13]

Methodism was good both for Bethune-Cookman and for Bethune who soon, at age fifty, switched her own religious affiliation away from Presbyterianism back to the Methodists, the denomination of her early childhood. This was another indication of her own ecumenical religious tendencies. She viewed herself primarily as a Christian, apparently with little regard for doctrinal denominational differences. More importantly, however, she did not choose to join the independent all-black African Methodist Episcopal (AME) denomination whose services she often attended, but opted instead to affiliate with a black Methodist church tied to the predominantly white denominational structure that helped fund her school. She became a member of Stewart Memorial Methodist church, an all-black church within the white Methodist denomination, and maintained her membership there until her death.[14]

Black religious people outside the black Baptist, AME, and AME Zion churches faced a particular set of difficulties as members of black churches within the larger white denominations. The Methodist denomination, like other white Protestant churches, had split along regional lines in the nineteenth century over the issue of slavery. When the denomination moved to reunite its Northern and Southern branches, a move that partly stimulated Woodson's arguments for a United Negro Church, the question of what to do with black Methodist churches like the one Bethune attended took center stage.

The denomination moved to create an entirely separate jurisdictional conference for the black churches nationwide within the General Conference, despite the fact that all other conferences were based on geography and region. That plan, which in effect segregated black churches and their members, was endorsed by a group of two hundred black Methodist ministers within the denomination, including its first black bishop, Robert E. Jones. Their rationale was that the proposal allowed the black ministers to exercise self-governance, something they feared would be lost in an integrated conference. But this view was roundly condemned and ridiculed in the black press as a capitulation to segregation.[15]

When the Plan of Union, as it was called, was debated at the 1936 General Conference, Bethune, who was a delegate to national Methodist conferences for nearly three decades, strongly opposed it and spoke against it. "I have not been able to make my mind see it clearly enough to be willing to have the history of this General Conference written, and the Negro youths of fifty or a hundred years from today read and find that Mary McLeod Bethune acquiesced to anything that looked like segregation to black people." She was joined in her opposition by David D. Jones, who was chosen to represent a caucus of other black delegates. He was Bishop Jones's brother and the president of the Methodist-supported Bennett College for black women in North Carolina. All was for naught, however, as the final vote of 470 to 83 carried the day and created a unified Methodist church with a segregated, all-black conference within it. The newly formed Methodist Church was a victory for Southern white Methodism and for those black Methodists who believed that they would be better served by governing themselves within a separate segregated conference rather than integrated within the larger white fellowship.[16]

For the outspoken Methodist college presidents Bethune and Jones, racial contradictions and religious hypocrisy were not easily relieved or reconciled even within a denomination that provided much-needed financial support for black educational institutions like Bethune-Cookman and Bennett. As in the segregated armed forces, this separation into parallel and separate units was intended to thwart black authority over white people, a possibility within a denomination with presiding bishops, some of whom were now black. In addition, it was designed to prevent the appearance of an "integrated" institution, something that was as important to churches as to the armed services. It seemed to matter little that, unlike the military, the Methodist mission and its authority had been founded on notions of religious egalitarianism, cooperation, and communion.

Paradoxically, of course, at the same time that Bethune and Jones resisted efforts to create new segregated entities, they both proudly presided over all-black educational institutions. In 1943, both were among the black college presidents who helped to establish the United Negro College Fund which was designed to ensure the survival of private, mostly church-affiliated black colleges in an era when the legal campaign to end segregation in higher education commenced. Bethune persisted in her belief in the value of formal education that took place in settings infused with a religious ethos of service, something that would not occur in publicly funded institutions. This kind of training was especially important, she believed, for preparing race leaders who could survive the "spiritual animosities of the world." She explained that "only Christian education can have born into the mind of the Negro leader the optimism which will fight for his goal in spite of lynchings, social depravities, inadequate school facilities and injustices of various sorts." She saw black schools like hers not only as educating young black people, but as providing them with the spiritual armor and faith needed to lead and sustain the fight against racial injustices.[17]

Bethune remained convinced of the need for training black women in particular to assume positions of racial leadership. Even though she had agreed to make her school coeducational in return for Methodist support, she never gave up her original vision of a college dedicated exclusively to young black women. In 1938, she launched an urgent plea with the Methodist board, asking that the school be returned to that original mission. Bethune stressed that there were only two all-female colleges available to black women (the Baptist-funded Spelman and the Methodist-sponsored Bennett), although the number of black women who were prepared to enter college had overtaken the number of black men. More than that, Bethune emphasized the need for four full years of college training for black women, as opposed to the junior-college experience that Bethune-Cookman was limited to at the time.[18]

Bethune complained that the educational programs at black schools, "to avoid the semblance of effeminacy, have consciously or unconsciously been shaped to the interests and probable careers of young men." She pointed out that even though black women had equaled or exceeded the academic performance of their male counterparts, few efforts were directed at preparing them for careers as teachers, civic leaders, and skilled homemakers. For her, this was a waste of the leadership potential of "socially intelligent and spiritually alive" young black women. Bethune's pleas went unheeded by the Methodist board. Meanwhile, her colleague David Jones continued to preside over the all-female and Methodist-supported Bennett College.[19]

BETHUNE pursued her commitment to black female leadership by joining a network of Southern black women active in the women's club movement. In 1924, she defeated Ida B. Wells to become president of the National Association of Colored Women, a position she held for four years.[20] In her speeches and writings in the 1930s, Bethune spoke proudly about the achievements of black women since slavery and credited them with much of the progress made by the race as a whole. Looking back on the position of black women in slavery, she concluded that "the Negro woman embodies one of the modern miracles of the New World." Under slavery, a black woman was nothing but a "household drudge," an "animated agricultural implement," and an "automatic incubator, producer of human livestock."[21]

Bethune also challenged the history of black churches as it had been written by Carter Woodson, though she did this without naming him directly. She called the development of the churches since the Civil War a "modern miracle" that would have been impossible without the work of black women. "Throughout its growth the untiring effort, the unflagging enthusiasm, the sacrificial contribution of time, effort, and cash earnings of the black woman have been the most significant factors without which the modern Negro church would have no history worth the writing." In no field had the service and influence of black women been "felt more distinctly than in the Negro orthodox church." Yet even though she recognized the enormous contribution that black women had made to the church, she cast them largely as fundraisers and organizers, not as religious leaders.[22]

Bethune's account of the development of Southern black churches veered sharply from the one advanced by Woodson since her emphasis was on black women rather than on black male ministers. Surprisingly, she also disagreed with Woodson's assessment of the political function of black churches immediately after the Civil War. She characterized them not as sites of political resistance to white oppression but as a "steadying agency" that deserved credit for "the miraculous restraint it has exerted over the natural impulses of a horde of freshly-emancipated people." Similarly, though Du Bois embraced sorrow songs as modes of protest, Bethune offered a different interpretation. "'Take your burden to the Lord and leave it there,' has been the plaintive melody," she wrote, "the practical acceptance of whose sentiment has distinctly affected for the better, the history of Reconstruction in the South following the Civil War." In these ways, Bethune seemed to embrace the idea of black Christianity's ameliorating influence.[23]

Credit for the achievements of black men had to be shared equally with black women, Bethune argued, despite the fact that the "struggling clutch of die-hard tradition" created "certain social situations open to the Negro man to which the Negro woman may not be admitted." Black women still had to fight for leadership positions because "she has not always been permitted a place in the front ranks where she could show her face and make her voice heard." In recognition of Bethune's leadership of black women and at Bethune-Cookman, the NAACP awarded her its prestigious Spingarn Medal in 1935. Among the wide array of congratulatory notes she received was one from Adam Clayton Powell Sr. in which he teased her about the deeper significance of the award. "It is a long way from the rice and cotton farm of South Carolina to this distinguished recognition," he wrote, "but you have made it in such a short span of years that I am afraid you are going to be arrested for breaking the speed limit." Little did he know that Bethune was just beginning, or at least beginning the next phase of a long professional life which would build on her idea that black women were ready to assume broader political roles.[24]

It was Bethune's work within the black women's club movement that brought her into contact with prominent white women, including Franklin Roosevelt's mother and later his wife, Eleanor, both of whom helped her become an advisor to the president and in 1936 the director of minority affairs of the National Youth Administration (NYA). She held this position for seven years until the NYA was terminated. Bethune used her tenure there to build an expanded nationwide network of black educators and social workers interested in the problems of black youth.

Bethune's access to President Roosevelt, through her friendship with the First Lady, added to her aura of power. She was recognized as a national figure during that time and served on the boards of the NAACP and the National Urban League, and as president of the ASNLH, a position she assumed at Carter Woodson's request in 1938. These were very impressive achievements, especially for a Southern rural black woman born to newly freed ex-slaves in the Reconstruction period and with limited access to a formal education. All the more remarkable was the fact that it was she and not any of the more powerfully situated black men working for the Roosevelt administration who was often credited with holding the most strategic position in the administration on race issues and with crafting a clearly stated program of demands in this area.[25]

That Bethune was a woman seemed never far from the minds of black men who wrote about her in the press or talked about her privately. E. Franklin Frazier was amazed that a woman without a formal education or prominent family connections could achieve as much as Bethune had. He also accused her of having an "ego problem" and of becoming "more domineering and arrogant as she acquired power and prestige." This was and still is a familiar refrain about women in leadership positions.[26]

Even in crediting her with organizing black public officials into a working unit, one reporter described her assumption of power as a gathering of "everything and everybody under her very ample wing." Another black writer referred to her as a "modern matriarch" and introduced his profile of her with this lead: "Not once but many times will the thought of the ancient matriarchies of primitive Africa occur to one who comes to know of the life and work of Mary McLeod Bethune." Bethune was proud of her family's African heritage, but here the reporter connected it with her rise to power. "Her mother was a direct descendent of a ruling family in West Africa, where even today descent, kinship, and succession are reckoned through the mother."[27]

Bethune understood the symbolic nature of racial and gender politics in an age of photojournalism, especially in a period when black newspapers covered her Washington activities closely. She knew that she was a racial token, but she believed her physical presence as a representative of the race was an important influence on both whites and blacks. Writing in her diary after attending a tea at the White House, Bethune confessed, "While I felt very much at home, I looked about me longingly for other dark faces. In all that great group I felt a sense of being quite alone." But this was a sacrifice she was willing to make for the larger good. "Then I thought how vitally important it was that I be here, to help these others get used to seeing us in high places. And so, while I sip tea in the brilliance of the White House, my heart reaches out to the delta land and the bottom land. I know so well why I *must* be here, *must* go to tea at the White House. To remind them always that we belong here, we are a part of this America."[28]

By the 1940s, Bethune's political legacy was secured by her proximity to power and access, whether in her relationship with Eleanor Roosevelt or through her well-publicized trips to the White House as the only woman among a small handful of educated black federal officials. Bethune believed that her work as a member of the so-called Black Cabinet and as a representative of the NCNW benefited the race as a whole, and not just black women.

Bethune's experience as a national political figure in Washington convinced her that the political promised land for black people was not over the River Jordan, but on the northern shores of the Potomac. Her faith and belief in the power of the national state deepened as the state itself grew more powerful under Roosevelt's New Deal, including its limited outreach to African Americans. Bethune embraced a brand of liberalism that put faith in the national democratic state as a central tool in the improvement of the lives of black people. To her, the ballot, access to civil service and political patronage, and legislative advocacy could be used to bring the powers of the federal government to the cause of racial equality.

Those beliefs were part of the impetus in 1935, when Bethune, then sixty, had organized an umbrella organization in Washington that would link all black women's groups, primarily clubs and sororities, into a single political lobby. Her specific inspiration came during a visit she had made to a Woman's Convention meeting of the all-black National Baptist Convention. There she heard black women giving "a large group of reports from crude places, but it showed that they were blazing away for better things." More importantly, she appreciated the full extent of the local networks of women working within black Baptist churches, in numbers far exceeding those of organized secular women's clubs. That, and the limited inclusion of black women and their interests in the white-run National Council of Women, culminated in her idea for a National Council of Negro Women. Like Woodson urging consolidation among black churches, Bethune too seemed to be in search of some larger unified basis for collective racial advocacy, but in the secular realm and led by women.[29]

One aspect of the NCNW's history that is often overlooked, however, is its affiliation with several of the women's auxiliaries of major black religious denominations, including the Woman's Convention of the National Baptist Convention, and the corollary groups for the AME and AME Zion churches and the Church of

God in Christ, a major Holiness denomination. This attempt to unify groups of club women and church women, though there was overlap among the women's affiliations, had the potential to bridge the secular club movement with the religious work of those very large denominations. At the same time, these connections held the promise for greater class diversity within the NCNW and among women performing community work in venues outside women's clubs. The extent to which that promise was realized, however, appears to have been very limited.[30]

Bethune used her presence in Washington to speak in strong support of the political demands that African Americans were making during the Second World War, before and especially after she left her federal post at the NYA. This is made clear in Bethune's submission for the 1944 anthology *What the Negro Wants*. The book had its own political history, having originated with requests to a sample of African Americans from across the political spectrum for essays on the political, economic, and societal desires of African Americans. It had been hoped that the group's answers would refute Myrdal's bleak rendering of American democracy's racial dilemma. On the contrary, the writers all agreed that Myrdal's assessment was correct and that the time for change was now.[31]

Although Bethune was not the only Southerner in the group, she was the only woman. When she prepared her response, she answered the question "What does the Negro want?" in ways that were a startling departure from the more diplomatic political language she usually employed during the years she worked in the Roosevelt administration. Her essay began with an American history lesson comparing the race riots of 1943 to the Boston Tea Party, holding both up as examples of what can result from "a rumbling of anger and resentment." She cast these latest events as "uprisings" that were part of a world movement by repressed people, made more potent in the United States by the resentment of the mistreatment of black soldiers. Cries of "Go slow!" would no longer be heard, she warned.[32]

Black people now wanted, in her words, "what all other Americans want." They wanted equal opportunity and equal legal and civil rights. She emphasized the need for a strong federal government obligated to ensure that "the ideals of democracy and Christianity work for equality," especially in the armed services. Beyond this, she called for the protection of civil rights, an end to lynching, access to the ballot, equal access to jobs (especially publicly funded ones), and new federal programs of increased support for education, health, housing. These were all positions that the NCNW had supported as well. Indeed, these were ideas that Bethune and the black women associated with the women's club movement had proposed as early as the 1920s.[33]

Bethune characterized the rising militancy among African Americans as "a people's movement" and as "a march of the masses." "All of us must go forward with it or be pushed aside by it." She urged people to engage in open protest so the government would lift the restrictions on full citizenship: "We must take the seat that our ticket calls for and place upon the proprietor the responsibility of denying us. We must challenge everywhere the principle and practice of enforced racial segregation." In her answer to the question of what African Americans wanted, Bethune asserted that black women bore a "tremendous responsibility" in this struggle because they always had been essential to the race's progress, repeatedly rising out of their own despair "to help our men climb the next rung of the ladder." She linked the strength of black women to the "courage and tenacity" of their slave forebears as well as to the surge of politically and socially engaged women around the world.[34]

Bethune made no special pleas on behalf of black women or for their special political or economic needs as women *per se*, nor did she urge the use of their status as the ultimate barometer of the nation's commitment to its democratic ideals. This stance was consistent with her political philosophy which stressed the importance of moving educated black women into positions of power and influence, following the model that she had embraced and benefited from in her own life. This left her open to criticism that she was ignoring the needs of less well-educated or uneducated, poor, black working women and focusing too narrowly on opening opportunities for educated black women. Bethune also continued to place great faith in the democratic political system and paid less attention to economic disparities between the races. Voting rights and political patronage seemed to her a way to gain access to the enormous powers of the federal government. With that, she believed, the rest would follow.

IN HER final addresses as president of the National Council of Negro Women in 1948 and 1949, Bethune did something surprising. She told the women assembled that her initial aim in founding the council and her dream of creating an "integrated spiritual unit" representing black womanhood had been achieved. Bethune recommended that the council open itself to "any" woman who shared its goals, and that the "limiting adjective designating the racial origin of membership" be eliminated altogether. She proposed that the group be renamed "The National Council of United Women."[35]

As if to reassure her assembled black women listeners, Bethune predicted that "Negro women would always be represented in largest numbers in the organization perhaps, and none of the interest which has focused on the problems of our women in American life, would be deflected to other concerns, but this interest would simply extend itself to include all women of our own country, and

the world." As part of this move, the NCNW's long-running magazine, the *Aframerican Women's Journal,* also would have its name
changed to *Women United.* It would no longer focus exclusively
on black women but would strive "to promote justice, amity, understanding and cooperation among all women regardless of race,
creed, color or station in life" or as she emphasized, become a group
of "women united for human rights." Her proposal to rename the
organization did not succeed, but the magazine's name was
changed to *Women United.*[36]

These changes were consistent with her ideas about broad unifications and, more locally, with the prospects for all-black institutions in an age when black claims for an end to desegregation were
mounting. When legal challenges to racial discrimination in voting and in higher education began to meet some success in the
mid- and late-1940s, Bethune, like many of her contemporaries,
wrote about the broader implications of a possible end to legalized
segregation. In 1948, she had begun to write a weekly column for
the *Chicago Defender.* As public talk of the prospect of integration
increased, she felt compelled to join the discussion.

On the question of integrating colleges and universities, Bethune
argued that she would close all "segregated Negro institutions"
across the South if black students in return could attend any school
in any state in the South. In the interim, however, she urged
the maintenance and support of black institutions like Bethune-
Cookman because they still produced the vast majority of college-
educated youth. This was the group she saw as future race leaders,
writing that "we cannot stop the training of replacements for those
of us who are fighting Jim Crow today" and who would continue to
come from "the inadequate, segregated schools of the South."[37]

The fate of black institutions in an integrated world would be a
vexing question for many African Americans in the period leading
up to the *Brown* decision. If one were opposed to segregation, then

one would argue against the retention of those institutions. In a 1950 column, she did just that: "We shall have to dispense with the little monopolies which were the accommodations and partial compensations of segregation." In this case, the monopolies she referred to were black churches and black schools. To buttress her argument, she quoted approvingly from a speech given by Edwin Embree, director of the Rosenwald Fund. *"Negroes who protest discrimination sometimes are as guilty of it as their white neighbors,"* Embree said. "Some Negro preachers have a vested interest in segregated churches. . . . Some Negro teachers see a benefit to themselves in being secured positions in a segregated school system."[38]

Once the *Brown* case was in process, Bethune's discussions of the potential costs of integration to black institutions moved from the theoretical to the practical, including fears that black teachers would lose their jobs in the move to consolidate and desegregate school systems. Bethune tried to assuage those concerns by arguing, in effect, that only incompetent black teachers would suffer. "This may be a shocking point of view," she wrote, "but we must not support the walls of segregation because it gives us job security. To do this is to deny our children the highest type of education."[39]

In the months immediately preceding the Supreme Court's decision, Bethune began warning against expecting the decision to change things dramatically for better or for worse. "It will not even resolve segregation in education," she predicted. Yet when the decision actually was announced, the tenor of Bethune's writings changed dramatically, since she saw the court's action as preordained. Referring to the ruling itself, she wrote, "The words were those of the Court and the voice was that of conscience, but the truth was God's." In a speech one month after the decision, she confessed that "when I first heard of the Supreme Court decision, I lifted my voice to utter the first inspiration of my heart—and I said, 'Let the people praise Thee, O God! Let ALL the people praise

Thee.'" When she described black reactions to *Brown*, she again invoked a sense of inevitability. "I am proud of the quiet, modest way in which my people received the news of this decision. And why not? We have God and justice on our side."[40]

Consistent with her analysis of the role of black churches during the chaos and transitions of the Reconstruction era, Bethune urged other blacks to rely on a "religious frame of mind" in the days ahead when they would need to resist any temptation toward violence or any hesitation in embracing the opportunities she believed would be available. "It is our constitutional duty to enter now the doors opened for us. It is a false idea that 'we must take our time.' The time has now come."[41]

Bethune's enthusiastic response to the *Brown* decision was consistent with the NAACP's position, but some African Americans expressed reservations about the implications of the case. Among them was Bethune's fellow Floridian Zora Neale Hurston who created a flurry of controversy when she rejected what she saw as an underlying premise of the decision, that there was something inherently wrong with black schools. Having been raised in the all-black town of Eatonville and educated in its public schools, Hurston took it as an insult that the decision implied that schools controlled by whites were best able to educate black students. Gliding over the question of the lack of equal resources, which was the heart of the problem, Hurston rejected the Supreme Court's decision as an insult to black people and argued against "forcible association" with white people as the solution to racial inequality. To her, there was nothing magical to be gained from sitting alongside whites and she denounced such "forcible association."[42]

Hurston viewed the experience of being in an all-black setting as enriching and affirming rather than denigrating and demeaning, as the social scientific arguments for ending school segregation had claimed. Her ideas were consistent with her long-standing views on the vitality and independence of African American culture. Hurston did not oppose desegregation. "As a Negro, you know I cannot be in favor of segregation, but I do deplore the way they go about ending it." In this way, she was insightful about the potential negative impact of desegregation on black institutions. Yet hers was a minority voice and she was roundly criticized and dismissed by other African Americans for her views. She called instead for the investment of sufficient funds to improve existing black schools, a step that few states and localities, whether in the South or elsewhere, have yet found the political will to do.[43]

Bethune and other African Americans also worried about the impact of *Brown* on the continued existence and viability of black institutions, but they were less blunt about it publicly. In her role as a columnist, she wrote glowingly of the historic political role of black newspapers as "a real service to all the people of the country." In an argument similar to the one she had made about black colleges, she predicted the eventual demise of the black press "only when the Negro has found his full place as an American citizen and our society ceases to think first in terms of color." Until then, Bethune concluded, "minority groups must have a voice, an organ of expression." Her strong faith in black newspapers and magazines was consistent with that expressed by the authors of *Black Metropolis* and *An American Dilemma*. What neither she nor they could anticipate was that black weeklies would soon become vulnerable to competition from television and from white daily newspapers' coverage of the fight against segregation, despite the fact that racial integration itself remained elusive.[44]

At the same time that Bethune was concerned about the fate of black institutions in an age of desegregation, she was also committed to models for broader unifications of people around the world.

In the last decade of her life, Bethune turned increasingly to religious interpretations of contemporary political events and of the meaning of her own work. She had always been a person of strong private faith, but now she explicitly and eloquently credited her personal faith and spiritual practices with having given her the stamina and vision behind her own long life. "As I look over the years, I feel my faith and my work have justified each other. My life has been a spiritual thing, a religious reality, creative and alive. Whatever 'works' I have done have 'justified' my faith, as Saint Paul would say, for I have daily felt the presence of God in the tasks he has set before me in visions, and I have known His Divine Guidance and Presence through all the years."[45]

Bethune moved toward a racial, religious, and political universalism shared by other African American religious intellectuals and political activists in the immediate post–World War II era, although for different reasons and in quite varied ways. The combination of world war, the atomic bomb, the opportunities for world travel, and her participation in international gatherings paved the way for Bethune's expanded emphasis on human rights. Increasingly, she also reckoned with the limitations of Christianity itself.

The colossal death and destruction wrought by World War II and America's use of the atomic bomb jolted Bethune and other African American public figures. Bethune sought new mechanisms for peaceful coexistence in this period. The driving concern was not a false dichotomy of "human rights" versus "civil rights" that some have seen, but the palpable fear and deep anxiety of entering a Cold War with two new superpower nations capable of destroying each other and the world itself with technological ease. For Bethune and other black Christians, this was interpreted as a development with consequences of biblical proportions that had to be met by worldwide spiritual forces of equal strength. In the last decade of her life, this was her central spiritual and political quest. Her writings and speeches in this period were replete with references to the atomic bomb and the need for mechanisms to prevent war and conflict, because the consequences were too grave to imagine.

Those fears drove her fervent embrace of the idea of a United Nations. At her request, and over the objections of some within the NAACP, she begged her way into being appointed a United States delegate to the UN's founding convention in San Francisco, along with Du Bois and Walter White. She later described that experience primarily in spiritual terms. It was like seeing a new world order in action: "As the sessions continued, and the languages and voices constantly made articulate their common plea for world peace, world cooperation, world good-will, world freedom and world security—a spiritual something began to weld them together and to undergird their efforts as they worked on the development of a program for the common good. The leaven of democracy was at work."[46]

The "new world order" that Bethune hoped for found its model in Pentecost, a religious paradigm that she and some other African Americans turned to in this period. Although its origins are rooted in the Hebrew Bible, especially the Book of Joel, for Christians Pentecost symbolizes the hope for a church composed of diverse peoples. This is based on a story in the Book of Acts when the Holy Spirit came down among the followers of Jesus and allowed them to speak and hear as one body, despite their many languages and practices. Beginning with a quote from that biblical account, Bethune likened the United Nations to modern-day Babel but one aided by modern technology and simultaneous translations: "We are told that as the men sit around the United Nations Conference table in New York, the discussions are transported and translated over a mechanism which makes possible a modern Pentecost."[47]

During the five weeks of the conference, Bethune was especially encouraged by the interactions between the large numbers of African Americans and men of color from colonially occupied lands in the Far East, the Middle East, and Africa. Still, she was the only black woman who held official status at the conference and again she felt the heavy burden of representation, both as a woman and as someone sympathetic to the millions of colonial peoples who had no formal representation at the conference. When those peoples were denied any real protections, she joined with Du Bois and White in protest. While she was inspired by the potential for greater international unity represented at the gathering, she was not naïve about what had been actually achieved or about the work that still needed to be done. "'San Francisco' is not building the promised land of brotherhood and security and equal opportunity and peace," she said. But "it is building a bridge to get there by."[48]

Despite her realization that the ideal of a United Nations was far from being achieved, Bethune nonetheless remained convinced of the necessity for some mechanism for international recognition and cooperation. She was deeply moved by her own personal interactions within such a diverse gathering of people from places that she had only read or heard about but never had the opportunity to visit. For her, the meetings were especially spiritually invigorating because she saw the UN as a symbolic representation of universal religious concepts of communion and peaceful coexistence. In that way, the political and the religious converged. She came away from the UN gatherings even more committed to the principles of a common set of human rights that she saw under threat not just by economic and political oppression, but by the newly created technologies designed to obliterate and destroy on such a massive scale. These were the lessons that Bethune took away from her time in San Francisco, and they were ones that she pursued for the rest of her life.

Speaking in Montreal in 1946 about her experience at the UN conference, she cast that gathering in religious terms, reporting that "there was a spiritual something that undergirded their every thought and action." Bethune also bluntly warned that "the slogan today is not just simply 'One World' but 'One World or No World.' The atomic bomb which crashed into the Isle of Japan, less than a year ago, has brought us face to face with a realization of the world at our very door steps. . . . We must learn to live with these peoples peacefully or all perish within the twinkling of an eye." Bethune took a similar message a few months later to a national conference of the AME Zion Church in New York City.[49]

Two years later, when Mahatma Gandhi was killed in 1948, Bethune spoke in Washington at a gathering to honor his life. She framed Gandhi's life, work, and death in ways that reflected her own Christian beliefs even as she searched for a broader way of talking about him. "When Mahatma Gandhi fell mortally wounded in the garden of New Delhi," she began, "my heart trembled with the thought that here again is Gethsemane and Golgotha," referring to the death of Christ. Placing him in the company of other spiritual figures, she asked plaintively, "Could such a Spirit die? Did Buddha die?—or Christ?" No, she answered. Gandhi was a spiritual force who forged a political weapon "out of his love of God and of his fellow man," providing a living example for the United Nations as well as for a free and independent India and the Western world. "As mothers of the earth stand in awesome fear of the roar of jet planes, the crash of atom bombs and the unknown horrors of germ warfare," she said, "we must turn our eyes in hope to the East where the Sun of Mahatma blazes." She ended by declaring the lessons of the Mahatma and the Christ as the "only answers to the atom bomb that we have not yet tried."[50]

Her horror, shared by other African American Christians, at the destruction caused by the first atomic bomb aroused in her an even more fervent belief in the need for a unified struggle for world peace, a goal she saw as contingent upon the success of the fight to end racial oppression. "The advent of the Atomic Age flattened out a great deal of race consciousness among all peoples," she wrote. "It eliminated at one sweep, the zones of 'safe living,' the places where it was possible for one part of the world placidly to ignore any other part."[51]

While Bethune professed a continued faith in American democracy and institutional Christianity, she doubted that either could bring about world peace or end racial injustice. She admitted that when it came to the early appeals against racial segregation, the "government has bowed to the inevitable." "In some areas," she observed, "it has bowed graciously; in other areas, grudgingly."[52]

At the same time, Bethune predicted a political shift marked by the "gradual disappearance of the one-spokesman concept," of which she had been such a great beneficiary. Instead, black people were now beginning to listen "not to just one or two people who can 'speak for' them, but to many people who speak with authority, not from pinnacles, but from vantage points gained by mingling, observing and working with the masses." Her plea was not just for a new kind of mass-based leadership but also for a different kind of Christianity, one that "would call for an increase in religion not to 'drown our sorrows,' but to inspire our souls" and that would not act as an "opiate."[53]

Bethune's spiritual and political ideas in this period were deeply influenced by opportunities to participate in some international gatherings. In the 1920s Bethune had traveled as a tourist throughout Europe on a trip sponsored by an association of black doctors, and in 1930 she had visited Cuba. But the travel at this stage of her life connected more directly with her life's work and influenced her political and religious beliefs in new directions. The president of Haiti invited her to help celebrate the 1949 Haitian Exposition.

She traveled the countryside and was awarded the Medal of Honor and Merit, the country's highest honor, given for the first time to a woman. While she was there, Bethune made public her urgent recommendation that voting rights be extended as soon as possible to Haiti's women. Three years later, Bethune finally made it to Africa when she formed part of an inaugural delegation to Liberia. In a whirlwind of activity, she explored the country, including its many missions and churches, and met with women's groups, founding a branch of the NCNW while she was there. These trips to lands ruled by people of African and African American descent moved Bethune deeply.[54]

In what would be her last trip abroad, in the summer of 1954, Bethune traveled not back to Africa but to Caux, Switzerland, where she attended the World Assembly for Moral Re-Armament (MRA) at the invitation of the group's president, Frank N. D. Buchman. Bethune's experience there, rather than the ones in Haiti and Liberia, had the most profound effect on her political and spiritual beliefs at the end of her life.

Buchman, a white American Lutheran pastor, founded an organization in Europe in 1938 that called for a worldwide spiritual awakening. His work, known originally as the Oxford Group, generated considerable controversy and criticism. Buchman was adamantly anti-Communist and had been accused of being partial to fascism; only the group's efforts assisting the war recovery effort in Europe allowed Buchman's reputation as a right-wing sympathizer to recover, enabling the group's international influence to grow in the postwar period. Later accounts of MRA have mixed assessments. Some have accused the movement of being a right-wing "cult" while others have charted its influence on the founders of both Alcoholics Anonymous and Amnesty International and on white Americans drawn to its Cold War racial liberalism.[55]

Buchman's philosophy rested on four principles that, if accepted, would transform human relationships, individually and globally. The principles themselves were disarmingly simple: absolute purity, absolute honesty, absolute unselfishness, and absolute love. If large groups of people joined together and practiced these principles in their own lives and in their interactions with others, then they would be empowered to dismantle oppressive regimes, for example, in South Africa where he was focusing some of his organizing.[56]

The principles could be applied by anyone regardless of religion, race, class, or color. Buchman's group had given special attention to including colonized people of color in its campaigns, especially in Africa where it offered itself both as an ideological alternative to Communism and as a way to heal the hatreds of colonial oppression. Those were the claims that had first attracted Bethune's attention to the Moral Re-Armament movement in the late 1930s. She later devoted several of her newspaper columns to the movement and its work in South Africa which had gained the support of the African National Congress.[57] The invitation for Bethune to attend an international MRA conference came as part of the organization's devotion of considered energies to recruiting African American supporters for its work, an aspect of its American program that has been overlooked. Although she was no longer at the height of her political powers, Bethune's towering stature as a leader of black women and as an educator convinced MRA officials that her support would heighten their visibility among black people.

Bethune's attendance at the conference in Caux came as she entered her eightieth year but her accounts of her time there and its meanings for her are lucid, powerful, and poignant. She spent two full weeks in meetings, meditation, and services high in the Alps at the palatial resort that served as the movement's headquarters. There, Bethune had "a soul shaking experience" as one of her colleagues called it. "As I sit 3,000 feet above sea level overlooking

Lake Geneva, surrounded by the snow-capped Swiss and French Alps, at the World Assembly for Moral Re-Armament," Bethune wrote in the *Chicago Defender*, "my heart reaches out to all the readers of this column with a sincere desire that every single one of you might be as privileged as I am these days to sit with 800 from 30 nations gathered from all over the world." The power of the setting and the gathering convinced Bethune that Moral Re-Armament was the best and only way to achieve global peace, human rights, and an end to discrimination against people of color all over the world.[58]

Bethune's attendance at these meetings was very well publicized in black newspapers because she still elicited such attention. But the coverage was enhanced because the Re-Armament Movement had an extremely sophisticated public relations machinery in which Bethune was treated, and used, like a star. She also took her enthusiasm for the movement to radio, telling an interviewer that her trip to Caux had been the "greatest experience of her life" and that it was "like opening a new door." Bethune found hope there for improved race relations in the United States. "I could not help realizing as these men spoke that here was the spirit that could implement the recent legislation on segregation and make it work. Laws alone can never remove the hates and bitterness from the human heart." She also was deeply affected in particular by the large numbers of delegates from Africa and Asia.[59]

More than the global ramifications of the meeting, Bethune took to heart MRA's emphasis on absolute unselfishness and the diminution of the ego. In her address to the assembly at Caux, Bethune went to great lengths to apologize publicly to her son, Albert, whose needs she believed she had neglected in pursuit of her work, her ambition, and her school. "I think first of my son, my only son, my only child," she said, "how I had to leave him in the care of others as I tramped all over America looking for nickels, dimes, dollars, and quarters," despite his repeated pleas to her not to leave him again. Although she rationalized that her work was for a broader good, she also regretted that her public commitments had blinded her to her son's emotional needs.[60]

In the privacy of her personal letters, Bethune also expressed herself passionately and powerfully about her newfound belief in Moral Re-Armament which preoccupied her in the final months of her life. In a letter to a friend and colleague, Bethune explains how she had been affected by attending those meetings, again with echoes of Pentecost: "All of the assemblies were glorious. The peoples of the world were there. The silent hours, the testimonials, the listening for the guidance we need in all that we do are so enriching." After a lifetime of working for a collective response to the problems of injustice, Bethune became captivated by the notion that individual devotion to four simple tenets could change the world. "I am striving day by day to live up to the four standards of Moral Re-Armament—first, absolute purity; second, absolute honesty; third, absolute unselfishness; fourth, absolute love. If we can gear ourselves to these standards and can bring those that surround us to a change of heart and determination we will soon belt the world where we shall have brotherhood and peace and freedom without war and bloodshed." In another letter to a friend, Bethune emphasized how changed she had been by the experience of attending the conference. "It was a wonderful gathering of people from all over the world uniting their strength and their spiritual awakening to help build a new world, a better world in which to live—a world where mankind will be brethren everywhere, where we will have peace and happiness and freedom, where no war and bombshell will be needed but where the spirit of the fatherhood of God will dwell and we will forever abide in him."[61]

In addition to the assembly at Caux, Bethune also attended and publicized other Moral Re-Armament meetings held in subsequent months in the United States, including a small one in Mount Kisco, New York, and two much larger gatherings, the first at the Grand Hotel on Mackinac Island, Michigan, and the other in Washington, D.C. Bethune pleaded with Claude Barnett of the black newspapers association to devote press coverage to the events. "The most important Assembly of our time is being held now at Mackinac Island under the auspices of Moral Re-Armament," she wrote him from the Grand Hotel. She emphasized to him that the movement "has the answer to the conflicting problems of America and the world. Our public relations department would like to send you a daily coverage of what is going on here, so that the Negro people of America may know more definitely about the scope and importance of this Assembly." Some members of the black press expressed skepticism about MRA and raised questions about whether Bethune's ailing health and advanced age clouded her judgment about the group.[62]

The continued urgency and sincerity of her pleas were borne out in her public remarks at the meeting held at Mount Kisco where she once again talked about the power of individual transformation and the necessity for renewed humility. Saying that she had been "on the fringe of Moral Re-Armament for the past 15 years" but had resisted getting "into the deep water," Bethune spoke at length about her own life's work and her frustration that so much remained to be done. "In America we have suffered so in segregation. You can't sleep here; you can't listen to music there; you can't do this; you can't do that. As I looked I saw Frank Buchman with his army of men and women from all over the world touching one another, all God's children, all waiting for his voice to direct them, all banding together as one great army to go out to the world to preach justice." She felt that compared with this sense of a worldwide movement, her work had been too individualistic, too focused on "Mary McLeod Bethune" and her own legacy, which left her with no remnant of followers. And once again, she confessed her sense of failure as a mother whose only son had disappointed her because she had abandoned him emotionally, she feared, in her devotion to work.[63]

Yet even at age eighty, Bethune refused to be dispirited and presented herself as a "fit soldier" eager to embrace and advance a "new vision" with humility. She offered her own life from that point forward as an "illustration" of what it would mean to live the simple life, not driven by ego but devoted to a large unified struggle to "bring about the harmonious, peaceful world that God would have this be." Bethune began to incorporate the tenets and language of Moral Re-Armament, sometimes naming it and sometimes not, into explanations of her philosophy of life. When a young student wrote her as part of a school project on good habits of living, Bethune's response added something new, an endorsement of the movement's principles. "The attributes that I am trying now day by day to keep alive in my daily life are absolute purity, absolute honesty, absolute unselfishness, absolute love. These are the standards and attributes of Moral Re-Armament—an ideology that will save the world from war and strife and will make us brothers the world over."[64]

Bethune confessed her new philosophy to trusted friends and colleagues and tried to enlist them in bringing greater recognition to the movement. In a letter to her longtime friend Charles S. Johnson, then president of Fisk, Bethune wrote poignantly about its personal meanings to her as a spiritual practice: "It has done so much for me, Charles. It has strengthened me spiritually. It has given me power. . . . I hope that it may become more vivid to you." Bethune also urged Johnson and their colleague Horace Mann Bond, Lincoln University's president, to consider bestowing honorary degrees upon the movement's founder "as our stamp of approval of the great leadership that he is giving in this time when godly leaders are needed." Bond had been unable to attend the meeting at Caux but had his own relationship with Buchman, to whom he turned for financial support when the Presbyterian church withdrew funding for his school. Bond proposed that MRA establish an institute at Lincoln devoted to the movement's principles and linked to the school's program in international reconciliation and education. The following year, Bond would be among those supporting Buchman's nomination for a Nobel Peace Prize, citing MRA's support for the work of two Lincoln alumni, prime ministers Kwame Nkrumah of Ghana and Nnambi Azikiwe of Nigeria.[65]

In this way, Bond joined Bethune and a long list of other prominent African Americans receptive to Buchman, the MRA message, or its considerable resources. The publishers of *Ebony* and *Color* magazines devoted two pages of coverage to the MRA, emphasizing its work in Africa. Vivian Mason became such a devout MRA follower that her involvement was seen as a distraction from her duties as president of the NCNW and rumored to be part of the reason for her ouster from that position; her association with MRA extended into the 1960s. Leaders of the National Association of Colored Women's Clubs also embraced MRA, giving an award to Buchman in 1958 and participating in an MRA assembly in Caux in 1960.[66]

A number of other black public figures took a message of reconciliation and forgiveness from MRA teachings and meetings. Daisy Bates, an Arkansas journalist and NAACP leader who oversaw the campaign to integrate Central High School, credited the movement's tenets with lifting a hatred of whites from her heart, enabling her to meet with Arkansas governor Faubus with whom she had battled during the integration of Little Rock's Central High School. Jane Edna Hunter, a prominent African American reformer and activist from Cleveland, also spoke of MRA in terms similar to Bates's, explaining that she had experienced a deep spiritual change during her attendance of meetings at Caux: "I always hated the Southern whites because I thought they deprived me of so many things, and made my life so hard as a child. Of course I never told anyone how I carried this hate around for sixty years. Then, during my meditations, it dawned on me that they were all dead and times have changed and opportunities are fresh."[67]

Part of Bethune's attraction to MRA was her long-standing search for ways to move beyond what she saw as the perils of religious and racial exclusivity. In the last decade of her life, Bethune repeatedly emphasized the ways in which she had grown spiritually to embrace people who were quite different from herself. When President Harry Truman's Commission on Civil Rights issued its 1947 report, Bethune took that as an occasion to encourage African Americans to use its recommendations as a foothold for social and economic advancement. But she warned against the dangers of attacking others because of racial or religious differences. "While we insist—as we must insist—on full democracy for ourselves, are we teaching our children not to dislike the *color,* or the *nationality* or the *religion* of a person who has done wrong, but to dislike the wrong? Are we teaching them not to dislike Jews, but to regard the Jewish merchant with the same spirit of brotherhood that we feel for the great Jewish philanthropist?"[68]

Increasingly in this period, Bethune understood herself to be, in her own words, "strongly inter-denominational, inter-racial, and inter-national." She portrayed Jews, Gentiles, Catholics, and Protestants as part of one "universal expression of divinity" with no cultural barriers separating them. When she urged the formation of an interfaith coalition to fight discrimination, she emphasized that such a group "would not concern itself with theology" but commit itself to ending the immorality of segregation and discrimination. Calling herself full of "righteous indignation," Bethune interpreted her role as that of a "fighter for the things that are just and fair for myself and for my people, and my people are all mankind."[69]

Bethune's embrace of Moral Re-Armament was but one part of her own personal theological reinterpretation of Christianity to better enable it to serve as a basis for a universal worldwide unifying political movement. When "we look to the *religion of Jesus,*" she wrote, "rather than the *religion about Jesus* we have the foundation of world unity." Those familiar with the writings and philosophy of the black theologian Howard Thurman will recognize his influence in her definition of true Christianity. Bethune was a longtime friend and supporter of Thurman, a Daytona Beach native; she also had worked closely with his wife, Sue Bailey Thurman, at the NCNW. While he was dean of the chapel at Howard University, the couple had traveled to India and met with Gandhi. Through correspondence and frequent meetings, Bethune continued her relationship with them when they moved to San Francisco in 1944 to establish the Fellowship Church of All Peoples, a path-breaking interracial, nondenominational church, and later to Boston in 1953 when he was chosen as dean of the chapel at Boston University. Thurman was among those to whom Bethune shared her excitement over the MRA meetings in Washington, D.C., which she declared "glorious."[70]

In one of her last talks at Bethune-Cookman, given during religious awareness week in 1955, Bethune spoke about the power of daily meditation, a practice long embraced by Thurman and one to which she had rededicated herself as part of her new commitment to Moral Re-Armament. She also was advocating at the time that a Meditation Center be built on the campus. "Young people, begin now to give a special portion of the day to meditation, so that your spiritual lives may be fed and your soul enriched and the fruit of your lives multiplied through your sincere devotion to what is highest and best. May every one of you join with me as I strive daily toward absolute purity, absolute honesty, absolute unselfishness, absolute love through God's guidance."[71]

A month before her death in 1955, Bethune's column in the *Chicago Defender* lauded Frank Buchman and his movement, saying she had been a follower for over eighteen years. She supported his philosophy, she wrote, precisely because it escaped the boundaries of race, creed, color, class, and region. "It makes effective our religious beliefs; it broadens and unites," she explained.[72] By using the word "creed," Bethune also opened the way to religious faiths quite different from her own. Similar ideas drove a Bethune essay entitled "My Philosophy of Christianity" in which she placed the four principles of the personal credo of Moral Re-Armament at the center of her own religious beliefs:

> Am I pure in heart? Do I give myself daily cleansing through prayer, scripture reading and quiet times with myself and God?
>
> Am I honest in all my thoughts? Am I honest in my dealings with others? Do I forgive and seek forgiveness so that my heart is free from prejudices and biases and little ugly impressions?
>
> Am I unselfish? Do I think of others first? Is my heart attuned to the needs of others? Are my desires directed toward the good of others?
>
> Am I motivated by absolute love as I work and serve others. Is love the underlying spring rising up within me for creative good in whatever I do?
>
> Do I listen for God's direction and give myself wholeheartedly to His guidance? These questions help me to live freely, happily and abundantly. . . . I believe I have entered the kingdom of Jesus Christ right here on earth—for, I believe, "For me to *live* is Christ."[73]

Such a vision of Christianity did not limit itself to those who believed in Jesus or worshiped him, but extended itself to all who would embrace an ethos of love in their personal and political engagements. For those who were able to transform their own lives into ones of service to humanity and a commitment to the ideal of equal human rights, the reward would come here in a peaceful reign among all peoples on earth. There was no talk of sin or of Christ as personal or humanity's savior, but only of his life as an example of loving embrace of others. Also at work was a belief that the commitment to a personal set of beliefs and behaviors could be translated into a collective and transformative collective spiritual and political power. When Martin Luther King, also under Thurman's influence, publicly embraced the concept of a "beloved community" and love over hate, he was articulating what Bethune and others, including black Mississippians in Hortense Powdermaker's study, already believed.

Bethune was no longer limited by Christianity's vision of Pentecost, which imagined a common body of unified Christians spanning many colors, nations, and languages. She grounded herself in Christianity but reached beyond it to commune with others regardless of their own religious faith or lack of it, so long as they believed and practiced the four moral principles of the movement's founder. The concept of a church universal was too limiting at a time when Bethune believed that a larger, more open, and more encompassing personal, theological, and political framework was needed. In Moral Re-Armament, she believed that she had found Pentecost and exceeded it at the same time.

A FEW months before her death in 1955, Bethune wrote to her friend and fellow educator Charlotte Hawkins Brown that "we have planted the philosophy of our lives in the hearts of men and women" and that time now required the two of them to "watch the great procession of growing young leaders." As Bethune sensed the end of her life, she issued a public call for new leaders of great moral strength and ability who were "informed and militant, brave and astute," listing Nannie Burroughs as one of her models. She portrayed her own life as an embodiment of the "Christian ideal of helping others" and of "selfless service to humanity." At the same time, she warned that "we need more than religious faith, however important that is. We need to have faith in ourselves." She argued that African Americans should "help to further the process of integration, but we must continue to *integrate with ourselves*" by pooling the race's growing internal economic strength.[74]

Bethune concluded with a reminder of current realities. "The tragic fact is that the mass of our people is still underprivileged, illhoused, impoverished and discriminated against." Those were the people that her friend Brown and others had accused her of neglecting in her own life's work. Even after living long enough to see the *Brown* decision, the ever-optimistic Bethune was forced to acknowledge "that death will overtake me before the greatest of my dreams—full equality for the Negro in our time—will have been realized." She ended with the avowal that she was "still full of a powerful faith in God, in my people and my country," full of hope that her unrealized dream "will yet come alive—after I have passed on."[75]

In one of her final *Chicago Defender* columns, Bethune rejected the idea that African Americans were uniquely religious. "There are many false ideas about the spiritual glow which, in the eyes of the whites, is supposed to characterize the Negro soul." She urged black people to reject "revivalistic" and heaven-focused religion and suggested instead that they adopt a more mature religion that had at its center "social passion" and a "religion of life abundant here and now." Bethune also demanded that white Christianity rid itself of racial hypocrisy. "We must look to the church for the leadership that recognizes the 'pigment of the divine' in all the

Children of God, whether they are natives of the Kentucky hills, or the plains of India, or the backwoods of Mississippi."[76]

Yet so convinced was Bethune at the end of her life that Moral Re-Armament was a model for a new kind of religion that she asked that a marker at her planned gravesite read: "Moral Re-Armament. To be a part of this great uniting force of our age is the crowning experience of my life," a quote taken from her address at Caux. The story of her request was spread by MRA's formidable publicity arm which, with the cooperation of Bethune's son Albert, would later produce a musical play and then a 1960 Hollywood movie about her life, titled *The Crowning Experience*. In that film, Bethune's life story as an educator and a political figure was used to advance the message that the MRA was an antidote to Communist and subversive appeals to activist black college students. Anti-Communism was never what had attracted her to Moral Re-Armament. Had she lived to see the black student sit-ins, it is difficult to imagine that she would have been anything but thrilled and proud. Bethune was once again serving as a symbol, but in death her image was no longer under her control. The entirety of her life story, with its many political and spiritual complexities, was grossly oversimplified to showcase a philosophy of world unity which had spoken to her as the final step in her life's work of pushing beyond boundaries, including those of her own Christian faith.[77]

After her death, editors at the *Chicago Defender* reminded their readers that Bethune once had been honored as the "Mother of the Century," calling her a "living symbol of the Christian ethic." Howard Thurman delivered the sermon at her funeral which attracted thousands to Bethune-Cookman, including leaders from the Moral Re-Armament movement. Writers at *Christian Century* interpreted Bethune's death as part of a generational shift. "Today a new race leadership must take the place of these potent figures who are passing off the stage." But they would soon be proved wrong when they made a prediction about the future of racial leadership: "It will probably be more immersed in politics, less identified with the churches, than has been the leadership of the past." They queried, "But will it have as sound a moral integrity, as deep a wisdom?"[78]

For Bethune, religious and racial leadership were entwined precisely because she saw religious diversity not as a barrier but as a conduit for civil rights and for human rights: "Our churches, our synagogues, yes—and our mosques—all of our places of worship and meditation; all of the myriads of words of religious leaders that find their way over the air waves—all must point the way, with courage and clarity and humility." Those who claimed religion, she concluded, "should be fired with a divine discontent" to lead the way forward.[79]

4

The Advent to Civil Rights

IN A 1961 letter to Nannie Helen Burroughs, Gordon Hancock, the Virginia journalist, scholar, and minister, lamented the recent death of Charlotte Hawkins Brown, just five years after Bethune's. "I believe it was the Romans who boasted of a great Triumvirate," he wrote, "and when I thought of you and Charlotte and Mrs. Bethune I always wanted to invent a Latin word, 'Trifeminate.' This may be bad Latin but it is mighty fine sentiment." He complimented Burroughs on her leadership abilities, drawing a contrast with what he called "the current debacle" among black Baptist men. "When I see how smoothly you lead the women," he explained, "and how roughly the men are being led, I bow my head in shame." Hancock's letter was more timely than he knew. Only months later, Burroughs, four years younger than Bethune and four years older than Brown, also would be gone, at the age of eighty-two.[1]

Brown, Bethune, and Burroughs have been grouped together as examples of black religious women leaders, but the common contours of their lives as educators obscure the fact that their differences were as vivid as their similarities. Like the two others, Burroughs was a child of the nineteenth-century South. She was born in 1879 in central Virginia to formerly enslaved parents. In contrast to the more politically and religiously agile Bethune, she focused her life's work on black Baptist women, especially the masses of black working-class women who, like her, devoted their time, talent, and treasure to the churches they called home.

Burroughs spent six decades in that work and brought to it a fighting spirit, a keen intellect, a gift for language and for organizing, and a storehouse of creativity, verve, and conviction. A religious intellectual excluded from the pulpit and the academy because she was a woman, Burroughs lived out a public career as a religious leader and an educator who ministered to the needs of other black women and the churches and communities they helped build and sustain. She lived with and strove to reconcile the tensions and contradictions that working within a religious tradition entailed. She did this out of a conviction that black religious institutions had primary responsibility for training black political leaders. Yet her focus was not on the clergy, but on training women to assume leadership. Burroughs worked inside the National Baptist Convention to reform it and to redirect resources toward the education and training of women. She allied herself with the fight to dedicate the convention's work to the campaign for civil rights, a battle that concluded without success after her death.

WHEN Burroughs was a young child, she and her mother moved to Washington, D.C., but her father, an itinerant preacher, did not join them. Her mother raised and supported her on a domestic's wages, enabling her to graduate in 1896 from the prestigious M Street High School. Yet Burroughs and her family were not part of Washington's black elite. It had been her plan to teach in the public schools, but the position she coveted went to another woman with more political connections and lighter skin. After this disappointment, Burroughs vowed that one day she would have her own school which would be open to training women who had no political pull or money, and without regard to color. "It came to me like a flash of light," she recalled years later, "and I knew I was to do that thing when the time came. But I couldn't do it yet, so I just put it away in the back of my head and left it there."[2]

Having acquired stenographic and bookkeeper skills, and seeking a job in line with her deep religious faith, Burroughs found work with the Foreign Mission Board of the National Baptist Convention. In 1900 she gave a riveting and impassioned speech at the founding meeting of its Woman's Convention Auxiliary. Though only twenty-one, Burroughs was elected corresponding secretary of the auxiliary, a position she held until 1948, when she became the group's president. At her death, she had been president of the auxiliary for only thirteen years, but had served it for six decades. Burroughs fashioned an organization that reached black women in individual churches, districts, and state conferences and that functioned largely outside the control of the parent convention. An auxiliary in name only, this group of women derived power from their fundraising abilities and from their dominant presence within local church memberships.[3]

Burroughs used her position as a pulpit and an organizing forum from which to speak and write bluntly on a wide range of matters, including the weaknesses of both black and white Christianity, and black ministerial leadership in particular. In annual convention meetings, speeches, and a variety of Woman's Convention tracts, she relentlessly prodded women to assume greater leadership within their churches and communities. She urged them to use their Baptist faith to help sustain the spirits and morale of the masses of African Americans who remained poor, uneducated, and exploited. Burroughs led the Woman's Convention through the shifting political demands caused by migration, the Great Depression, World War II, and black political activism in the 1950s. She repeatedly prodded black Baptist men and women to embody a Christianity that was both protest- and service-oriented, that engaged with the political issue of race, and that used its human and financial resources to help black people escape demoralization and hopelessness, conditions she saw as by-products of poverty and racial discrimination. At the same time, she challenged the hypocrisy of white Christianity and a segregated and racially unjust America, advocating for an end to Jim Crow.[4]

In 1909, as part of her work with the Baptist Convention, Burroughs founded the National Training School for Women and Girls, an institution she presided over for the rest of her life. Commitment to the dignity and value of labor and to the pursuit of fair wages for domestic work was part of the school's mission. For that reason, the school is commonly represented as primarily a vocational training school for domestic workers. But this description is somewhat at odds both with Burroughs' intended design and with what the school actually did.

From its founding, Burroughs envisioned the institution as a place to train women for effective lay religious work and to better prepare them for the heavy responsibilities that women had already assumed in the operation, governance, and financing of black churches. The school's first goal was to train women to be politically and publicly engaged Christian lay leaders who would transform churches into what Burroughs and others wanted them to be: community centers, social welfare agencies, and a means of racial uplift. Its dominant drive was toward training black women for "work" that had an expressly religious purpose, in effect for Christian social service.

Situated on eight acres on a hill northeast of the Capitol, the

National Training School was funded primarily by black Baptist women. It received no direct subvention from the National Baptist Convention and no substantial funding from whites. For these reasons, despite a constant struggle for resources, the school remained a valuable asset and a source of the pride of ownership for her and the women of the convention. Their efforts to build something of their own made the school the subject of recurring and heated disputes between the Woman's Convention and the larger male-run National Baptist Convention.

Like Bethune, Burroughs took an interest in party and electoral politics, but the political careers of the two women diverged in the 1930s, largely because Burroughs lived in Washington, D.C., a city then as now without national political representation. As important, Burroughs remained in the Republican party even after Franklin Roosevelt's repeated presidential victories, serving at one point as head of the National League of Republican Colored Women. Under fierce attack from some blacks who switched to the Democratic party in that period, she accused her critics of political opportunism: "I am not a political rat running from party to party." She would never ally herself with a Southern-dominated Democratic party that still used all-white primaries, the poll tax, and other repressive measures as ways of denying black citizens the right to vote.[5]

The Republican party was excluded from the White House for twenty long years, from 1932 to 1952, but this did not convince Burroughs to change her position. She remained a lifelong Republican, watching from her home in the nation's capital as Bethune and many other contemporaries benefited from their Democratic party affiliation. Stubborn and sometimes rigid, Burroughs occasionally sacrificed pragmatism for principle. She firmly believed that access to the ballot could be used to improve the lives of black people, yet she was skeptical about the degree to which white-controlled institutions, including the federal government, would ever fully commit to that goal.

Burroughs' writings and speeches moved so fluidly between her moral, religious, and political sensibilities because her deeply held Christian beliefs brought them into a unitary whole. The political commentaries she sent to her Baptist colleagues in the 1920s and 1930s read like a rolling review of the most pertinent political issues affecting black people in that period. She was an avid supporter and board member of the NAACP; she urged her listeners and readers to agitate for antilynching legislation; and she lent vigorous support when the NAACP succeeded in blocking the confirmation of a controversial nominee to the U.S. Supreme Court. She vehemently protested the continued segregation on trains, arguing that Jim Crow cars and the so-called Iron Curtain that separated passengers on first-class cars by race were both schemes designed "to crucify our racial self-respect." She led protests when President Herbert Hoover acceded to segregationist demands by sending black Gold Star Mothers, those whose sons had died in World War I, on a ship separate from the one carrying white mothers when they went to visit battlefields in Europe. "We are all in the same boat when it is time to go to die on the battlefield," she wrote, "but we cannot go in the same boat to see the battlefield on which the heroes of both races died."[6]

Burroughs was never hesitant to engage in intraracial warfare, and unlike Bethune she bluntly accused black men of failing in their responsibilities in many areas, whether as race leaders or as ministers. This was unusual for black women in her era, actually in most eras, but Burroughs did not conceal or soften her racially specific gender-based political critique. At a time when black women were denied access to most professional education and to most positions of authority, Burroughs argued that the men who had a monopoly on power and privilege had special duties to the race that they were not executing well.

Perhaps for this reason Burroughs was especially attuned to the implications of the Twentieth Amendment, which guaranteed women the right to vote. The ballot box was now accessible to black women, or at least to those who lived in states where racist policies and practices did not impose barriers. "Negro women are in politics to make a new name for themselves," she predicted, "and a new place for the race." Burroughs accused black men of having squandered their early opportunities to vote by exchanging them for petty patronage payoffs during the Reconstruction era. "Negro women are in the game to emancipate their race from the political bondage into which their men sold them, and the party that will contribute the most to that glorious end will get their support—whether it be Republican, Democratic or Progressive! If it takes all three (and it does seem at this time that it will take all three to make one, so far as we are concerned), they will be in all three parties."[7]

Here again, ideas about the Reconstruction era serve as a backdrop for views about political strategies in the 1920s and 1930s, just as they had for Woodson and Bethune. Burroughs' reinterpretation of the postbellum period accuses black men of failing the race in their role as newly empowered leaders and voters. This view contrasts sharply with the usual Reconstruction narrative, certainly the one proffered by Woodson, which exalts that era and portrays its black men, especially black ministers, as ready and able political operatives who were thwarted only by federal abandonment and white supremacist reclamation. Burroughs' opinion echoes the view expressed by Bethune that black men had not done a good job of representing the race after emancipation.

Even as she was critical of black male leadership, Burroughs never spared women, especially elite black women, from criticism when they engaged in frivolities instead of racial uplift. But her condemnations of black men, in particular the charge that they were failing as race leaders and as fathers, by definition also were accusations that they were falling short as men. This way of thinking, applied to black men in politics and in the pulpit, was a central aspect of her political philosophy throughout her life.

For better or for worse, Burroughs' work within the Baptist Convention was rife with opportunities for judging men's work and women's work separately, since the functions of the organization and the churches rested on a clear demarcation of gender-specific work. This in turn reinforced her own views on gender differences in the stewardship of the race both inside of and outside of churches. More than that perhaps, she took very seriously her identification with the plight of black women, including working-class women who, like her mother, had suffered under slavery, labored as domestics, lived on low wages, and raised children alone. Both personally and professionally, she empathized with black women's burdens and responsibilities.

Those themes took on even greater urgency during the Great Depression, when the already impoverished state of African Americans greatly deteriorated, both in the rural South and in the newly concentrated black communities in the North. The nadir of black American history is often said to be the period around the turn of the twentieth century, but for those who lived through the 1930s that designation seems as apt for the depths of despair of that decade. To read Burroughs' accounts of the widespread suffering during this period and to hear her ardent pleas for help for the masses of black people is to enter a world where fear and near-helplessness are palpable. "We face our darkest days since freedom," she wrote, labeling the impact of the Depression on black women in particular as "tragic." The loss of jobs for black men left black women to bear the economic burden of the race almost alone. Burroughs' school responded by adding additional classes for girls aged eight through twelve, so as to meet the needs of mothers who went out to work every day.[8]

Troubled as well by the economic plight of black men, Burroughs warned that job losses would have long-term consequences for the race. "The manhood of the race is going to weeds—going to waste. Go up and down the streets in Negro ghettos and see for your self. Social deterioration has set in." She feared that long-term unemployment would have deleterious effects on the men and their communities. "Negro men are entirely too idle and they are entirely too satisfied at being idle. They are doing too much sitting down, hanging out and hanging around. Men cannot be made under these conditions, they are unmade."[9]

The likelihood that black men would reassume family and other responsibilities after the Depression was lowered by well-meaning, protective impulses. "Mothers and fathers are responsible for much of the laziness and lack of manliness. They have not taught their sons to be industrious." But Burroughs also blamed black women for coddling black men and not demanding much in return. "Then too, young and old women ruin men. They ruin good men and make bad men worse. They run after them, support them and let them sling them around as if they were rags."[10]

Burroughs feared that a lengthy economic depression would exacerbate a loss of self-respect and undermine belief in hard work among black people. "No race can live on schemes, odd jobs, the meager earnings of hard working women, number playing, gambling, room renting, and bootlegging." She searched for a collective response from black people that could save them as a group from this crisis. "'What shall we do to deliver them from the bondage of this death?' should be the burning question before every Negro church, convention and welfare organization." She demanded that black church leadership come to their aid. "The masses have been the backbone of our churches; the hard working horny-hand men and women have either bought or built nine-tenths of the churches now occupied by Negro congregations; they have supported the ministers, taken care of current expenses of the church and helped thousands of ministers to educate and clothe their children. . . . It is the plain duty of Christian leaders to pool their brains and find a way out. The masses have never failed the churches; will the churches fail them in this hour of need? That is the question."[11] Burroughs turned to the one institution in the community that she believed had the moral responsibility to lift impoverished people out of economic depression and the ability to find or create jobs for them. This institution was the church. She expected the churches to help sustain families materially and spiritually during this crisis in return for the decades during which the members had sustained the churches.

Burroughs never had much faith in the federal government as an ally or a source of help for black people. This was one way in which she differed from the Democratic party stalwart Bethune. Even in this period of great need, Burroughs expressed deep suspicion and hostility toward public welfare agencies and relief monies not tied to work. She feared they would breed dependency and idleness among African Americans, especially men. To her mind, relief without work represented as great a vice as hustling or gambling or selling bootleg liquor. "So far as the Negro is concerned, America's present plan of economic recovery makes him a parasite, a degenerate, a pauper, a confirmed loafer."[12]

Burroughs feared that the Depression had mired African Americans in their worst plight since the end of what she called the "ungodly" institution of slavery. "Now millions of Negroes are sitting down waiting for somebody to deliver them, waiting for their second emancipator—and millions of others are happy and satisfied to live below the common level of decency." She thought that conditions were even "worse off inside—in our *hearts* and *minds* and *spirits*." African Americans had accepted a new form of "moral slavery" that deprived them of all desire for freedom and for better lives. Fearful of an "army of enforced idlers," Burroughs demanded that the federal government simply guarantee black people equal opportunities for jobs, for training, and for fair play.[13]

This political conservatism is consistent with Burroughs' faith that black people could take care of themselves once legalized racial barriers were lifted. These views were driven as much by her belief in the fundamental abilities of black people as they were by a refusal to trust any permanent state commitment to economic relief efforts. She was also convinced that self-sufficiency and pride in work, combined with religious faith, would strengthen the moral fiber of black men and make them once again able and engaged community members and leaders. Burroughs was an admirer of Booker T. Washington's emphasis on black self-sufficiency, even as she parted ways with him by insisting that the federal government enforce the political rights of black people.

Burroughs also interpreted the magnitude of the economic downturn in providential terms, as a punishment that the United States deserved for its immoral treatment of black people. "America is reaping what she has sown. Twelve million Negroes have been crying for justice and protection—for a chance to be men and women—for a chance to earn their daily bread—educate their children and build their homes, but a rich Christian nation has withheld these common blessings." The Depression would lift only when the nation entered a new moral order requiring its leadership "to purge its own heart of hatred; to wash its hands of blood-guilt; and to apply the principle of justice in giving every man an equal chance to earn his own bread in the sweat of his brow."[14]

In these ways, Burroughs political agenda was framed by her religious outlook. For her, only massive individual and collective personal sacrifice could help black people survive the 1930s. She demonstrated this in her own life, forgoing a salary, cashing in her life insurance policy, and pleading for coal sufficient to keep her school open through the harsh Depression winters. Despite these steps, the school went into debt and was forced to curtail its operations. Still, she believed that however limited black institutional resources were, black leaders, especially the men, needed to make similar sacrifices for the benefit of the people whom they were called to serve and who had served and supported them. This was the obligation of leaders, to be moral exemplars willing to forfeit personal gain for the benefit of the collective good.

BURROUGHS' outspokenness and effectiveness as a leader, orator, and organizer were apparent throughout the protracted and venomous disputes over the ownership and control of her school. The leaders of the National Baptist Convention tried to lay claim to it and its valuable real estate in the nation's capital. They wanted to bring the women's fundraising abilities back under their exclusive control. Burroughs was successful in fighting off these attempts because most of the women in the convention were on her side, as were a small but committed minority of politically progressive ministers. The law too was an ally, but the incessant conflict took its toll on her and on the school's mission.

At the time the school was purchased, chartered, and incorporated, Burroughs had shrewdly made sure that its deed established no legal connection to either the National Baptist Convention or the Woman's Convention. She had not wanted the school to be placed under the legal ownership of the Woman's Convention, because she feared this would make it vulnerable to satisfy the financial obligations of the National Baptist Convention. She also wanted to avoid putting the school under the umbrella authority of the larger male-controlled group. She had refused earlier offers from the National Convention to help pay off all of the school's considerable debts in exchange for amending its charter to bring the school under the convention's control. The men of the convention did not want such a valuable enterprise that was dedicated to training women to be outside of its reach.[15]

In 1938, this recurring tussle for control of the school's property erupted into a big public fight. Leaders of the National Convention, with the cooperation of Mrs. S. W. (Willie) Layten, the often compliant president of the Woman's Convention, engineered a surprise resolution designed to derail fundraising for the school in Baptist churches.[16] At the same time, leaders of the National Convention announced that it planned to open its own religious training school for women in Nashville. This resolution was aimed at redirecting the women's fundraising efforts away from Burroughs' school for women and girls to this new institution, which the male church leaders would control.[17]

Although there had been previous attempts to bring the school under the larger convention's authority, a precipitating event for this particular action was a rumor that the white women of the Southern Baptist Convention were preparing to make a $10,000 donation to the school. The rumor was fed by the general knowledge that Burroughs had forged a supportive working relationship and friendship with Una Roberts Lawrence, a prominent member of the Women's Missionary Union, auxiliary to the all-white Southern Baptist Convention.

Male leaders of the National Baptist Convention and the Southern Baptist Convention had their own relationship. In 1913, the black Baptist leaders wanted to establish a seminary to train black ministers and sought the support of the white Southern Baptists for this purpose, since they had insufficient funds acting alone. In 1924, the American Baptist Theological Seminary opened in Nashville, with the joint support of the two conventions and with substantial amounts of funds coming from the Southern Baptists. In 1937, the Southern Baptist Convention agreed to share equally

with the black Baptists in the operation of the school, an agreement that obtained until 1996, when the Southern Baptists relin-
quished their ties to the school. It was in conjunction with the
seminary and its campus that the black Baptist leadership moved
to establish its own National Baptist Training School for Christian
Workers, an institution for women that would compete with Burroughs' school in Washington.[18]

These complicated arrangements between black and white Southern Baptists had their own tensions over governance, authority,
and money. Moreover, there were recurring accusations and suspi-
cions that the seminary's theological conservatism was designed to
thwart the development of an activist black Baptist ministry. Certainly, in their missionary work among black Baptists in this period, white Southern Baptists had their own anxieties about some
of the differences between black and white Baptists—and not primarily about differences in liturgical practices. Rather, there was
concern about the differing political and social functions of white
and black churches.

In 1935, Noble Y. Beall, a white Southern Baptist missionary
who did fieldwork in black churches, wrote a report in which he
expressed his fears about what he called the "real dangers of the
American Baptist Negroes." Having just spent a year attending annual conferences, conventions, meetings, and local church services, Beall concluded that black Baptist churches were engaged in
a kind of "socialism," not the kind associated with communism but
something quite distinct:

> This is what I mean: the American Negroes are keenly con-
> scious of their slavery, emancipation, suppression, and disen-
> franchisement, they are putting forth every effort to bring
> themselves up to equality with White Americans. . . . I have
> seen poor, illiterate, helpless, old men and women give their

last dime to representatives of agencies working to "Elevate the Race." Possibly that is all right within itself; but that is not all. The great danger lies in this fact. They are converting their churches into social agencies and the chief note in practically all of their deliverances is "Elevate the Race. . . ." But, the "Elevating the Race" must come as a by-product of the Gospel, and never [be] the chief object of it. Therefore, as I see it, the real danger lies in prostituting the churches and their organizations for illegitimate ends: "socialism."[19]

Beall warned that white Baptists needed to contribute to and to control black educational institutions or risk having them too become places where the "chief emphasis" was "Elevate the Race." He noted, quite astutely, that those who took comfort from the fact that one-half of blacks were church members were missing the larger point, "that there are about 5,000,000 unchurched among the 10,000,000 Negroes of the South." Most white people, he argued, took it for granted that "all Negroes are religious," but this guaranteed nothing about whether they would become or remain Baptists, and Baptists devoted to the Gospel rather than to elevating the race. His recommendation was that Southern Baptists focus on black Baptist leaders as the "best approach to the masses. It will be a long time before we shall be able to command enough missionaries to reach the millions of Negroes. Therefore, if we would reach them, we must utilize the Negro preachers, churches, institutions and organizations."[20]

This was part of the backdrop for the debate that emerged about Burroughs and her school. Just as the men of her convention had established relationships with the men of the Southern Baptist Convention, Burroughs developed connections with Una Lawrence of the Women's Missionary Union. As members of the women's auxiliaries to larger conventions, they sympathized with each other

over their struggles with the "brethren." Burroughs worked strate-
gically with Lawrence on specific projects, such as the publication
of newsletters and educational materials for black and white Baptist women. Their relationship was not without its own recurring
racial tensions, but they managed to maintain a working partnership that lasted for decades. Their work together progressed to the
point that in 1936 Burroughs wanted members of Lawrence's group
to serve on her school's board of trustees.[21]

Burroughs often confided in Lawrence about the ineffectiveness
of the women in leadership positions within the Woman's Convention and about her battles with the men within her larger
convention, especially its president, the Reverend L. K. Williams.
When one tense episode in the contest for control of the school
erupted, Burroughs reported to Lawrence that the fight was the
work of men like "Brother Williams," who wanted to "pull the
women off from their very own project" simply to "help the men."[22]
A female informant inside the convention but loyal to Burroughs
warned her that "the devil is mighty mad about your success with
the Southern Baptist women." Undaunted, Burroughs vowed that
she would simply forge ahead with her work. "I am going right on
serving the Lord, unless they tackle me, and then I am going to
serve Him with one hand and fight them with the other."[23]

And fight she did. Though initially blindsided by the latest move
against her authority, Burroughs and her allies quickly rallied. In a
statement issued in conjunction with the National Convention
meeting where the issues were to be resolved, Burroughs laid out
her defense in explicitly gendered terms, even though men and
women were involved on both sides of the issue. She argued that
the training school was a woman's institution that had been "conceived, developed, managed, owned and controlled by Negro
Christian women" and that this fact made the school unique and
successful. She conceived of the school as the life work of women,

by women, and for women and "too sacred to be desecrated." She yielded no ground on this point. "I want Negro women to have absolute control of this property—which is what was originally intended—that is what it has been—and that is how it must always remain."[24]

Because women were refused membership on the board of directors of the National Convention, ceding control of the school to the directors would be tantamount to denying women any authority over it. Burroughs called this move "undemocratic and reactionary," especially because "Negro women are carrying almost the entire burden in our churches." To her, the school was a valued asset precisely because it symbolized the independence of black women and their commitment to the Baptist enterprise. She ended her appeal with two curt statements, the second one comparing her with Jesus and her opponents with his killers. "(1) God is not dead. (2) Father, forgive them."[25]

Burroughs and her women allies were not alone when they characterized the fight over the school as a struggle by the men for control over Baptist women's work and fundraising. So too did a group of progressive Baptist preachers who helped to resist the takeover effort and defended the good works of Baptist women. The Reverend J. H. Jernagin, president of the National Baptist Convention's National Sunday School and Young People's Union board, appealed directly to Lawrence, although they did not know each other, asking her to publicly disavow the rumor that white Southern Baptist women were providing funds to the school. This gossip, he wrote, had been the cause of the most recent, hurried attempt by the men to take over the school, even though the men's organization had never made any financial contribution to Burroughs' work. "What money was raised," he explained, "came through individual pastors, the Woman's Convention, and by Miss Burroughs' own effort," as well as from individual white support. "I don't think there is a colored woman in America who has made greater sacrifices for her race and denomination, or one who is more greatly loved."[26]

Jernagin reported that the men were resentful of Burroughs' capacity to raise money, especially if she was now reaching out for support from white Southern Baptists. "May I say as a Christian, confidentially to you, that the bottom of it all has been a deep-seated jealously on the part of the president of the Woman's Convention, and the president of the men's convention has always fought this school. I hate to have to say this, but in justice to all that is right and righteous, I must tell the truth."[27]

This intra-Baptist fight over the school spilled into the public domain when writers in the black secular newspapers and in the *National Baptist Voice* traded barbs over the controversy which touched on the issue of men's and women's roles in black churches and the dependency of black political institutions on those churches. William Pickens, national field secretary of the NAACP and a longtime supporter of Burroughs and her work, came to her defense and lambasted the Baptist leaders. He accused "little men" and "some weak and envious women" in the Baptist Convention of trying to gain control of the school for more than twenty years, portraying them as a "wolfish pack" that could not "even wait until [Burroughs] is peacefully dead to tear into her life's work." He reminded his readers that "without these women, the pastors would not even get railroad fares to go and attend the conventions." Pickens acknowledged that Burroughs was "hard-headed and firm-jawed," characteristics she needed to "fight her race and fight for her race at the same time." She had to "fight both the treachery of race in America, and the treachery of sex in her own race and Church."[28]

Although Pickens wrote in his capacity as an individual and not in his role as an NAACP official, leaders in the Baptist Convention did not read it that way. Russell Barbour, editor of the convention newspaper, the *National Baptist Voice*, attacked the NAACP and instructed its member churches to withdraw all cooperation and support for the group. "They use our churches for their annual sessions, beg us for money for their salaries, use our workers, and in return call us jackasses and grafters." Barbour accused the NAACP of being a "dead" and "godless organization" and an enemy of the masses of black people; he urged Baptist church leaders to exclude the organization from their sanctuaries. "We are going to organize our own social movements, and support men who have at least a little sympathy for our religious leaders and the masses they lead."[29]

Walter White, the NAACP's executive secretary, contacted several prominent progressive Baptist preachers seeking their advice on how to respond to the controversy Pickens had created. These exchanges and White's deep concern over them illuminate the ways in which the NAACP's leadership respected black churches as allied institutions, perhaps not only its best but its only conduit to the masses of black people. He feared that Barbour's call for denying the NAACP access to Baptist churches, if followed, would "destroy the organization." White's fear of offending Baptist supporters was conspicuous and reveals the extent to which his organization, despite its secular imprimatur, depended on church people and church resources.[30] This is similar to the way Carter Woodson relied on black churches for support of his work popularizing black history, while he remained a vociferous critic of black churches in general.

When the controversy erupted, Burroughs quickly contacted White and jumped to Pickens' defense. She felt that White was too "excited" and worried by Barbour's response, and confidently predicted that Barbour's opinion would never be heeded. "Believe it or not, nine-tenths of the Baptists of this country are with Nannie Burroughs."[31] Yet the dispute was serious.

The belief that Burroughs had received funds from white Southern Baptist women was so deeply held by men in the leadership of the Baptist Convention that it persisted nearly a decade later even though no $10,000 gift was ever made. In 1947, at an interracial religious meeting in St. Louis, Lawrence was seated next to Dr. David V. Jemison, by then the president of the National Baptist Convention. "You can imagine how I felt and how I was somewhat speechless for a moment when he asked me about the $10,000 we gave your school in 1938," she wrote Burroughs. "When I got my breath back I told him I knew nothing of any $10,000 or even of any $1,000 that the Woman's Missionary Union had ever given your school in any way whatsoever. I was so astonished and dismayed to find this so fixed in the mind of the President of the National Baptist Convention, that I could not jar it loose."[32]

In the end, Burroughs maintained the independence of her school, but the battle was not without consequences. In 1938, the National Baptist Convention severed its formal relationship with the school and abrogated all formal connection between it and the Woman's Convention, making it much more difficult for the school to raise money from Baptist women. At the same time, the convention moved to establish its own school for training Baptist women near its headquarters in Nashville, and diverted its fundraising efforts to that work.

Burroughs remained defiant about the way the National Baptist Convention had treated her and the school, but in a letter to a friend she made it clear that despite all the strife she was not defeated in spirit. "I know how to cooperate graciously (no personal compliment), but I do not take domination. God, himself, doesn't try it on 'us worms,' and no human with sense would attempt it."[33] The public nature of the dispute had stirred up support for Burroughs and her work, including fundraising campaigns, as well as for commitments from Baptist supporters who worked independently of the larger convention.

At the end of the 1930s, Burroughs felt herself shunned and under attack by the leaders of the National Baptist Convention but still in communion with black Baptist women through her work in the Woman's Convention. Despite attempts to replace her in the convention, she emerged buoyed by the fight and by the overwhelming support she received from the women, from progressive Baptist ministers, and from the larger public. She would need all of this when she subsequently faced the challenge of ensuring the survival and growth of her school without the benefit of formal fundraising channels though the conventions.

The contest over the school is significant because it represents a dispute over the power of men and women within black Baptist churches where women were the primary fundraisers and organizers but were denied access to positions of authority and governance. Those positions were reserved for ministers. Since women were excluded from the ministry, they also were forced to accept male leadership in the administrative as well as the spiritual realm.

One of the reasons Burroughs was so committed to training black women to assume even greater responsibility in black churches was that by the 1940s she had lost faith in the idea that a college-educated elite would take on the work of racial uplift because they had turned away from religion. Mays had shuddered when he found evidence that young black educated people were rejecting religion, but his primary concern was for the future of black churches themselves. Burroughs was more concerned about the larger communal consequences of that shift and searched for ways to encourage a return to religion and religious training. "Most assuredly there are a few great souls somewhere in Negro colleges 'hid among the stuff' but somebody will have to make it their business to find them and challenge them to come forth and help deliver the Negro masses 'from the body of this death.'"[34]

For Burroughs, it was imperative that progressive women be trained to assume greater responsibility for the future of the race through their work within churches. "It would be more profitable to invest something in the training of the women who are already engaged in the service," she advised. Her conclusion was that "the church had better do something with what it has," rather than concentrating so much effort on a handful of male ministerial prospects or unproven educated young people.[35] This is why the fight for her school took on such importance for her, for the women who supported it, and for those who were trained in it.

LIKE most other African American public figures during the World War II years, Burroughs linked fascism abroad to domestic racial injustices. She condemned the tyranny in Europe under Hitler, warned the United States to cure itself of race hatred, and called for a unified political front among black people at home. She also wondered out loud about the racial aftermath of the war.

> White Americans with visions of the Czechs and Poles, German and Austrian Jews languishing in concentration camps or standing, unflinching, before Nazi firing squads were moved to go to battle for freedom. Negro Americans, too, have deep sympathy for these enslaved peoples. Only yesterday, our race was in the slave pen. We know what it is. But, we confess that our sympathy is mixed with sadness, fear and suspicion. We wonder if when the Czech and the Pole and the Jew, of all nations, eventually achieve freedom from fear, will they join the rest of the white world in appropriating and reserving for themselves this freedom for which black men, too, have fought, bled and died? Freedom for all men, everywhere, is the only thing worth fighting for.

In these and other ways, she was quick to express concern about the postwar conditions of African Americans and other people of color. "Negroes and the dark races are not going to pay, sacrifice, fight and die—simply to make the world safe for Britons, and white Americans."[36]

Burroughs railed against segregation and discrimination in federal employment, job training, and especially the military. She cautioned that "freedom, like Charity, should begin at home" and that "the war will not be over until Negroes are given their rightful chance to be all-out Americans." Her final warning was that "when this war is over, we shall not go back to live on husks and in hovels, simply because we are Negroes."[37]

Even as the demands of the war and the postwar period required her to address the new ways in which the federal government was imposing racially discriminatory policies, Burroughs never let up in her pleas to black churches and educated black people that they help their less fortunate black brothers and sisters escape poverty and demoralization. Her political philosophy was grounded on the idea that privileged black people were responsible for helping those less fortunate and that the fate of black people as a *collective* depended on this. She continued to reject the notion that success by a few blacks was meaningful or that a talented tenth held the fate of the race in its hands. "Our real progress now depends upon two-tenths of the race that have climbed to middle ground by their own boot-straps; the clean, plain, honest, dependable, hardworking class; the back-bone of the race." The remaining seven-tenths were living in a "complete social economic and spiritual blackout," no longer possessed of the burning desire or the opportunities needed to make that ascent.[38]

Burroughs seemed to be advocating the modern notion that a psychological depression and a sense of hopelessness had fallen on the masses of black people as a consequence of their lack of progress since slavery. "If they cease hoping, believing and toiling upward," she warned, "the race is done for." The responsibility for preventing this rested with the churches because black people had nowhere else to turn. "The improvement of the Negro masses should be the dominant concern and responsibility of every Negro church."[39]

In 1948, Burroughs finally ascended to the presidency of the Woman's Convention, an organization which she had managed to dominate for four decades from the position of corresponding secretary. Once she assumed the new office, she increased her outspokenness on a variety of political issues both within and outside the Baptist Convention. As in her earlier years, Burroughs attacked what she saw as the sorry state of black political leadership in postwar period, especially in view of the mounting legal challenges to segregation and integration. "What we need at this hour of crisis and challenge is a leadership to match our mountains—not pygmies to match our mole hills." Looking at black Baptist churches in particular, she reminded her audience that churches had "a tremendous educational, moral, social and spiritual responsibility" toward the women in their congregations, who constituted the large majority of their members.[40] More adamant than ever about the need for black churches to engage in public service missions, Burroughs ridiculed efforts to build elaborate church sanctuaries, calling them a waste of precious community resources. Churches should use their buildings to serve as teaching institutions and community centers, not just for church members or black people but for humanity in general.

Such pleas to help lift up the masses of black people seem at first to be a simple continuation of the uplift ideology of the early twentieth century. Yet something more interesting was occurring. The 1950s gave rise to a dramatically shifting political reality that unsettled and complicated notions of racial progress. By then, Burroughs, like Bethune and many other black leaders, could see that the judicial challenges being mounted by the NAACP would soon topple the legal barriers to segregation, especially in education. The prospect that an end to legalized segregation would open new opportunities for black people brought feelings of joy mixed with apprehensions that this was an opportunity as fragile as it was rare. A palpable anxiety began to set in due to fears that neither blacks nor whites would be prepared for such a change in the legal and political landscape: whites because their belief in their racial superiority was so ingrained and blacks because they lacked the skills, self-confidence, and self-respect needed to take full advantage of the new opportunities.

Burroughs predicted that legislative and judicial reforms, however far-reaching, would be inadequate to improve the conditions of impoverished blacks. She worried that the masses of black people were deeply demoralized, their spirits being so broken by racism and oppression that they no longer had the self-respect necessary to engage in the most basic acts of bodily and domestic cleanliness, pride of person, and physical modesty. The attention that Burroughs paid to the importance of cleanliness and self-care were not about a sense of racial shame or class pretensions or about what white people thought. Rather it was more about healing the demoralization that she believed had set in among many poor black people. She did not reproach the people themselves or anything innate to them; rather she blamed racism, poverty, and oppression. "The moral breakdown in the Negro masses stems from the fact that laws, practices, and attitudes that are basically unchristian and undemocratic are practiced in race relations with impunity and defiance."[41]

Burroughs feared that people so long denied the basic rights of human worth had simply lost their desire for self-improvement and their faith in the possibility of a better life. She saw race pride and personal pride as inextricably linked. Blacks had lost hope in the future for themselves and for their children, had lost the motivation to learn and the will to work. Many had turned to self-destructive behaviors, including addiction to alcohol and drugs. It was with this rationale that she admonished black churches and a growing post–World War II black middle class that they had a basic obligation to reach and teach the masses of less privileged and less educated black people in urban and rural areas.

Burroughs specifically warned more privileged black people against racial abandonment in the rush toward a desegregated world. She urged them to help bring poor black people back into a racial communion that would restore their faith in themselves and the future. In these ways, she was warning against any politics of respectability that would hamper racial collectivity and cooperation, or that would privilege those who were wealthier and better educated. "If these leaders had interest, ability and influence enough to get Negro masses integrated in their own race," she wrote in 1950, "they would get full credit for performing the miracle of this century." Once again, she assigned the church the central role of bridging those intraracial class differences, arguing that "the improvement of the Negro masses should be the dominant concern and responsibility of every Negro church."[42]

Burroughs' entreaties about the political responsibility of black churches took on even more passion after the *Brown* decision. She worked to bring women in the Baptist conventions closer to the reality of unfolding political events. In addition to her long-standing ties to the NAACP, Burroughs also demonstrated her personal support for the work of the Legal Defense Fund by making financial donations to it.[43] She also invited the NAACP's Thurgood Marshall to speak at the Friday night plenary session of the 1954 Baptist Convention in St. Louis, making him the first NAACP official to receive that honor. Marshall was warm and enthusiastic in his acceptance letter. "I know that you know that all of us are forever indebted to you for the long hard fight you have made for our people. You will forever be an inspiration to all of us."[44]

It was not the first time, Burroughs reminded him, that women had led the way in inviting political leaders to address the annual convention. She mentioned her efforts earlier in the century to bring in Booker T. Washington, setting the precedent of reserving the convention's Friday-night session for an appearance by a national leader. In a letter written after Marshall had delivered his address, Burroughs told him that women were still prodding the men along politically. "I think our men caught on at St. Louis. Bless their hearts. I hope they will have genuine interest to hold on—and give." She followed up his appearance with a $500 contribution from the Woman's Convention.[45]

For Burroughs, the prospect of a post-segregation world seemed fraught with both anticipation and anxiety. When she spoke at the 1954 convention, the implications of the *Brown* decision aroused not joy but a deep sense of unpreparedness. "Neither race is ready for integration," she warned in her presidential address: "For nearly a hundred years, with not enough exceptions, parents, teachers and other adults in the white race have been teaching their children that the Negro race is innately inferior, and that the white race is innately superior—that just being white makes them superior. This doctrine has been taught in the home and in the school and practiced by American Churches by separation and silence." As for blacks, they had been "bruised, broken, strangled and made bitter as a result of mistreatment, discrimination, injustice and segregation." In her view, members of both races were psychologically unprepared for the transition to a desegregated society.[46]

That year, Burroughs also had the Woman's Convention host an appearance by the relatively unknown new minister of Dexter Baptist Church, the twenty-seven-year-old Martin Luther King Jr. Although this was only a year before the start of the Montgomery bus boycott and his association with it, Burroughs was not acting out of prescience about King's emergence into national leadership. Rather, she was operating out of her long acquaintance with King's family, including his maternal grandfather, who had served as treasurer of the National Convention. More important, she was friendly with both of King's parents and especially his mother, Alberta, who was very active in the Woman's Convention and an admirer of Burroughs and her work. When Burroughs assumed the presidency of the Woman's Convention, she appointed Mrs. King to its music division as the organist for the annual meetings.[47]

In the early 1950s, the relationship between the two women grew closer. Mrs. King offered encouragement when Burroughs began to chafe under the national organization's demands for greater control over the Woman's Convention. Part of Burroughs' complaint was that women had no representation on the policymaking committees of the National Convention. "It is much better for me to quit than it is for me to mark time or be hamstrung because some folks fear that I am usurping authority." It was during this struggle that Mrs. King reiterated her ardent support for Burroughs and her work. "You really are *the one* person to head the Woman's Convention; I know of no other who could do the job you are doing with those women," she wrote. She ended the letter by thanking Burroughs for creating a "new day" for Baptist women."[48]

Mrs. King's letters to Burroughs span the 1950s and convey well the meaning of the annual Woman's Conventions for women who, like King, subsequently returned to work in their home churches and communities. The letters brim with enthusiasm and repeated expressions of inspiration, joy, and strengthened commitment from being in the presence of thousands of other Baptist women, hearing about the work in their churches, listening to political reports, and worshiping in such a large communion. Music was no small part of this experience, and even though she was an accomplished and experienced church musician, Mrs. King was deeply moved by the songs. "I shall always remember how those hundreds of women would sing each morning at the convention, till their souls were stirred and they would nearly lift the roof off the house as their voices rang out in one accord." She remained very modest about her own contributions to the musical program.[49]

It is no surprise that when Burroughs wanted to invite Martin Luther King Jr. to speak at the Woman's Convention, she approached him through his mother. "Nothing could have pleased me more than for you to deem the best way of contacting my son was through me," Mrs. King wrote. Her son's speech, delivered on a Thursday at noon, was titled "Vision of a World Made New." He spoke of those who suffered from a "divine discontent" with the old order and who were working to realize a vision of a "new order." He juxtaposed the old and the new through pairings of "injustice" and "justice," "darkness" and "light," "an old Jerusalem" and "a new Jerusalem," and endorsing John's Gospel revelation of a "new heaven and a new earth." He reserved his speech's high point for a condemnation of the Christian church and its alliances with the colonizing orders in South Africa and India, and with segregation in the United States.[50]

Burroughs was as committed as King to remedying global injustices, but the "new order" that concerned her most immediately was the one made possible by the promise of the *Brown* decision. Her speeches and writings in this period reiterated that the institutions most capable of helping African Americans prepare to compete and survive in a desegregated world were black churches. She worried that too few of the race lived day-to-day lives that were connected to religion, or at least to the Baptist faith. It was estimated that the overwhelming share of black religious people were Baptists, but by her calculation "our four million Negro Baptists are but a fourth of the race." How could the churches even reach and influence their own members, let alone the rest of the race, and especially black men, who were vastly underrepresented in all black churches? The stakes at this crucial time were high, as the possibility of real racial progress drew closer.[51]

There were too few ministers being trained to lead black churches, and too little likelihood that a ministry dedicated to social welfare would ever emerge. Burroughs estimated that the population of religious African Americans produced "a little over one hundred ministers a year for over fifty thousand Negro churches." For this reason, unlike Mays and Woodson, she was intent on preparing the women within them to assume even larger leadership roles and to do so more effectively with assistance from her school in their training. "The courses which we propose to offer are the only answers to the present embarrassing leadership situation in Negro Churches." She wanted her school to meet the "actual needs of women and girls who are determined to prepare for efficient leadership in Christian Social Service."[52]

Consistently and emphatically, Burroughs reserved her harshest criticism for those African Americans who were educated and succeeding financially. "The time has come for the educated, well-advantaged Negro to become concerned about the mass in his own race and unite in a crusade of redemption and uplift." The movement toward desegregation had brought the promise of greater economic and residential mobility for better-educated blacks, but Burroughs feared it would lead to a literal and psychological distancing of the middle class from poorer members of the race. For her, the question was how African Americans would maintain a sense of collective purpose when segregation's restrictions began to lessen and when class fissures continued to widen.[53]

During the following years, the emergence of direct-action campaigns in Montgomery and elsewhere in the South gave Burroughs reason to hope, because the goals of the new movement and its union of poor, working-class, and more privileged blacks were consistent with ideas that she had been espousing throughout half a century of public life. She used her position in the Woman's Convention to support the bus boycott and King's family, sending letters of support and contributions to his parents. "The enclosed is my personal expression of interest in the calm, sure way that Junior is standing up for right and righteousness," she wrote. Mrs. King thanked Burroughs for her "encouraging and uplifting" letter. "It came at a time when such words had added value for as you know, we have been and are still deeply concerned over the Montgomery situation and our son, thinking of the safety of him and his family. Though in the face of danger he says he cannot recant, he cannot walk off and leave the people now, so I feel, as has been done before, God will protect and deliver him from all harm."[54]

In September 1956, the tenth month of the boycott, which would take more than a year to resolve, Burroughs and Martin Luther King Jr. appeared in Denver for the annual Baptist meetings. Burroughs' speech reveals the contradictions and conflicts in her thinking about the relationship between classes of black people and about the nature of black religious leadership. "The only continuous, sacrificial support Church leaders have ever had has come directly from the masses," she maintained, but still she saw most black people as "sheep without shepherds." African Americans of all classes from all over the country should unite "to deliver the masses from the bondage of their death and to awaken the classes from their lack of real interests in mass improvement and smug sense of escape and security."[55]

At the same time, Burroughs made it clear that King embodied exactly the kind of ministerial leadership she had been calling for all of her life. "The race has seen a matchless example of leadership in the Montgomery, Alabama, situation. We have had nothing comparable to it, in handling the mass, in a serious and challenging situation." King, she believed, set an example for other young educated African Americans. "It is the business of the educated Negro to write, teach and guide the masses—not only into understanding—but into the way of standards. Above all, it is the business of Negro Church leaders to stop trying to—LEAD FROM BEHIND."[56]

"Your remarks after my address were magnificent," King wrote in his letter thanking her for her speech. "You said in a few words more than most people could say in hours. . . . I can assure you that your moral support and financial contribution have given me renewed courage and vigor to carry on."[57] In December 1956, King invited Burroughs to speak at the event marking the first anniversary of the start of the Montgomery bus boycott. Linking her to other women leaders of her generation, King explained: "Without Mary McLeod Bethune, we must depend on you. Your position as a leader among Baptists also increases the tremendous contribution it will make." He emphasized how important her appearance would be to the women who were stalwart supporters of the boycott, the many domestics who refused to take the buses to work. "As the first leader of Negro women in America, it is imperative that you come to give hope to the thousands of women who are paying the price of sacrifice in our struggle."[58]

Inspired by the Montgomery resistance, Burroughs redoubled her efforts to speak to the issues of the day and to keep the members of the Woman's Convention engaged with the beginnings of what would turn into the civil rights movement. Working from within the convention, she launched tracts and other publications designed to encourage blacks to support the movement and to prepare themselves and their communities to take advantage of opportunities as they developed. She also addressed herself to white people, issuing a tract entitled "Twelve Things Whites Must Stop Doing" in which she deplored the hypocrisy of white men who rallied against desegregation and social equality while continuing to engage in clandestine sexual liaisons with black women. "Stop making social excursions into the Negro race, depositing white offspring and then crying out against social equality" and "stop fighting integration in public education in the daytime, and practicing social equality anytime they want to."[59]

As for advice to African Americans, Burroughs emphasized

themes that had been hers since her earliest speaking days. It was as if the situation in Montgomery had offered a glimmer of the potential of a unified church response, especially if a majority of churches were prepared and willing to step into political leadership. Burroughs remained deeply worried about what she saw as misdirection and decline in black churches as a whole, despite the involvement of churches in the Montgomery campaign. Her address at the 1958 Woman's Convention included her assessment of the current situation. "We have entirely too many store-front churches. We have entirely too many empty churches. We have entirely too many meaningless churches. We have too many manless churches—(churches without Christian laymen)." As a result, the "masses" were "as bad off as if they were living in a land without Christianity."[60]

This of course was the same litany of complaints that Mays and others had made two decades earlier, but in 1958 the declining influence of religion and churches meant something different. Burroughs predicted that implementation of the *Brown* decision would be "delayed indefinitely by open defiance, political chicanery, subtle devices and all sorts of schemes, to delay and prevent the application of the law." But blacks had to be prepared to take full advantage of any new doors that opened. This is where she saw a failure of black leadership, especially from the pulpit, faulting preachers for "not doing enough ground work to enlighten, inspire and enlist the masses in their own salvation. Equal opportunity for education is our only hope, but that hope is dim without the united dedication of our leaders to the task of arousing the masses in interest of their own salvation through proper education." She continued to believe that the "main problem is inside the race" and that "class indifference to mass conditions has contributed largely to the present chaos."[61]

For all her penetrating intellect and political courage, Burroughs never completely escaped certain nineteenth-century prescriptions that implicated the shortcomings of the masses of black people as factors in their lack of social, economic, and political progress. Dedicated though she was to helping black people, when the likelihood of public interactions with whites increased, the more she reverted to an emphasis on physical cleanliness, sensible dress, good public conduct and manners, work skills, and personal responsibility. By then in her seventies, Burroughs was again preoccupied with the body, especially black women's bodies, as she had been early in her career. She was driven to exasperation by the fact that women had begun to wear pants and other revealing attire in public. "The scanty covering of their bosom is doubtless held up by faith, because there are no straps in sight." Her disgust with these changes in fashion and the moral laxity they represented was visceral. The new clothing styles came to represent all that was wrong with the women whom she was most interested in helping but who lived their lives outside the arc of her influence.[62]

A different set of issues also linked Burroughs back to ideas held earlier in the century. In 1953, extending her commitment to foreign mission work, she proudly developed a retreat center for missionaries returning from their work abroad. Decorated with elaborate African motifs and murals by the artist Lois Mailou Jones, the center's walls celebrated ancient Africa and its postcolonial future, portraying modern leaders of Egypt, Ethiopia, Liberia, Ghana, and Kenya. The mere existence of this building captured the contradictory set of ideas that Burroughs held about Africa. Like the young Bethune, she revered Africa as an ancestral home, but she saw her primary obligation to it as that of Christian missionary work. Burroughs held ideas about Africa and mission work that were entwined with her commitment to Western Christianity and its potential as a civilizing influence in a place she still judged to be in dire need of such help. That she did not view this as a conflict but as something to be celebrated is another indication that Burroughs still harbored notions forged in the late nineteenth and early twentieth centuries. Yet it also shows that she still believed in Christianity, despite its hypocrisy and abuses, as a force for good in postcolonial Africa.[63]

That was a belief reiterated by Mary McLeod Bethune when Burroughs hosted her at a visit to the new retreat center. Writing later in her *Chicago Defender* column, Bethune lauded the center "as a headquarters for mission work, for interracial effort, and as a place of rest and retreat for foreign missionaries." But more than that, Bethune celebrated it as an institutional achievement for black women. "It is the finest single accomplishment of its kind that I know of resulting from the unselfish efforts of a group of women of Negro descent," Bethune wrote in praise. "I am so proud of them, and of what they have done to promote the work of the missions and the cause of self-help in attaining our goals."[64]

By the end of the 1950s, Burroughs was becoming excited and moved by the early days of the civil rights movement. She was not by nature an optimist and rarely expressed idealistic or utopian thinking, but the emergence of effective direct-action strategies made her wish they could be used more widely. She issued a plea for "a peace force drawn from people of every country and race and color, and from every religion and none, who will be the pioneers of a new and undiscovered country." People joining such a movement, regardless of their religious beliefs, needed to have a "divine enthusiasm for tolerance and forgiveness." She called for an army of people who would not be afraid of breaking unjust laws or of using boycotts and noncooperation to end laws and customs that "prevent people living in peace and friendship with one another and, where they wish to, being educated together and worshipping with one another." The watchwords of that army would be prayer and action, always in conjunction. Shifting her tactics, she diagnosed a race crisis in America which she blamed on three causes, related not to the personal behavior of black working-class people but to the failings of whites. The causes were "unchristian practices, undemocratic attitudes, and unconstitutional application of laws."[65]

These were the ideas and commitments that drew praise for Burroughs from the influential civil rights activist Ella Baker, who was thirty years her junior but who knew of her work through her family's long-standing connections to the National Baptist Convention. Baker contacted Burroughs in 1959 to ask for her help organizing a series of protest hearings in Washington. Burroughs responded with great enthusiasm, finding a place to hold the hearings when the church Baker had booked for the event withdrew its invitation at the last minute. Baker's grandfather and great-grandfather had been prominent Baptist ministers. As a child, she had often traveled with her grandfather when he preached, and she had attended meetings of the North Carolina state Baptist Woman's Convention with her mother. There she saw, in the words of her biographer, "confident, competent, and committed African American women" who were living out an "activist, woman-centered faith." At fourteen, Baker was sent to Shaw Academy, a Baptist boarding school attached to Shaw University in North Carolina, where she would graduate from college in 1927. In a high school essay she argued that black churches had both spiritual and political missions, but she apologized for the gradualist approach to reforming churches that many of its leaders embraced. At the same time, she highlighted as a teenager what Mays, Woodson, and Du Bois had ignored: the economic fragility of black communities and the churches within them. "The group's economic resources," she wrote, "would not be adequate to carry out a radical program." Like her parents and grandparents, Baker believed that there was humility in service to others. She choose to do her service outside religious institutions and, beginning in the 1930s, through her work in coalitions that were more leftist and politically radical.[66]

In 1957, Baker had been hired as the first staff director for the Southern Christian Leadership Conference (SCLC) when it was formed in the aftermath of the Montgomery bus boycott. Her work within its ministerial leadership model left her discontented with both the sexism of the organization and its antidemocratic leadership model. She recognized its gendered patterns from her own immersion in Southern black religious life where the role of women was "that of doing things that the minister said he wanted to have done. It was not one in which they were credited with having creativity and initiative and capacity to carry out things." She also resented the moral hypocrisy of those black preachers who engaged in illicit sexual activities. In the end, she concluded that she and the ministers at the SCLC had a conflict over the definition of leadership. They saw themselves as "saviors" while she advocated more humble, grassroots, collective approaches.[67]

Burroughs' support for Baker's request was evidence of her active interest in the unfolding events of the civil rights movement. Writing in her column for the *Pittsburgh Courier*, she fearlessly entered the controversy that erupted when Robert Williams, the president of a North Carolina branch of the NAACP, was suspended by the national organization for advocating to blacks that "we must fight back" if attacked by whites. Although she eschewed violent self-defense, she also sympathized with Williams' impulse not to cower, saying that this was not "the time for Negroes to cringe or to take low." Yet if blacks followed Williams, she argued, they could be walking into a "death trap" because she feared that the overwhelming powers of the "enemy" would annihilate black resisters. At the same time, she criticized the NAACP's action against Williams. "This is the time for the NAACP to teach the people," she wrote, "what the right weapons are and how to use them effectively." She warned against the sense of divisiveness that the NAACP's action had created. Instead, Burroughs turned to biblical lessons for guidance. "In this crisis, fight back with 2nd Corinthians, 10th chapter, fourth and fifth verse, and do it like it's nobody's business, but yours and God's—'for the weapons of our warfare are not carnal but mighty through God to the pulling down of strongholds' of prejudice and injustice. Intelligence, calm and a faith that will not shrink are the weapons with which to fight."[68]

Burroughs' engagement with this and other aspects of the civil rights campaign stood in marked contrast to the prevailing ethos within the National Baptist Convention. Since the 1950s, disputes had been simmering over the autocratic nature of convention leadership and over its lack of commitment to the new civil rights movement. The Reverend David Jemison, old and blind, had stepped down from the presidency of the convention in 1953 and was replaced by the Reverend Joseph H. Jackson of Chicago. Burroughs had refused to be drawn into the contest for leadership, and chastised Jackson for asking her to endorse him. "We must certainly pray that Negro Baptists shall not be drowned by ungodly ambition of any leader, for empty honor and selfish power."[69]

Both King and his father had supported Jackson's election, but soon became disenchanted when in 1957 Jackson eradicated a new provision imposing a four-term limit on the presidency. At that point, the younger King became more actively engaged in coalition with a group of other ministers who resented what they viewed as Jackson's autocratic and antidemocratic style, as well as his refusal to rally the convention in support of the civil rights movement. These disputes over the leadership of the Baptist Convention were the subject of considerable public attention and a source of much distress to black Baptists.[70]

In 1956, Alberta King told Burroughs she was relieved that the women's meetings had not been ruined by the controversies. "The

Woman's Convention (unlike the Men's) affords so much inspiration, information, and offers so many challenges, til all who attend, always leave with great intentions of rendering much service when back home and *many of them do*." The next year, she seemed to dread the larger convention as much as she looked forward to the Woman's meetings, predicting to Burroughs that it would be terrible and full of "much confusion, disorder—in other words—pandemonium."[71]

King's son and a group of young, politically active preachers were preparing to unseat Jackson as president. They wanted to institute more democratic procedures within the convention and insisted that the organization be more centrally involved in the civil rights movement. King and his allies rallied behind the candidacy of Gardner Taylor, who promised to transform the convention into an organized arm of the civil rights movement. The convention delegates overwhelmingly elected Taylor, only to see Jackson mount a court challenge that reinstalled him in office.[72] Undeterred, King and Taylor tried once again to defeat Jackson at the annual Baptist meetings in Kansas City in 1961. Pandemonium did break out, as well as violence and confusion, resulting in the accidental death of a minister when Taylor's forces tried to seize the podium. Afterward, Jackson summarily ousted King from his position as vice president of the convention's Sunday School Board. Perhaps more damaging were the published rumors that Jackson held King personally responsible for the death that had occurred.[73]

A week later, unable to dislodge Jackson or to take over the convention, King and Taylor and thirty-two other Baptist ministers left the National Baptist Convention. In September 1961 they formed a rival organization, the Progressive National Baptist Convention (PNBC). When King went, so did his parents and his wife, Coretta. By the next year, 1,200 black Baptist ministers representing twenty-two states had joined this new group. Today, the group claims 2.5 million members but remains much smaller than the National Baptist Convention, which boasts 7.5 million members. After the split, Jackson served as president of the National Convention until 1982, longer than any other holder of the post.[74]

As part of its founding principles, the PNBC imposed strict tenure limits on officeholders and made all convention offices open to any member, lay or clergy, male or female. In the official account of its history, the PNBC emphasizes that the organizational split had two equally important causes, namely the dispute over democratic self-governance and the imperative of linking black Baptist churches more closely to the civil rights movement and the quest for human rights in general.

NANNIE Burroughs did not live to witness these developments. In the spring of 1961, her advanced age and failing health took their toll. Burroughs died in May, just weeks before the dedication of her last project at the National Training School, a new chapel where her body lay in state before her funeral. In her last days, she had instructed colleagues to request that people make donations to the school instead of sending flowers in her memory. Her funeral was held at the church she had attended all her life, the Nineteenth Baptist Church in Washington, and drew a crowd of thousands of people, including the Reverend J. H. Jackson and his rival Gardner Taylor, who would emigrate to the new denomination.[75]

Although she had insisted that she never wanted anything named after her, in death, although rarely in life, Burroughs' wishes were disregarded and the trustees of the school renamed it in her honor. Eventually they ceded control of the institution to the PNBC. Today, the Nannie Helen Burroughs school operates as a private coeducational religious school, on a campus that also houses the headquarters of the denomination.

The split from the National Baptist Convention and King's role in it illustrate something much larger than denominational politics. They remind us that there was continued disagreement, even at the height of the civil rights movement, about whether and to what extent black religious institutions and their adherents ought to be engaged in direct political action, even in a campaign that sought the most basic of rights. As King himself would say, it has almost always been a small "creative, dedicated minority" that has made the world a better place.[76]

Black churches, their members, and their ministers were crucial to what the movement achieved, but it never involved more than a small minority of black religious people. These few are what Burroughs at one point called a remnant of the larger whole and a remnant as well of the descendents of slavery and of those who still called themselves people of faith. They believed that religion belonged in politics and that the moral impetus for social change could come from within black Christianity, despite its flaws. They were part of a new generation, one that succeeded Bethune and Burroughs and the many church women who remain nameless and that found its public voice in King.

At her death, Benjamin Mays began his commentary on her life this way: "But before paying a tribute to Nannie Burroughs, I must mention Mary McLeod Bethune and Charlotte Hawkins Brown." For Mays, the salient link between these three black women leaders was that none was "college-bred." It was his plea "that those of us who have been privileged to go to college will do as much in our day as Nannie Burroughs did in hers." Recounting his last visit with Burroughs, when she had summoned him to Washington, Mays emphasized that despite her age, "her mind was young." Indeed, she asked to meet with him out of her commitment to the student-led sit-ins and demonstrations that were taking place in Atlanta in 1960 and 1961. Burroughs told him that she "wanted to be sure that the sit-in demonstrations were not a fly-by-night thing" and "she wanted to know what was being done to guarantee the continuation of the sit-ins until every vestige of discrimination in eating establishments and lunch counters had been abolished." She remained focused on the work yet to be done.[77]

"That indefinable thing that we call time travels so fast that the past is gone and the present becomes the past even while we attempt to define it," Burroughs wrote early in her life. "And like the flash of the lightning, it at once exists, and expires."[78] Burroughs spent her entire life working within black churches, where she always placed her faith. She cast her lot with all-black institutions, even when racial homogeneity failed to avoid conflicts. For Burroughs, there could be no political progress for black people without the leadership and sacrifice of black religious and educational institutions and the men and women who devoted themselves to their survival.

5

Southern Black Liberal Protestantism

IN HIS 1971 memoir, *Born To Rebel*, the religious scholar and educator Benjamin Mays wrote that it would be "a sad commentary on our life and times if a historian writing in the year 2000 can still truthfully say that the most segregated institution in the United States is the 'Church of the Living God.'"[1] A Southern black man born in the late nineteenth century, Mays experienced the eras of Jim Crow, both world wars, civil rights, and Black Power. But he did not live to see the new millennium or the failure of his own prophecy.

Mays had an unusually rich background that included the Southern black rural religious world in which he was raised, the Northern mostly white liberal theological institutions in which he thrived as a scholarship student, and the Jim Crow South to which he returned and where he worked for all of his life. Earlier in the twentieth century, W. E. B. Du Bois had warned of the weariness that resulted from black double consciousness, from the effort to reconcile being both black and American. Would that it were that simple. For Mays, the challenge was far more complicated because he was a Southern black religious liberal, an identity described by terms normally held in juxtaposition and rarely joined. In fact he was all of that, as were many other men and women of his region and his race and his faith and his politics.

Perhaps the advantage of a multiple consciousness is a learned aptitude for abiding with irreconcilable contradictions. Mays advocated a church universal that could build a worldwide movement for social justice; at the same time, he understood the inherently local nature of religious and racial policy and practice. He argued that Christianity ought to be color-blind and desegregated even as he adhered to a belief in the political need for black-controlled institutions, especially churches and colleges. Still, Mays did not believe only in the power of the sacred or of private institutions; he coupled that with a faith in an interventionist egalitarian state, believing that both church and state were essential to achieving racial equality.

Toward the end of his life, Mays came to understand better that local churches, black and white, served not only as religious sanctuaries but as racial and political ones as well. Neither blacks nor whites wanted to sacrifice institutions with distinctive cultural, theological, and political natures. Born and bred in segregation, each group's churches had developed in distinctive ways, and neither group wanted them to be subsumed in a quest for liberal universalism or color-blind Christianity.

An early and eager engagement with global religious organizations provided Mays with opportunities to travel the world. In this respect, his life is more emblematic than it is unusual. Many other prominent politically engaged African American religious intellectuals in the pre–civil rights era arrived at a notion of global politics in just this way, through travels to and participation in ecumenical world gatherings. For that reason, our understandings of African Americans and international politics must make way for religious universalism as one route to a compelling critique of colonialism and of the oppression of people of color around the globe.[2]

Mays clung to his faith in the potential of international religious enterprises, but he repeatedly confronted the difficulty of convincing local religious organizations to embrace the lofty tenets of a church universal and of global ecumenism. Putting those worldviews into local practice proved extremely difficult and often impossible. Indeed, a full half-century after the civil rights movement and well into the twenty-first century, racially separate Christian churches still dominate the landscape. The reasons for this are rooted in the complicated history of race, religion, and politics present even before the founding of the republic but here presented through the narrative of another politically and religiously engaged black twentieth-century life.

MAYS'S thinking about the hypocrisy of American Christianity was deeply influenced by his travels outside the United States. His tenure as dean of Howard University's School of Religion from 1934 to 1940 provided him with the opportunity to participate in several international, ecumenical conferences where world race relations was a central topic of discussion. He attended the World Conference of the YMCA in Mysore, India, and the Oxford Conference on the Church, Community and State, both held in 1939. He also traveled to Amsterdam for a 1939 conference of 1,500 young Christians from around the world.

What struck Mays as most remarkable about these gatherings was that "members of different races and nations met on a plane of absolute equality" where they could take communion together as Christians and where they imagined themselves to be part of a "universal church that transcends all national, racial or class barriers and cuts across all theological presuppositions." He witnessed many vigorous debates on resolutions urging Christian churches to end segregation on the basis of race or color in worship and in more informal fellowship activities. The resolutions passed with majority support, but only after white delegates from South Africa offered a spirited theological defense of segregation in both church and state.[3]

Traveling broadened Mays's exposure to issues of color, class, and religion beyond the American example. In 1937 he made the first of his three trips to India and met with Gandhi whose nonviolent-protest work he had long admired as did many other black Americans in the late 1920s and 1930s. Leaders and intellectuals as diverse as Du Bois, Marcus Garvey, and A. Philip Randolph embraced Gandhi's anticolonialist and, later, anticaste positions. African American newspapers and journals across the political spectrum devoted extensive coverage to Gandhi's life and campaigns in South Africa and India. The journeys of African Americans to India and the visits from Indians to African American communities were closely covered.[4]

African American Christians like Mays were especially drawn to the example of Gandhi and his spiritual and political commitments. Apparently without hesitation, they found in this Hindu a twentieth-century embodiment of the teachings of Jesus. Mays was but one in a long line of black theologians and religious leaders who made the journey to India. In a ninety-minute meeting with Gandhi in 1937, Mays came to understand more clearly that nonviolence was not simply passive resistance but rather an "active force." It had to "be practiced in absolute love and without hate." After returning to the United States, Mays published a series of essays arguing that African American Christianity was especially compatible with the principles and strategies endorsed by Gandhi.[5]

As Mays traveled through the Middle East on that same trip, Arab Muslims challenged him to defend his belief in Christianity in the face of white American Christian hypocrisy and racial segregation in the United States. Mays vividly recounted a conversation on a train from Jerusalem to Cairo with an Arab who criticized American racism and American Christianity's role in it. "When I kept telling him that we were all Christians," Mays recalled, "he was bewildered. Finally he said, 'In my religion when once one embraces the faith of Islam, race makes no difference. That is why I cannot understand how you Christians behave as you do towards each other.'" In the end, the man "expressed little faith in our Christianity and little in our democracy" and challenged Mays to rethink his commitments to both.[6]

Although these early opportunities for international travel were formative factors in Mays's intellectual, political, and spiritual growth, he realized that the world conferences to which he traveled had little influence over local beliefs and practices in the United States and elsewhere. The Oxford Conference passed strongly worded resolutions against racial segregation, but Mays knew that churches in South Africa and the United States would largely ignore them. The conference also produced an outline for a World Council of Churches, which was later established and in which Mays would participate.

Despite these developments, Mays experienced feelings of "futility," since it seemed unlikely that such efforts would advance the cause of justice, peace, and racial equality. "Nothing we said at Oxford will have any influence on the governments of the world with respect to their armament plans. . . . Nothing we did at Oxford will change Hitler and Germany in their ruthless warfare against the Jews and nothing we did there will destroy Italy's ambition to reestablish the Roman Empire. The communists and fascists in Spain will continue to fight despite what we said at Oxford. Segregation in God's church will continue in America and in South Africa after Oxford."[7]

Mays connected the issue of racial injustice in the United States with political persecution around the world and called on Christian churches to combat both. "The persecution of the Jews in

Germany and Poland, the complete subjugation and exploitation of the Bantu in South Africa, the disfranchisement and economic prescriptions of Negroes in the United States, the treatment of Aborigines in Australia, the Anglo-Indian problem in India, and the struggle of suppressed peoples everywhere—all these must be the immediate concern of God's Church."[8]

In the end, what did give Mays some hope was his feeling at these ecumenical gatherings that there was "such a thing as a *Universal Church*" which could stretch across national, racial, class, and theological divisions. And, again, he got that feeling from the sheer power of the experience of sharing worship and communion with groups of people from all around the world. This fed his belief in "interracial fellowship" as both a symbol and a practice of a Christian church engaged in common work for the greater good.[9]

IN THE United States, the desire and the prospect for interracial fellowship were weak among blacks and whites alike. Mays recognized this even as he put the idea of such fellowship to good rhetorical use in his attacks on segregation. While he chastised white churches for closing their doors to black worshipers or explicitly restricting membership to whites, he defended all-black churches and denominations by explaining that they had developed only as a necessary response to the exclusionary practices of white Christians. This historical vision of the founding of independent black denominations veers sharply from more traditional and more nationalist claims about this development as an act of political defiance.

Mays acknowledged that the proliferation of segregated black churches was driven by a "growing racial consciousness" and by "the desire of the Negro to manage and direct his own religious activities." He cautioned that even though black churches would never turn away white worshipers, "Negroes themselves would question the motives of white people if they sought in large numbers to join Negro churches." What he called the "dual religious system" was actually a very complicated issue that would be difficult to resolve. This was especially true once one ventured beyond his call for all Christian churches to open their doors to all regardless of race, about as limited a version of interracial fellowship as one could imagine.[10]

Despite his own persistence on this topic, Mays was not particularly optimistic about the prospects for interracial fellowship or for a more progressive, politically engaged, and unified American Christian community. Two formidable ideas stood in opposition even to the ideal of an interracial fellowship. The first was the apprehension among both blacks and whites that it would eventually eradicate churches in which their own race predominated. The second was a stated fear among whites that it would lead inevitably to interracial sex and marriage.[11] When Mays was asked in 1939 to predict the state of American Christianity a decade later, his most optimistic prediction was that "by 1950 Negroes and white people who want to exercise Christian fellowship will not have to sneak and hide as much as they do now," an unfortunate choice of words for those already afraid that church integration would bring interracial marriage and sex.[12]

Indeed, even the most "liberal" white Protestants were unwilling to confront the question of interracial marriage at that time. In the mid-1940s, Mays and other African Americans served on several committees convened by the Federal Council of Churches to study race and religion. One of those, the Commission on the Church and Minority Peoples, convened in 1943 with the aim of gathering facts about the relations between blacks and whites, between Jews and Gentiles, and between recent immigrants and other Americans. When the commission held a series of regional conferences on race relations, the fear of intermarriage, especially between black men and white women, emerged as the biggest source of tension and resistance to any change in race relations. This was true for every region and not just in the South.[13]

The most optimistic conclusion from the commission's meetings was that "it is not necessary to want a man for a brother-in-law before treating him as a brother." For whites, that distinction affirmed a notion of equality while strictly maintaining marriage and sex prohibitions as if the incest taboo applied to fraternal relations between the races. The commission urged churches to declare intermarriage "not a sin, but perhaps unwise."[14]

Mays and others proposed language to strengthen what they perceived as a weak position on the legality of interracial marriage. "In a democratic and Christian society such as we dream of in America," they wrote, "there can be no legal limitation, based on race, creed, or national origin alone, upon free relationships among people." In 1946, when the council adopted its final commission report on the conferences on race and religion, it included no mention of the intermarriage issue. All references to it had been marked out by hand in the penultimate draft with the simple notation, "Eliminate." The final statement merely condemned segregation as "a violation of the gospel of love and human brotherhood" and proposed more study to "work on an unsegregated Church and an unsegregated society."[15]

The evidence of sexual relationships between the races was inescapable for black Southern men and women of Mays's generation, most of whom were the children or grandchildren of slaves. Family memories of the frequency and consequences of coerced sexual relationships between white men and black women under slavery were plentiful even if routinely silenced among many Southern African Americans. For these men and women and their female children, the fear of forced interracial sexual relations at the hands of white men was not a mere relic of the slave era but something that persisted. Mays's memoir, which offers few emotional revelations, contains powerful descriptions of interviews Mays conducted that reveal how hard Southern black parents had to work to protect their daughters from "the sexual demands of any lecherous white man" and how they taught them to defend themselves.[16]

When Mays married Sadie Gray in 1926, her family's history brought this issue even closer to home. "Like my father, my wife Sadie's father, James Gray, was born a slave," he explained in his memoir, but "unlike my grandfather on my father's side, Sadie's grandfather was white, and her great-grandfather on her mother's side was also white." Born in Georgia in 1900, Sadie was college educated, like Mays, and earned a B.A. and a master's in social work from the University of Chicago.[17]

Despite the secrecy and the silence that often enveloped the place of white men in black family histories, Mrs. Mays broached this subject publicly and used it to defend her own race pride and her insistence on equal rights for black women. In a series of vignettes from a talk entitled "Hallelujah I Am Not White," Mrs. Mays recounted the tangled web on her father's side of the family: "I've heard that my paternal great grand mother had a strain of Indian blood. I do not know what else, my paternal grand sire was of Scotch Irish descent, I was told. He was the county's most influential citizen who never married, never owned slaves unless he secretly owned his children, and whose children were all born slaves."[18]

When Mrs. Mays turned to her mother's side of the family, a different narrative emerged. "My maternal Great grand mother was an Eboe [sic] and taught her son, my maternal grandfather, to be proud of his African blood even though my grand father was sired by an outstanding slave holder, his mother's master. My Eboe Great Grandmother, who I remember, was proud of her great tribe and was never subdued." That grandmother had been sold in Virginia and taken to Georgia because her white owners believed she "needed rougher treatment to manage her." But, in Mrs. Mays's words, "she was never managed."[19]

Things were different on the other side of her mother's family however; Mrs. Mays reported that her "maternal Grand mother had a Negro mother and was sired by a kindly slave holder who kept an interest in her." Mrs. Mays expressed relief that her own life was different from that of her foremothers and that "there are some cruel fates I do not have to suffer." Her repeated use of the verb "sire," a term associated with the breeding of horses, is jarring. It denies white men their place as "fathers" in her family, and implicitly argues that there was no consent on the part of the mothers.[20]

These and other aspects of Mrs. Mays's family history were featured in a 1952 cover story of the *Negro History Bulletin;* a photograph of Sadie and Benjamin appeared on the cover of the issue. Emma Gray, Mrs. Mays's sister, wrote the long accompanying article that traced their family history back to the 1850s; she was blunt about the presence of white male figures in their legacy and about the varied responses accorded them by male members of their family. Emma and Sadie's father was the son of a prominent white man who never married but who had three children by an enslaved woman; their father adored this man and defended him by saying, "I was a slave in the system and he was a slave to the system." Her grandfather on her mother's side also was the son of a white slave-owner, but he despised his white father for having taken sexual advantage of his mother. When Sadie neared her teen years, that grandfather warned her to tell him if any white man approached her, promising that he would fight to the death to protect her. "Our mothers were slaves," he said. "They could not protect themselves. But you do not have to take insults from anybody." Her grandfather, she reported, had seen so many of the injustices of slavery that "he never joined the church because he did not believe that God exists."[21]

The marriage between Benjamin and Sadie Mays should have made him more sensitive to the particular strengths and struggles of black women. Their relationship always had to accommodate the fact that she was professionally active and publicly engaged. They had met in the late 1920s at South Carolina State College where they both taught. Their decision to marry cost them their jobs despite their protests all the way to the governor, because an unofficial rule barred married women from continuing to teach.[22] Mrs. Mays later worked as a social worker in Atlanta and at the National Youth Administration in Washington when her husband was dean at Howard University.[23]

In 1940, when Sadie and Benjamin Mays moved back to Atlanta and onto the Morehouse campus, she took an active part in student life even as she continued her own community activism despite the many demands on their household. She founded and chaired the board of a nursing home that served indigent black residents of Atlanta; the facility was renamed in her honor after her death in 1969. Even though her husband was a Baptist presiding over a Baptist-affiliated college campus where they lived for twenty-seven years, as another measure of her independence, Sadie Mays remained an active, loyal Methodist all of her life. She was also a devoted fundraiser for her alma mater, the CME-affiliated Paine College, and a participant in many activities there.[24]

Mrs. Mays credited her father for instilling her with racial pride, but she disagreed with him about the appropriate role of black women. "I was blessed with a father," she wrote, who raised his children to overcome the handicaps of race, but "even he felt that a woman should accept positions different from men." She explained that he "wanted women cared for, protected, and kindly treated," and that "he wanted leadership roles for his boys and soft protected roles for his girls."[25]

Obviously, Mrs. Mays rebelled against her father's expectations and held strong views about the disadvantages that faced women,

especially black women. In 1943, Sadie and Benjamin Mays participated in the annual Institute on Socio-Religious Affairs held at
Paine College. Speaking on a panel on the position of Jews, blacks,
and women in America, she told the group that she had been a victim of racial prejudice based on both race and sex. But she said that
in her opinion the effects of the latter were more serious: "Men ask
women to do more work for less pay. Men see to it that women do
not get jobs unless there is no man available or the work deals entirely with women. Women have been in this inferior position so
long they tend to accept it. Some even have a technique of trying
to make men feel superior. Many refuse to reach heights that they
could because they fear men will not approve." An audience member asked, "If women are fortunate enough to get married, should
not they be willing to make their homes their career?" "Some
women may be content to do this," Mrs. Mays replied, "but most
women with minds want more. They want an equal chance in professions and in business."[26]

Her views seem to have influenced and been shared by her husband. On the Sunday morning of the institute meeting, he preached
a sermon in which he addressed the plight of women. "Every right
gained by woman has been wrung from the hands of her father,
brother, or husband. Men will not voluntarily relinquish their position of dominance." He then urged black people to be more democratic in the areas over which they had control, namely "the home,
the church, the school."[27]

In 1950 the *Pittsburgh Courier*, as part of its midcentury com-
memorations, asked Mays to assess the progress of black churches
over the previous half-century and to predict what their status was
likely to be at the turn of the next century.[28] Sharing in the optimism of the immediate post–World War II period, Mays forecast

that the next fifty years would be "decades of integration." He actually predicted an end to black churches, a change that he represented quite surprisingly as a sign of progress and a good thing:

> There will be no Negro church in the year 2000 and there will be no white church. There will exist only Christian churches in the year 2000. . . . In the year 2000 the names of all denominations with Negro or colored designations will have been changed. The words "Negro Baptists" will not appear in the Federal Census of Religious Bodies in the year 2006. Nor will the designations CME, AME, and AMEZ. If we become Christian enough, avoid war and survive, racial designation in matters of religion will be history in the year of our Lord 2000.[29]

This prediction was more than a mere exercise in millennial prophecy, for Mays continued to call for a fully integrated church throughout that decade. In a lecture on the Christian's duty in race relations given at Yale's Divinity School in 1952, he broadened the political nature of his appeal and urged all Christian churches to integrate, to support the NAACP, and to instruct their members to disobey unjust laws related to segregation. Although he did not retract his prediction of the inevitability of an integrated church, he did seek to mollify and reassure those who were uneasy with some of the practical consequences of such an outcome. He predicted that "there would be little change in the membership of congregations if racial restrictions were completely removed" but still that "over a relatively long period the racially designated church would disappear, and Christians would cease to think in terms of race or culture."[30]

Here, Mays was acknowledging that a move toward integrating churches would bring real difficulties. Although he believed that

black congregations on the whole would be more willing to welcome whites into their churches than vice versa, he also knew that
many black people would oppose the full integration of churches.
"Many fear that their leadership would be threatened if the racial
church were abolished." But Mays had little patience for that view,
concluding that "the Negro church may be just as un-Christian
at this point as the white church."[31] He seemed most interested
in seeing black churches and white churches united as a way of
modeling interracial unity and desegregation, even at the risk of
weakening or destroying black churches as independent black institutions.

The notion of a church universal remained a driving force not
only in Mays's advocacy of a desegregated American church but
also in his early embrace of the movement toward a world council
of churches that had evolved out of the 1939 World Conference in
Oxford that had made such a profound impression on him. When
the First Assembly of the World Council was held in 1948 in
Amsterdam, Mays was elected to a five-year term on its Central
Committee. When the council convened in the United States in
fall of 1954, in Evanston, Illinois, Mays was given the honor of delivering an address to counter one given by a representative of the
Dutch Reformed Church of South Africa who defended segregation and apartheid as practical necessities defensible within Christian doctrine.[32]

In his rebuttal speech, entitled "The Church amidst Ethnic and
Racial Tensions," Mays offered a scholarly theological and historical case against racial discrimination and segregation within Christian institutions. He based his argument on a reading of early
church history, the Bible, and the findings of modern science. In
many ways, this speech expanded on ideas that Mays had been
preaching for decades but that now drew more attention because of
his and the council's growing prestige, symbolized by the spectacular pageantry surrounding the event itself.

Mays laid out a complex series of connected arguments taken from a report prepared by the council's working group on race. He relied, in part, on the fixed nature of the physical characteristics of color and race. "Segregation on the basis of color or race is a wicked thing because it penalizes a person for being what God had made him and for conditions over which he has no control." But even as Mays adverted to notions of immutability, he said modern science had proved that physical markers used to categorize people according to "race" did not rest on any deeper biological or human difference. "At long last science has caught up with religion," he teased, "for it was Paul who declared on Mars Hill nineteen centuries ago that God made of one blood all nations of men."[33]

Advancing a line of historical reasoning that presaged constructions of race theories, Mays told his audience that the racial bar in the church had not arisen out of Christianity's early history but was of modern origin. "It was when modern Western imperialism began to explore and exploit the colored peoples of Africa, Asia and America" that racial segregation and discrimination began. Only then did color became associated with "inferiority" and whiteness with "superiority." So, Mays asked, "how can segregation and discrimination in the Church be justified" if there was no basis for them in the Bible, church history, or theology? For him, segregation was the great scandal in the church, especially in South Africa and the United States.[34]

Mays was interrupted by applause ten times and was given an extended standing ovation. His World Council address was reported on and reprinted widely; it was issued in pamphlet form, and excerpts were broadcast or quoted on local and national radio. Coming as it did only months after the Supreme Court's *Brown* decision, Mays's talk generated considerable attention in the United States and abroad. Some listeners interpreted the speech as yet another radical attempt to move the country too rapidly into a post-segregation world. This surprised Mays because every world assembly since 1928 had condemned segregation and racism through speeches and resolutions. Indeed, the repetition of the condemnation year after year without meaningful change had led him to write about the futility of such work.[35]

The fact that the 1954 world assembly was held on U.S. soil made a difference in the reach and reception of its message on race. Some white Americans objected not just to the message but to the race of the messenger. Mays would later recount that he received "more vilifying letters" after that speech than after any other in fifty years of public life. One listener took up Mays's immutability argument and twisted it to ask, "Why can't a Nigger just go on bein' a Nigger like God dun made 'em, and be happy?" Despite this, Mays judged the meeting to have been a great success; but he resigned himself to the fact that, just as with all the other world assemblies, "the character of the local churches was hardly changed by any of the activities of the conference." Here again the global and the local had collided.[36]

The *Brown* decision's outlawing of segregated public education added fire to Mays's arguments against what he called the "voluntary" segregation in religion which he contrasted with secular practices. Mays argued that it was even more scandalous for Christian churches to maintain their racially exclusive policies since as completely private institutions they had the freedom to impose such policies and to lift them.[37] He urged churches to open their doors to all as a way of supporting the morality of the Supreme Court's edict even though the law did not apply to them. In an article in the liberal Protestant magazine *Christianity and Crisis*, Mays countered scriptural and historical justifications for segregated churches and implored Christian churches to assume a leadership role in the pursuit of racial justice. "If the Churches needed a *legal* basis for doing what the *Gospel has ordered* for nineteen centuries, they have it in the recent decision of the Supreme Court."[38]

The distinction Mays drew between the law that governs the state and the law that governs moral relations points to the difficulty of calling on churches to act as if they were public or political institutions, rather than private and religious ones. Public institutions were subject to legal edict, even if only reluctantly so, but the churches were not. The wall separating the public sphere of law and policymaking from the private sphere of worship and religious freedom was not porous, since it was designed to protect and divide two worlds when they were in conflict, or even when, as in the case of racial segregation, they were in harmony.

In the decade following the *Brown* decision, Mays defended the continuing existence of private black colleges like Morehouse, where he presided. In 1943, Mays and Bethune had been among the presidents of similar institutions who had formed the United Negro College Fund (UNCF) which dedicated itself to raising the necessary funds for preserving those schools. Like Morehouse, most of the affiliated colleges were in the South and had been founded with religious support.

In 1958, Mays began a three-year term as the president of the UNCF. By then, the really important practical question was why white philanthropists and others should continue to support private black colleges and universities in the face of legal decisions that opened the way, in principle, for black students to seek enrollment in white institutions. Even before the *Brown* decision Mays and his colleagues in the UNCF had begun to argue that the best way to protect black colleges from extinction was to make them as good as comparable white institutions, enabling them to compete equally for students.[39]

Mays tried to reassure black institutions that they would not perish but would flourish in an integrated society. But he was prescient in his concern that integrating blacks into white higher education would rob historically black colleges of some of their best students and thus deprive those institutions of needed resources.[40] This is the argument that Mays and other supporters of black schools made not only immediately after the *Brown* decision but in the 1960s and 1970s as well.

His predictions about the effect of integration on higher education proved far more accurate than his many prophecies on integrating churches. He reiterated this idea in 1962 as part of a funding appeal on behalf of the UNCF. "The prestige colleges and universities in America are not interested in providing a program that would take the most disadvantaged Negro students and prepare them for graduate and professional training. This is our task and if the UNCF colleges do not wrestle with it, nobody else will." Mays warned that "without these colleges thousands of Negro students would never be trained" and the race and the nation would lose large numbers of "qualified leaders."[41]

Mays made essentially the same argument in 1965. "The white institutions in this country are not greatly concerned about improving the quality of education for all Negroes." Using a term that Du Bois had coined for other purposes, Mays argued, apparently without irony, that white institutions "are concerned only about the talented tenth."[42] The possibility of ceding the training of the race's leadership class to white institutions disturbed Mays greatly. So too did his growing realization that any significant move toward interracial churches might have practical consequences for black ministers. Mays continued to be concerned about the relatively limited numbers of educated and seminary-trained black clergy, a subject on which he had been writing and speaking since the 1930s.

Mays used the specter of church integration to add fire to his arguments for increasing the black educated clerical class even as his protégé Martin Luther King Jr. was emerging as a national figure after the Montgomery bus boycott. In a 1955 column entitled "Who Will Preach to Negroes in 1980?" Mays combined his concern about the declining numbers of educated black clergy with the fear that as a consequence, educated black Christians might turn to white churches or to white ministerial leadership of black churches. Saying that he was not opposed to either on principle, a view consistent with his other public stances, he explained that he would still "like to see Negroes have their share of the ministerial leadership in the desegregated tomorrow." Mays ended with a call for black churches to rid themselves of an "illiterate ministry" and for black religious and educational leaders to unite around a common goal of preparing educated preachers.[43]

In 1959, Mays argued that a demand for highly educated black ministers would "speed up the process of desegregation" by discouraging unenlightened, uneducated black preachers from founding small or storefront churches. His wish for an educated ministry was often coupled with his continued discomfort with small, mostly Holiness and Pentecostal churches. He maintained his early belief that the leadership and proliferation of those churches somehow played a part in holding the race back.[44]

To believe, as Mays did, that black churches were essential to black political advancement required reconciling this belief with the fact that those local institutions were male-led but dominated by women in membership and financial support. For him, it seems, the problem was not the overwhelming presence of women, but the relative absence of men in the pews and the unpreparedness of the men who ascended to the pulpit. Mays longed for an educated black male clerical class that could double as local political leadership and whose work would complement that of the dedicated black church women.[45]

In his view, it was not the case that men led and women did not, but rather that leadership was one of the defining characteristics of black masculinity. This sentiment remains central to the mission of Morehouse College. Before, during, and after the era when King,

Morehouse's most famous graduate, was providing a heroic example of an educated young black Southern religious political leader, Mays was lobbying hard for black men to take up the mantle of leadership. To his mind, well-educated black ministers were needed to preserve and further the gains then being made through litigation and changes in the laws of segregation.

Although Mays must have known that an educated black male clergy was a demographically unattainable dream in those days, he did not acknowledge the fact publicly. It was impossible to create enough college-educated and seminary-trained black ministers to shepherd thousands of local black churches, even if one excludes those black churches that would not have wanted a minister with that training, or that would have lacked the resources to support one.

In 1958, after fifteen years of groundwork, Mays's vision of creating a trained black ministry culminated with the founding of the Interdenominational Theological Center (ITC) at Morehouse College. The center brought together under one administrative umbrella four black seminaries affiliated with Methodist, AME, CME, and Baptists denominations, and later added two others linked to the Presbyterian church and the Church of God in Christ. Here, Mays was able to model his ideas of institutional consolidation and ecumenical cooperation, at least among African Americans. The ITC also welcomed men and women who sought clerical training, subject to denominational practices.[46]

THOUGH increasingly concerned that an integrated Christianity might adversely affect the black ministry, Mays continued to promote interracial and ecumenical alliances during this period as he had done throughout the previous three decades. He felt especially honored to be asked to chair the Conference on Religion and Race held in Chicago in January 1963. The conference, which gathered more than 700 hundred religious leaders, marked the first time that Protestant, Catholic, and Jewish religious bodies had convened for the express purpose of attacking racism in the United States at all levels of society and within the religious bodies themselves. Mays hoped that the consolidation of religious forces would at the very least encourage local communities to accept changes in the law and to "work against racial bias at the local level," including individual congregations.[47]

There were those at the meeting, however, who were fearful of the broader political consequences of sacrificing black churches at the altar of interracial Christianity and integrated fellowship. This complaint was raised by Anna Arnold Hedgeman, a savvy African American political activist with a long record of experience in various religious, women's, labor, and government positions. At the meeting, Hedgeman observed Catholic, Jewish, and Protestant leaders speaking about their faiths and their moral responsibility for helping to solve the racial crisis. But she was disturbed that there was "no presentation of the Negro church" depicting its achievements and strengths.

Mays spoke at the conference, as did King, who gave the closing address. Though Hedgeman praised their oratory, she wanted them to say more. Since Mays was one of the organizers, it was his speech that most disappointed her. "Dr. Mays could easily have indicated that there would be need for much conversation between Negro and white church leaders, for the only real power the Negro leader has ever had was within his own church. Would the Negro be willing to play a secondary role if churches merge? Could he have confidence in the leadership of the white churches? These questions were not discussed."[48]

Although she had worked for decades in ecumenical work among blacks and whites, including among white women's religious groups,

Hedgeman feared that African American churches would be imperiled if they were silently subsumed under the broad political umbrella of "Protestantism." For her the conference was "really the same old story." She issued a press statement to that effect, saying that "again we were the porters of the conference and not really having our great religious experience properly related to the whole thing." Ironically, Hedgeman was soon to be approached by the National Council of Churches, for whom she successfully organized the outpouring of 40,000 white Protestants at the March on Washington.[49]

Mays experienced the year 1963 and the remainder of the decade as many did: a rollercoaster ride of promise, achievement, and trauma. In the months following the meeting on race and religion, Medgar Evers was assassinated in his driveway in Mississippi, the March on Washington was celebrated as a triumph, four little girls died in a church bombing in Birmingham, and John Kennedy met a sniper's bullet in Dallas. At that point, Mays wrote a letter to his former student King in which his grief for Kennedy and his fears for King were palpable. "President Kennedy's death was almost more than I could take. If they hated him, you know they love you less. I hope that you will take every precaution as you move around."[50]

By 1964, Mays had tempered his earlier optimism that American churches might lead the fight for social justice. He resigned himself to the notion that in the decade since the *Brown* decision, white American churches had failed in their leadership through silence and inaction. If local white churches had acted in a moral and religious way, he argued in the *Christian Century*, years of "turmoil and bitterness" would have been avoided. "We might not have had Little Rock, Oxford, New Orleans. Even the sit-ins might have been unnecessary." He saw white churches now doomed to follow rather than to lead in the moves already underway toward desegregation in public arenas.[51]

Mays's vision of an integrated church did not fade entirely. He continued to imagine a world of black and white co-pastors and a day when "Negro and white Christians will worship together, sing together, pray together, share each other's joys and sorrows." But he continued throughout this period to chide white churches for their silence on the race question though "the false god segregation is dead." He began to see churches primarily as private racial sanctuaries held immune from any legal claims from a desegregated secular order. Mays feared that, as a consequence, "the haven of exclusion will be in God's house."[52]

The 1960s came to a close with little news that would stir any sense of hope in Mays. This pattern of joy and despair continued in the years that followed with the passage of civil rights legislation, the killing of Malcolm X, and, in 1968, the assassinations of King and Robert F. Kennedy. Mays delivered a eulogy for King at Morehouse, admitting that losing him was like losing a son for the childless Mays. The summer that followed was marked by violent outbreaks in the nation's cities, including protests in the streets of Chicago during the Democratic convention. This was also a period of other personal transitions for Mays. In 1967, after more than a quarter of a century at the helm, the seventy-two-year-old Mays retired from the presidency of Morehouse. Sadie Mays died in 1969; her death robbed the couple of the leisurely retirement they had expected to share, after more than four decades of marriage.

The emergence of Black Power in this period challenged the notions of interracialism that were so much a part of Mays's political and moral philosophy and that marked the generational chasm separating Mays from younger, vocal advocates of black nationalism, those on black college campuses like Morehouse and increasingly on white campuses too.[53] Like King, Mays became a vocal opponent of the Vietnam War and predicted that no military victory was possible there. "But we must get a victory that will wipe out poverty, disease, and ignorance here in the U.S. in urban areas and in the rural areas. If we can spend enough to kill one enemy, we can spend enough to build a society where none will be hungry, none will suffer from malnutrition, and none will be poorly housed." In this period, Mays began to add a strong economic critique of poverty to his traditional emphasis on racial inequalities.[54]

THE EMERGENCE of politically visible black preachers in this period reinforced Mays's decades-old belief that an educated ministry was the key to black progress and that more politically committed preachers were needed. A gendered conceptualization of racial leadership was an implicit part of his commitment to building strong, black male clerical training and leadership, as was his dedicated work as president of the all-male Morehouse.

Mays's overwhelming faith in the imperative of black male leadership meant that his writings, which were mostly prescriptive, did little to highlight the many female political and religious activists with whom he worked closely and cooperatively throughout his long public career. These included both Mary McLeod Bethune and Nannie H. Burroughs, and most intimately, his wife Sadie who, despite her duties alongside him at Morehouse, was active in many national and international political and religious networks. The centrality of women to black church life remains invisible in his large body of speeches and writings about religion, as if it is assumed or a given.

For someone as concerned about the future of black people as Mays most certainly was, his meager attention to black women is troubling and reflects as much about him as about the era in which he lived. Like Burroughs, who held on to Victorian notions about the propriety of women's dress, Mays had not shed the patriarchal attitudes which were dominant for most of his life. His primary professional commitments always were devoted to the training of black men in the same way that Burroughs was dedicated to black women. In his search for solutions to the problems of the church, men and the absence of the right kind of male leaders were the big problem. Black women were already doing their part and more and Mays did not criticize them for this, or fault them in the way that Burroughs explicitly criticized the failures of black men. If anything, his writings are preoccupied with a relentless search for able black men to fill the pulpits and the pews. His silence on women does not seem to reflect a disregard for them or their role; on the contrary, it reflects his assumption that it was the men who needed to be invigorated in their commitment to black churches. Without the help of men, the work of women would be insufficient in the long run to build an institutional black church positioned to do all that needed to be done for black communities.

Indeed, Mays continued in the 1960s and 1970s, as he had in the 1940s, to express political views on women's place that were remarkably progressive for a man of his generation. He was consistently supportive of women's rights at a time when this position would have generated controversy in many quarters, including among African Americans, both male and female. He supported women's rights in several political columns in the *Pittsburgh Courier* but in ways that mirror the often bifurcated thinking about the political categories of "women" and "black." For the most part, when Mays spoke of "women" he seemed not to include black women under that rubric; that is, "women" in those contexts really meant "white women."[55] In 1973, he wrote in support of the proposed Equal Rights Amendment. There again, he compared the plight of "women" with that of "Negroes" but made no mention of the possible importance of the amendment for black women.[56] Later he wrote a staunch defense of "women's lib," but in keeping with popular perceptions of that movement he portrayed it as if "women" and "Negroes" were categories with no constituent overlap.[57]

When Mays did speak or write directly about black women, he was sympathetic and sensitive to issues affecting them. In 1964, in a long speech on Mother's Day delivered at North Carolina A&T College, Mays paid special homage to black motherhood and womanhood. Surprisingly, he spoke bluntly about the history of their sexual exploitation. "All during slavery her body was not her own. She was property and if the master wanted her body he had it. The Negro male [was] also property and could not protect her."[58]

Moving from slavery to the contemporary, Mays criticized absentee black fathers who left the responsibilities of childrearing to women. "Even to-day the Negro mother takes a terrific beating. Go thru the student body at Morehouse, A&T, Bennett, and any Negro college in the U.S., and the number of students who do not know where their fathers are is enough to wring tears from your eyes. So many trifling good-for-nothing men have run off and left the burden upon the mothers."[59]

Mays honored the commitment of those mothers to their children. "It is she who is stuck with the child when fathers desert and when irresponsible men leave their illegitimate children uncared for and unclaimed. It is often the mother who has to sacrifice alone to help her children thru school." Unlike many then and now, Mays did not blame black women exclusively for their predicament, but praised them as good mothers willing to make sacrifices for their children. Both of these topics touched on issues of sexual exploitation, implicating first white men and then black men. In the early 1960s, these were touchy subjects to raise so directly, but he did it.[60]

In the same speech, Mays launched a defense of chivalry, distinguishing it from a belief in sexual inequality or chauvinism. "I do

not believe in the complete equality of the sexes," he teased his audience. "Women should have the opportunity to develop their
minds to the ultimate. They should be allowed to have any job
they are capable of doing. They should receive equal pay for equal
work." But he also hoped that "the time will never come when I
look upon a woman the way I look upon a man. I hope the days of
chivalry will never die." For him, this meant that he still wanted to
be a "gentleman" in his relationships with women, that he still
wanted to avoid vulgar language in their presence, that he wanted
to rise when a woman entered a room, and that he wanted to pull
her chair back at the dinner table. This combination of beliefs reflected how much his complicated conception of black masculinity
was tied to shifting beliefs about gender difference and deference
and sexual and personal mores.[61]

Mays wrote on the politically charged issue of sexual violence
against black women in a contemporary setting. In 1975, he published a column in which he lauded the jury verdict that acquit-
ted Joanne Little after she murdered a rapist prison guard in self-
defense. The case represented several things for Mays, including
evidence that justice could be rendered in the South by an interracial jury even in a sexually charged case. But the case also stood
for more for him, as he used it as evidence of the freedom black
women now had to fight the sexual transgressions of white men.
"The black woman is freer now," he wrote, "to live her life as any
other woman."[62] Again, his comments reveal sensitivity to the
larger racial, sexual, and class issues raised by the case.

These speeches and writings treat issues of gender and the subject of black women in powerful and politically savvy ways. Yet
Mays's work is also marked by a perplexing lack of attention to
black religious women and their work. It is as if Mays's focus on
the failings and the indispensability of black men rendered those

women invisible in his vision for the reformation of black churches, so concerned was he with Morehouse's mission of developing a male leadership class, both inside and outside of the clergy.

MAYS'S views on integration began to shift in the 1970s as he grew more skeptical that it would be achieved at all and more concerned about its possible impact on black communities and black leadership. Mays began to warn black audiences not to be "swept off their feet by the glamour of an integrated society" and urged them not to integrate themselves out of existence. The problem, as he saw it, was that integration meant "you move from black to white and never from white to black." This pattern could have grave consequences for black institutions, especially educational ones.[63]

Mays's long-standing commitment to education drew him back into public life. In 1969 he was elected to the Atlanta school board, and later assumed its presidency.[64] This experience gave Mays a firsthand view of the difficulty of integrating the public schools, even under the duress of court orders directed at state-financed public institutions. He also saw many experienced black teachers, principals, and administrators lose their jobs or be demoted as a consequence of school integration. In an article entitled "Integration Not All Gain," Mays observed that "I have not heard of a single white teacher losing his or her job because of integration."[65] This prompted Mays to ask whether black leadership had been asleep when it failed to anticipate the discrimination that would ensue in the process of desegregation.[66]

Even as Mays was wrestling with the challenges of the Atlanta school system, he became increasingly alarmed by the poverty and despair facing many black urban communities, as shown in statistics and exposés on unemployment, drug use, black-on-black violence, inadequate health care, and poor housing conditions. "I have a great fear for the future of black people," Mays said at a black ecumenical conference in 1971. "We cry 'Black is Beautiful,' we sloganize 'Black Power,' we go around calling each other 'sister' and 'brother,' [but] until black people stop killing themselves and stop fighting themselves, the salutations 'sisters' and 'brothers' are sounding brass or tinkling cymbals."[67]

Mays's most pressing concern was black poverty, both in cities and in rural areas. This is what moved him to reassess some of his earlier positions concerning the role of black churches in black communities. He continued to lose faith in white churches, writing in 1971 that "the white church belongs to the powerful ruling majority and it serves for the most part the privileged in our society."[68] Du Bois had held this view in the 1930s but extended it to all churches, both black and white.

More than ever, Mays embraced a service model in which he called on "affluent black churches" to minister to the needs of the black poor. "If the black church does not wrestle incessantly with and minister daily to the needs of black people, no other church group will." He called those institutions the "church of the living God," which had to serve as the "bridge to connect the middle class blacks and the poor blacks" and perhaps also act as a bridge to affluent white churches that might want to offer assistance. But most emphatically, Mays called on the black middle-class church to "cast its lot more and more with the black poor, the semi-illiterate, the under-employed, the unemployed, those who live on the brink of poverty, the boys and girls who have no father."[69]

Mays was moving away from his earlier emphasis on a prophetic messianic vision of black churches as the savior of American Christianity or as a balm for American political wrongs. Here, he endorsed a vision of black churches dedicated to social services that in the 1930s he had believed them to be incapable of support-

·ing financially. Now he directed black churches to help poor black children by adopting schools, setting up dropout programs, and establishing mentoring programs. He had lost faith in the state's commitment to help or to help enough. "If the black church does not do it," he warned, "it will hardly be done."[70]

But even in the post–civil rights period, Mays did not entirely abandon his vision of a broad role for religious leadership, black and white. "The Negro church is still the most segregated or separate institution Negroes own," Mays wrote in 1968. He then asked but did not answer this question: "Should it remain that way?"[71] He still preached a gospel of racial reconciliation in which Christian churches would take the lead in stabilizing communities where attempts to integrate schools and neighborhoods were met by white flight to the suburbs.

Mays urged black religious leaders to try to heal and unite the deep economic and political divisions he perceived among black people. He still believed that only the churches could do what most needed to be done. "If the church, Black and White, cannot bring Black and White, the rich and the poor, the educated and the ignorant together as brothers in order to establish a just society for all, we are not the church but a series of social clubs." Mays saw the civil rights movement as a triumph of black church leadership, but evidence of continued white resistance led him to conclude that ultimately it also bore witness to a failure of white religious leadership. "For the most part," he concluded, "the churches were conspicuous by their absence in speech or action."[72]

The central problem, which Mays had acknowledged after his attendance at World Council meetings, was that religious institutions are among the most local of organizations. If they were to act as moral and political agents, then this had to happen locally at the congregational level where community intervention was most needed and most effective. National religious organizations were endorsing an end to segregation, but without local follow-up and commitment this sentiment rang hollow.

"It is at the local level," Mays observed in 1974, "where implementation of the Gospel of Christ is most difficult." By then, he was urging all local churches to join an even broader fight against war, poverty, and racism. Evidence of local resistance was not hard to come by. His friend and fellow Georgian Jimmy Carter had been working since 1955 to get his own church to delete a color bar to membership from its policies; in 1976, as president-elect of the United States, Carter mounted the fight again, and this time prevailed, with his congregation voting to abandon the exclusion of anyone from worship or membership based on race, but not without considerable dissent in a vote of 120 to 66. Mays praised Carter but observed that "the churches in the United States are still the most segregated spot on Sunday at 11 o'clock in the morning."[73]

In 1979, four years before his death, Mays published an article revisiting his experiences at the international conferences he had written about so eloquently four decades earlier. In his search for evidence of progress in uniting black and white churches during the intervening years, Mays claimed that white churches no longer refused entry to black worshipers. But he also admitted that "so far as integrating the churches by merging them, I see no chance of that taking place in the twentieth century." This was an acknowledgment of the failure of his earlier predictions; he blamed institutional resistance from both black and white church bodies for the continued existence of segregated churches.[74]

At the same time that Mays bemoaned the lack of progress in integrating churches, he lavished praise on black colleges and universities, stressing their importance in training black leaders and strengthening black communities. He ended his 1979 article with the hope that by the middle of the twenty-first century the country would have moved "further along the road to a truly democratic America."[75] But he made no new predictions about the integration of black or white churches or about their potential for uniting in the arena of race relations.

The keenest irony is that the end of legalized segregation had the least immediate effect on the racially segregated sector of society that Mays cared about the most: churches. Other institutions, including black newspapers, black colleges, black schools, and black small businesses, were disadvantaged or destroyed by the forces surrounding the drive toward desegregation. In some cases, state intervention played a key role, as with the schools, and in others, as with the press and small businesses, market forces caused major losses. Being voluntary, private nonprofit institutions, churches were immune to market forces and legal edicts. By their very natures as culturally and politically specific entities and the most local of community-based institutions, they lend themselves to independent, idiosyncratic self-perpetuation from generation to generation.

In the post–civil rights era, the growth of a larger and more stable black middle and professional class did bring new financial resources to many urban churches. Such growth and financial stability have enabled some of those churches to better meet the social-service needs of black communities. Black megachurches, whose origins Mays traced back to the black urbanization of the Great Migration, have proliferated; they can be found in cities and in suburbs, and include churches that embrace a prosperity gospel rather than the social gospel. Regardless of their size or their theological orientation, their ever-increasing numbers refute Mays's predictions of the disappearance of black churches into an integrated Christianity by the year 2000. One consistency, however, is the dearth of other black institutions, preserving local churches as unrivaled community and political resources now as in the 1930s.

Mays lived out the complexities of being a Southern black liberal Protestant who believed that black and white churches should function as progressive political agents, resting on the moral foundation of global Christian universalism and an enduring faith in American democracy. In his vision, claiming a central, crucial role for black institutions, black religious leaders, and black religious discourse addressed these linked issues in politically and philosophically astute ways. Yet in his lifetime and in ours, the continued existence of the "race church," whether black or white, continues to be a fact of American life. As well, the search for a progressive politics of religious globalism remains as elusive today as during Mays's long life.

6

A Religious Rebellion

FANNIE Lou Hamer was born in the Mississippi Delta in 1917 to a large family headed by two sharecroppers. Her parents were devoutly religious and they taught her that hatred would destroy her spirit if she gave in to it, a warning designed to blunt the impact of the racial violence and injustices which brought so much suffering into their lives and their community. Forced to leave school and go to work, Hamer joined the Strangers Home Baptist Church where she improved her reading skills through Bible study. After 1942, when she married, she and her husband Perry worked as sharecroppers, but her literacy and her facility with numbers led to her duties as timekeeper for the plantation's other workers. In that position she saw firsthand how the white plantation owner cheated black workers out of their wages sometimes by under-weighing the amount of the cotton they had picked. She counteracted that, at great risk to herself, by using her own set of hidden weights to balance the scales in favor of the workers. "I didn't know what to do and all I could do is rebel in the only way I could rebel," she recalled years later.[1]

In these and other ways, Hamer established herself as a community leader and as someone willing to fight for what she thought was right. When she heard an announcement in her church in 1962 about a mass meeting with a group of young people who had come to the Delta to help African Americans register to vote, she was intrigued but cautious. The meeting was to be held at another church, Williams Chapel Missionary Baptist Church, the only one that would open its doors to such a gathering. Hamer went to that meeting where she heard members of the Student Nonviolent Coordinating Committee (SNCC) and the Southern Christian Leadership Conference (SCLC) explain that as adult citizens, black people in Mississippi had the right to register and vote. "Until then I'd never heard of no mass meeting and I didn't know that a Negro could register and vote." A young James Bevel of the SCLC preached a riveting sermon calling on his listeners to heed the biblical imperative to recognize the signs of the times as one would prepare for a storm, and urging people to act to secure their rights. Hamer was inspired by the sermon, and was motivated to register to vote to try to set some things right. "I could just see myself voting people outa office that I know was wrong and didn't do nothin' to help the poor."[2]

The meeting ended with a call for the first set of volunteers, and Hamer stepped forward to lead the group of eighteen who would go to the courthouse in Indianola, Mississippi, to claim their right to register. Their claim was refused and retaliation was swift; Hamer and her family were driven off the plantation where they had lived for many years and were forced to go into hiding. After a few months, Hamer felt religiously and politically compelled to return to continue the fight that she had helped to begin. Aware of the dangers and risks, she came back to Ruleville and eventually succeeded in registering to vote.[3]

That success brought further violence and threats, which in turn emboldened her to do more civil rights organizing. She encouraged other blacks to support the movement, including preachers whom she believed to be lagging in assuming leadership. She often broke church protocol by challenging preachers while they were in their own pulpits, relying on her own deep knowledge of the Bible to argue for their involvement. As one of her friends recounted: "See you really ain't supposed to ask no preacher no questions in the middle of a sermon. But see Mrs. Hamer would get up and disrupt the sermon and want to know certain things that he didn't talk about in terms of how it related to our daily survival."[4] Hamer saw herself as rebelling not only against white racism but also against traditional black leadership, both religious and secular, which she considered more a hindrance than a help.

Eventually, Hamer's work would lead to her arrest in a Winona bus station as she and a group of women were returning from a citizenship training session. She and two other activist women, June Johnson and Annelle Ponder, were beaten savagely while in police custody. The jailer's white wife and daughter took pity on them and secretly gave the women cold water and ice. Even as she was suffering tremendous pain, Hamer remained defiant and committed to teaching a larger lesson:

> And I told them, "Y'all is nice. You must be Christian people." The jailer's wife told me that she tried to live a Christian life. And I told her I would like for her to read two scriptures in the Bible, and I tol' er to read the 26th Chapter of Proverbs and the 26th Verse ["Whose hatred is covered by deceit, his wickedness shall be showed before the whole congregation"]. She taken it down on a paper. And then I told her to read the [17th] Chapter of Acts and the 26th Verse ["Hath made of one blood all nations of men for to dwell on all the face of the earth"]. And she taken that down. And she never did come back after then.[5]

Religion, realism, and rebellion dominated Hamer's life, as they guided the lives of those who constituted the fluid political collective that we know as the civil rights movement. Southern black churches provided a common culture and a sanctuary to a movement that represented a coalition of Southerners and Northerners from different economic and social backgrounds, different generations and political philosophies, different races and religions. Regardless of their spiritual orientation, few of them were unaffected by the power of the black religious faith they encountered in small churches and in the sit-ins and marches that fueled the movement. They all became a part of an activist minority, including "religious rebels" like Hamer whose courage and persistence and faith fomented a racial revolution and a religious movement.

Many of the college students who joined were religiously motivated, but even those who were not felt the power of faith among the people who spent their lives on the battlefield where the campaigns were waged. In their own accounts of their time in the movement, those students bear witness to that faith and its role as a central source of political sustenance and power. They also confronted recurring questions about the relationship between religion and the quest to end racial inequality, concerns that had figured in the writings of scholars like Du Bois, Woodson, Frazier, Hurston, Fauset, and Powdermaker and that vexed the lives of Bethune, Burroughs, and Mays, and those like Hamer who were there when the movement arose and there when it receded.

Student activists in the movement have written themselves into history by publishing their memoirs. Read together as a collective biography of the movement itself, their accounts preserve for us the traumas and the triumphs of that time. Their memoirs are as much spiritual as political autobiography. Working in communities alongside black Southerners like Hamer, this generation of students found themselves inside not a revival or a great awakening, but a religious rebellion. They became part of a remnant that rebelled against those who rejected ecstatic religion as primitive and antithetical to activism, against those who believed that men led and women merely followed, against those who believed that fear would overpower faith. In their own words, they bring to life compelling evidence that the civil rights movement was itself a religious movement and a religious revolt.[6]

MARIAN Wright Edelman has vivid childhood memories of Mary McLeod Bethune and Benjamin Mays. Like them, she was born in South Carolina, not in the nineteenth century, but in 1939 on the cusp of World War II. Raised in her father's Baptist parsonage, Edelman was named in honor of the black contralto Marian Anderson who only a few months before Edelman's birth had given her historic concert at the Lincoln Memorial. Edelman's parents worked to instill a sense of self-worth and collective obligation in the children of their community, and her descriptions of their efforts are rendered with religious and political inflections. They made sure she had opportunities to hear black public figures like Bethune and Mays, with her father often driving long distances to make this possible.[7]

Such encounters made a strong impression on Edelman. She remembers that Bethune seemed "confident about who she was, proud of what she had achieved, and never ashamed of where she came from. . . . The power of her forceful personality in a room— even one mostly full of men who listened very attentively to her— never left me." Edelman's parents welcomed Benjamin Mays and his wife, Sadie, into their home when he came to deliver a sermon at their church. Later, when she went to Spelman College on a scholarship, after her father had died, she looked to Mays, president at the adjoining Morehouse campus, as a father figure. She remembers him as being "ramrod straight of posture, of unwavering principles and caring, keenly intelligent and elegant in speech," and credits him with inspiring her with "a passion for excellence and service."[8]

As a college student in the late 1950s and early 1960s, Edelman was filled with intellectual curiosity and spiritual yearning. She struggled to reconcile her ideas about religion and political struggle into a sense of service and vocation. A far wider range of opportunities were available to her than had been open to her mentors, those earlier generations of black men and women whose examples so inspired her, including figures like Bethune and Mays, and those from whom she would learn in the movement itself, such as Hamer, Septima Clark, and Ella Baker.

A year abroad in 1958 expanded Edelman's sense of service and obligation, as had been the case for Mays and Bethune. Her travels gave her the feeling that she was part of a global community and strengthened her desire to do something meaningful. She had read the news of the Montgomery boycott from afar but it had struck a nerve, making her feel both proud and angry as a "long-suppressed rage bubbled up within me." When she returned for her senior year at Spelman in the fall of 1959, she faced a crisis of purpose, faith, and meaning. She was searching for a "call," a meaningful and politically relevant vocation, at a time when the civil rights movement was erupting all around her. Had she been born male, the ministry might have drawn her to follow in the footsteps of her father and brother. Or perhaps not, because at the time, she was searching for her own spiritual place. She attended chapel service at Spelman and Morehouse, but she stopped going to churches in the community because they were not politically engaged. "Too many Black preachers acted as if the last pharaohs to get in the way of God's people lived in Egypt three thousand years ago."[9]

While at Spelman, Edelman became an activist. She joined fellow students in staging sit-ins against segregation in Atlanta, the actions that had drawn Burroughs' attention at the end of her life. The students published a newspaper ad that explained their actions. "We want to state clearly and unequivocally that we cannot tolerate, in a nation professing democracy and among people professing Christianity, the discriminatory conditions under which the Negro is living today." She attended the founding meeting of SNCC. Against her family's wishes, she decided that she wanted to go to law school and become a civil rights lawyer, inspired by the example of Howard University law professor Charles Houston and other black lawyers who had been the architects of the *Brown* case.[10]

Yet Edelman was still searching for a deeper sense of spiritual mission and call. This changed dramatically the first time she heard an address by Martin Luther King Jr., at the annual Founder's Day speech in Sisters Chapel at Spelman. It marked the beginning of a relationship that changed her life. "From April 19, 1960, until his assassination on April 4, 1968, he was a continuous, personal, important presence in my life and in that of so many other young people."[11]

King, who was only ten years older than Edelman, deeply impressed her with his intellect, his spiritual maturity, and his political commitment. She scribbled long passages from his Founder's Day address in her diary. "He was great! There was something almost holy about him—powerful—assured. He has found the meaning of life in God. Hope and pray by the time I'm twenty-nine I will have done half so much for people and the world." That speech put her back in touch with a sense of God and reaffirmed her faith that there was a way to be both religiously and politically active. She recast her own student activism in language that reflected this. "We are making history. We are taking upon ourselves the problems of the time and what a good burden. Help us to be worthy of our great call!"[12] The next time Edelman heard King speak, in an Atlanta church, she found him to be "almost Christlike." Eventually she met with him, briefed him on the Atlanta sit-ins, and invited him to one of the student rallies. When a thousand students held a sit-in on the capitol grounds, "Dr. Martin Luther

King, Jr., came out of nowhere and the place went wild." *Time* magazine devoted a cover story to the Atlanta protests.[13]

In the fall of 1960 Edelman became one of ten women in the entering class at Yale Law School, but she maintained her prior political commitments. There, she threw herself into working with the Northern student movement to support SNCC. She begged to join the Freedom Riders who were aiming to challenge the segregation laws in the South, but Yale's chaplain, William Sloane Coffin, sent a black male student instead because he thought the confrontations would be too dangerous for a woman. In August 1963, just before entering her third year of law school, she attended the March on Washington. She underwent training at the NAACP Legal Defense Fund headquarters in New York City, and in 1964 made her way south to handle cases generated by the Mississippi Freedom Summer project, something she once again cast in religious terms. "God was headed south to Mississippi and Alabama and Georgia and Louisiana and North Carolina, and I went along for the scariest, most exhilarating, most challenging years any human being could hope for." She spent four years in Mississippi and in all that time she never saw another local female attorney, black or white.[14]

In Mississippi, Edelman was most impressed by "the strength and resiliency of the human spirit and the ability of determined people to resist and overcome evil through personal and collective will." It was their religious faith that empowered them, she felt, and this inspired her. "Never have I felt the company of such a great cloud of witnesses for divine and human justice willing to risk life and limb and shelter so that their children could be free and better educated." She was especially grateful to Fannie Lou Hamer for her "faithful practice of the hard message of Christianity which kept us from hating when we wanted to hate," though Hamer also criticized "'chicken-eatin' Black preachers" who refused to support the movement.[15] Captured in Hamer's ideas were distinctions that had been expressed by participants in the social-science studies of the 1930s and the 1940s, as well as evidence that a Christian ethos of love was surviving despite the brutality of Southern racism.

After 1964, as younger black student activists were becoming impatient with the country's lack of progress toward racial justice, Edelman's work in Mississippi shifted to issues of hunger and early childhood education, efforts that King joined in supporting. Although she is reluctant to take the credit, her testimony in front of a Senate subcommittee investigating hunger brought Robert Kennedy to the Mississippi Delta in 1967. That work on poverty and hunger was the genesis of the Poor People's Campaign, which lobbied for housing, food, and jobs on behalf of poverty-stricken Americans of all races.[16]

The planning for a poor people's march on Washington was well underway when King, just days before his assassination in Memphis, gave a sermon at the National Cathedral titled "Sleeping Through a Great Revolution." He emphasized that "human progress" depends on "the tireless efforts and the persistent work of dedicated individuals who are willing to be co-workers with God." It was this speech rather than the oft-quoted one he made the night before his death that Edelman most associates with King's death and his life. "Four days after his impassioned plea for America to help the poor he was dead." Her account still evokes the trauma of that death and the anguish felt by people within the movement. "Our dark, deep despair at Dr. King's death was leavened only by the fact that we still had Robert Kennedy who if elected president might not only end the war in Vietnam but finish the needed war against poverty." But eight weeks later, Kennedy too was assassinated.[17]

Edelman turned her energies toward founding the Children's Defense Fund, which today advocates for federal and state legislation to meet the basic health, nutritional, and education needs of poor children. By basing her work in Washington, D.C., she embraced Bethune's model of a political presence at the national level. Her attention to the needs of the young carries on commitments made by both Burroughs and Bethune, even as Edelman's work encompasses all poor children without regard to race.

Her view of King's role in the civil rights movement accords with that of Andrew Young, who has called King "a very reluctant and reactive prophet." In keeping with her focus on those she looked to as mentors, Edelman gives primary credit to black women activists. "The movement might never have realized its enormous potential to transform Southern politics if Ella Baker and Septima Clark had not picked up where Mrs. Parks left off. . . . And there might have been no movement without the preaching and mass meetings and music like Mrs. Fannie Lou Hamer's singing 'This Little Light of Mine, I'm Going to Let It Shine' that held us together as a community of ragged and often scared activists, giving us courage and spiritual nourishment." She saw the work of Hamer and others as a continuation of the central roles black women had long played in their communities and churches. "I understood that if Black women had not done what they always do—most of the organizing and scut work—while men got most of the credit and publicity, our families and communities would not have held together through slavery and segregation."[18]

Edelman is echoing Burroughs, Bethune, and Baker when she says, "Women are the backbone of the Black church without whom it would crumble. As in the Civil Rights Movement, Black women in the church are often asked and expected to take a back seat to the men who depend on but disempower them." These tensions persisted decades after the movement ended. "An old friend who is a prominent Black Washington lawyer astounded me not long ago by proclaiming that he and a leading Black preacher 'do not like women preachers' after I promised to send him sermons by two great women preachers I'd recently heard." To Edelman, the lawyer's remark "spontaneously revealed an attitude that too many men still hold, regarding women as instruments of their desires and needs and not as human beings of equal status due equal respect and opportunity." She concluded that men "often are unwilling to share power or control or to understand that a woman affirming herself is not disaffirming them."[19]

LIKE Edelman, many students who joined the civil rights movement were religiously motivated although their religious experiences were as diverse as their racial and political backgrounds. Mary King, a white woman from the North who worked for SNCC in its early years, had her first encounter with the organization when she took a Methodist study tour to the South in 1962 as a college student. Although she met SNCC's chairman John Lewis on that trip, what she remembers as most significant was her encounter with two women who deeply inspired her. They were Casey Hayden, a young white Texan already active in race relations work, and Ella Baker, an older and powerful black Southern activist who was instrumental in SNCC's founding. Mary King has characterized this trip and her exposure to these two politically committed women as the turning point in her life.[20]

Although King immediately felt drawn to join SNCC's work, she felt like an outsider because she was neither Southern like Hayden nor black like Baker. She did, however, have a deep religious faith that fueled her commitment to SNCC. She joined the movement after studying, as had her father, at Union Theological Seminary in New York. There she was deeply influenced by the life and writings of Dietrich Bonhoeffer, the German theologian who had studied at Union and who was hanged by the Nazis because of his resistance work. Inspired by Bonhoeffer, King felt that she needed to take a stand in the struggle for black civil rights.[21]

It was this religious commitment to working for social justice that King believed she shared with others who were drawn into SNCC in its early life. She realized that "an astonishing number" of those working in the organization were the children and grandchildren of ministers, as was true for her, Edelman, Baker, and Martin Luther King. She claims Stokely Carmichael as a fellow Northern Methodist traveler, outing him and his family for being the only black members of the white church they attended in New York. American Methodism provided a theological impetus toward activism for Mary King and for Carmichael, as it had for Bethune, Sadie Mays, and Rosa Parks. King explained that the "shared background gave us something in common," including liberal Protestantism's belief that "the institutions of society can change." For her, a broad set of religious beliefs was the unifying ethos of the movement and something she could claim as her own. "Even if one were in rebellion against a church that provided insufficient witness or failed to challenge the status quo, still at work was the fundamental influence of the Christian tradition."[22]

Of course, most of American Protestantism, whether black or white, was not supporting the movement. However, the presence of black religious leaders such as Martin Luther King Jr., and of the black congregations that opened their churches to mass meetings, meant that it was Southern black religious culture that formed the vital center of the movement. In her 1987 memoir, King wrote movingly about the power of Southern black rural religious culture, in particular the centrality of black sacred music traditions to all she believed the movement to be. She chose *Freedom Song* as the title of her book "because of the prominent place held by songs about freedom in the American civil rights movement." For her, the movement was "fueled by the singing of black people" and by the "magnificence of black congregational singing, nourished as it was by a legacy of struggle, resistance, endurance, and faith."[23]

This reality challenged the idea that liberal Protestantism resided primarily in Northern white congregations or seminaries. On the contrary, it seemed best represented among black Southerners who were often poorly educated, religiously spirited, and living in rural areas. Yet King, like many people today, was intent on claiming a more central role for Northern white liberal Protestant influence in the movement. She did note, however, that "many brave priests and rabbis joined their Protestant colleagues." The fact that many Jews joined black Southern religious liberals in the movement unsettles explanatory narratives that focus primarily on Northern white liberal Protestantism. Indeed, King found it hard to understand why Jews would "go south to take part in a movement so entrenched in the moral suasion and spiritual force of a black Christian culture closely linked to resistance." Despite being a white Northerner herself, however, she felt she was part of that culture.[24]

By one estimate, Jews accounted for two-thirds of the 650 volunteers during the Freedom Summer of 1964, to cite just one example. Martin Luther King's circle of advisors and supporters included many Jews and many were present elsewhere in the movement. Whether they considered themselves religious or not, many Jewish activists saw theological links between Judaism and the prophetic strand within Southern black Christianity. They also realized immediately that black churches provided the center for the movement. The churches were "where you went to meetings all the time," said one Jewish volunteer, so they "became very much a warm and friendly part of the whole movement." Eventually, King and other volunteers viewed the churches as "the only safe havens for civil rights workers."[25]

Many of the Jews who came to the South, especially women, already considered themselves outside not only the political main-stream but their own religious and cultural communities as well. Their decision to volunteer was yet one more confirmation of that outsider status. "Although the Jewish community takes credit for participation in the civil rights movement," said one volunteer, "it was Jews on the fringes who actually did the work."[26] This is also a comment that applies to the African American religious community, since only a small minority of black churches and black preachers actually supported and engaged in the movement.

For students who joined out of what they called "intellectual" or "political" motivations, the presence of so many religious young people in the movement came as a shock. Said one, "I had no idea that so many people of the age and education of the people here had any serious commitment to religion in this country." Another was caught off guard when SNCC organizer James Lawson spoke on "Christian revolutionary nonviolence" to an audience the student believed was composed largely of "agnostic nonviolent technicians." Some of the white students initially harbored a deep suspicion of religion but came to understand how important it was to the movement's leaders and its followers. "When I came I thought that M. L. King and his 'love your enemy' was a lot of Christian mysticism. Now I can see it as a force and support, helping those who understand it. It makes me think that maybe I can take what is coming this summer."[27]

Most of the Northern students, who were encountering Southern black religious culture for the first time, not only respected its beliefs and practices but often found themselves, like Mary King, deeply moved by it. They also came to appreciate the interdependency of religious faith and political commitment. This is apparent in the letters they wrote from Mississippi in the summer of 1964 during a campaign which would cost the lives of three SNCC members. For the first time for many, they spent many hours in black church services or in political meetings held in churches. "It's just like the scene in *Go Tell It on the Mountain* but it's real," wrote one student. "There's a direct tie between every person in that church and God, and every person with me and I with them." Describing a sermon in which the preacher portrayed Uncle Sam as a present-day pharaoh, a white student reported that the minister had spoken loudly and earnestly "to the little fanning congregation, which answered now and then with a quiet 'oyeslord' and 'ain't it the truth' to the rhythm of their fanning." Students were also struck by the commitment to the movement shown by people who had few financial resources but who recognized its political significance. "There are the old men and women in old clothing whom you know have little money and none to spare, who stop you as you are leaving the church after addressing the congregation and press a dollar into your hand and say, 'I've waited eighty years for you to come and I just have to give this little bit to let you know how much we appreciate your coming. I prays for your safety every night, son. God bless you all.'"[28]

Like Hortense Powdermaker during her research in the Mississippi Delta three decades earlier, these students were surprised to find an ethos of love among people who had every right to be bitter and to hate white people. The students were reminded of what it meant to be, as one of them wrote, "with people who have not forgotten how to love." The persistence of love in the face of bigotry made many of them marvel that the majority of black people still had "a dream of freedom in which both races understand and accept each other." It also made many students ashamed to be white. When they visited Mississippi's white churches, they were met with hostility, rejection, and sometimes violence. When they told others about this, local black preachers would say, "Yes, that was a white man's church. It was not God's church." That emphasis on love had its converts among the students. "Perhaps love will come of all this. I'm not ashamed to use the word right now, for I feel very attached, very loyal to the common but infractable bits of passion and affection and desire and appreciation and enjoyment and loyalty that are what it comes down to, if one lives for any reason other than to keep from dying."[29]

Some like Mary King also believed that the movement rested on a "fundamental assumption of the 'redemptability' of America," confident that the "nation could experience shame and remorse and would repeal its history of oppression." This was not an uncommon characterization; Gunnar Myrdal's work depends on a secular version of it. But activists were unable to sustain a redemption narrative, particularly when faced with the brutality of white resistance and the continuing evidence of racism's political powers after it ended. King reminds us that Ronald Reagan opened his 1980 presidential campaign in Philadelphia, Mississippi, a town made famous only for being the site of the deaths of three civil rights workers. His version of the Puritans' "City upon a Hill," which he would promise in many speeches, rested not on redemption but on the resuscitation of old wounds and hatreds.[30]

Later, the waning days of SNCC and black nationalism's emergence included a rejection of the Christian forms of nonviolent resistance and the perceptions of passivity associated with them. King writes candidly about the pain and loss she felt when she left SNCC. Some of her disappointment stemmed from her earlier efforts, along with Casey Hayden, questioning what they viewed as a gendered hierarchy of leadership within the organization. In 1964, they wrote an anonymous position paper on this issue, prompted in part by gender disparities in work assignments and delegation of authority, something they expected from the preacher-led "patriarchal" SCLC but not from what they thought of as the democratic and secular SNCC. It was to King that Stokely Carmichael made a joking retort that the only place for women in the movement was "prone." She believes that the controversy over this remark was unwarranted, since Carmichael made it in a long playful monologue on a wide variety of issues. Indeed, she portrays him as being one of the male activists most responsive to her ideas on gender and leadership.[31]

When their paper was discussed within SNCC, King was not as surprised or as hurt by arguments that the issue of gender was a "diversion" as she was by the reaction of black women within SNCC. Their response was to not respond at all. She describes the antagonism white women often felt from black women, something she attributes in part to strains created by the sexual ties between some black men and some white women. But she offers a fuller explanation as well about racialized differences in the expectations toward gender roles of leadership. While formal leadership roles often went to black men, black women also maintained a great deal of authority and clout in community and political work and in the family. "If any generalization can be made," King observes, "it is that black women had too little support for the responsibility they carried." She quotes Andrew Young's eulogy of Fannie Lou Hamer, in which he praised women as the "spine" of the civil rights movement: "It was women going door to door, speaking with their neighbors, meeting in voter-registration classes together, organizing through their churches, that gave the vital momentum and energy to the movement, that made it a mass movement."[32]

Despite these conflicts, King's allegiance to SNCC was strong and enduring. She relied on Casey Hayden to provide an eloquent evocation of what the movement meant to both of them. The days of the campaign were a "holy time," said Hayden. "When I was no longer welcome there, and then when it was no longer there at all, it was hard to go on. Many of us in this situation, especially the Southern whites, only barely made it through. I count myself lucky to be a survivor. . . . We were living in a community so true to itself that all we wanted was to organize everyone into it, make the whole world beloved with us, make the whole world our beloved." Like others, King and Hayden found the "beloved community" in SNCC.[33]

After her time in SNCC, King pursued a life and career in human rights activism and the study of international politics. She headed the Peace Corps during the Carter administration, and wrote an account of the relationship between Gandhi and the civil rights movement. To her, part of the appeal of nonviolence strategies is their gender neutrality, that is, the tactic itself "favors a kind of gender equity because there is no supremacy, no inferior or superior weight on any of the human beings involved." She credits the people with whom she worked, especially local black Christian leaders, for helping her to understand the "interconnections of inequities" among race, class, gender, and region. This understanding came to her "from people who were not enshrined within priesthood, had no position hierarchically within a community, but who were simply regarded as effective or honest or discreet or trustworthy by others in the community."[34]

MARY King believed that John Lewis was elected in 1963 as the first chairman of SNCC because he was the perfect compromise candidate. "The sincerity of John's commitment and the ardor of his example made him acceptable to everyone, including those who were more impatient, less religiously oriented, and more sophisticated." King revered his courage, saying that he "personified the spirit of nonviolence" better than anyone else.[35] Implicit in this praise is a notion that was shared by many others in SNCC, that Lewis' upbringing as the son of sharecroppers in rural Alabama left him unprepared to defend the organization when savvier and better-educated black Northerners deposed him in favor of black nationalism and Stokely Carmichael in 1966.

Lewis and Carmichael respected each other despite their long-standing and fundamental disagreements. Lewis, born in 1940, and Carmichael, born in 1941, grew up in culturally and politically distinct worlds that gave them quite different philosophical groundings. What they shared was a deep commitment to ending racial injustice and to improving the lives of poor black people. They eventually came to represent the opposite ends of the political spectrum and of the civil rights movement itself. By the time each turned to prepare an autobiography, their paths had diverged farther still. Lewis was a congressman from Georgia and Carmichael, who founded the All-African Revolutionary Party, was living in Africa facing the prospect of his imminent death from cancer. Lewis' book was published in 1998, the same year that Carmichael died. Carmichael's account was published posthumously in 2003.

Religion was a formative influence for Lewis who remembers the richness and vitality of black rural church life in the 1940s of his youth. He grew up in a community full of those little country churches that social scientists viewed as evidence of "overchurching" and in need of theological reform. But for Lewis and his family, going to church after long stints of backbreaking farm labor was a source of "joy," of "relief," of "sweet inspiration," attributes that Zora Neale Hurston had also emphasized in her own analyses of rural black religious cultures.[36]

Like churches in those early academic studies, the ones in Lewis' community often held services only once a month. Rather than creating a religious void, this schedule allowed people to visit more than one church, oftentimes in different denominations. Lewis' family attended a Baptist church one Sunday and an AME church the next. The infrequency of the meetings and the isolation of rural life meant that church gatherings were not only spiritual events but social ones that made church "an exciting place, a colorful, vibrant place." The communal nature of those gatherings and the spiritual strength of the people there, including his parents, was "the same strength of spirit" that was at the center of the civil rights movement. It was the spirit of "simple people, everyday people, good, honest, hardworking people" struggling against the odds to make ends meet and to care for their families. "Is it any wonder that come Sunday their voices were lifted so strongly and so openly to God?"[37]

The Lewis family's faith in God was rivaled only by their faith in education and their drive to give their children the best schooling possible, despite the family's low income. Lewis attended a school built by the Rosenwald Fund on the grounds of an AME church. As he read and learned more, he began to question some of what he heard in church and to notice that the preachers said almost nothing relevant to the political and economic conditions of its members.

Lewis supplemented his formal education with what he gathered of the wider world from listening to the radio. In 1955 he heard a broadcast he never forgot, Martin Luther King Jr. preaching a sermon in Montgomery. "I listened, as this man spoke about how it wasn't enough for black people to be concerned only with getting to the Promised Land in the hereafter, about how it was not enough for people to be concerned with roads that are paved with gold, and gates to the Kingdom of God. He said we needed to be concerned with gates of schools that were closed to black people and the doors of stores that refused to hire or serve us. . . . This man was talking about dealing with the problems people were facing in their lives right now, specifically black lives in the South."[38]

Later that same summer the sad news of Emmett Til's death also reached him, but for Lewis it was King's sermon and the boycott in nearby Montgomery that "changed my life more than any other event before or since." That one radio sermon convinced Lewis that going into the ministry, an ambition he was already harboring, was exactly the right course for him. And King's activism during the boycott showed him that there were other models for the ministry than the preachers in his own rural community.[39]

Lewis wanted to attend Morehouse College, like King, but his family, unlike King's, could not afford it. One day his mother, who worked as a maid for a white Southern Baptist family, brought home a Baptist newspaper containing an ad for the American Baptist Theological Seminary in Nashville. "For Colored," said the advertisement, and Lewis applied. He considered it a blessing to attend the school which allowed its students to work to pay their room and board. Like many black Christians, such as Benjamin Mays, Lewis criticized white Southern Baptists for closing their churches to black people while claiming to adhere to Jesus' doctrine of brotherly love. Ironically, the seminary he attended was funded in part by the Southern Baptist Convention for the express purpose of training black Baptist ministers and had come under criticism for instilling political conservatism in its students, a charge that Lewis' later actions defied. During his years there, Lewis tried to organize a student chapter of the NAACP but was stopped by the school's president who feared losing funds from the convention.[40]

Fortunately, Nashville was also the home of Fisk University and Meharry Medical School, which had a large number of black students eager to challenge segregation. Lewis came to know a number of them during two years of political and religious seminars led by Vanderbilt divinity student James Lawson, a committed pacifist who introduced them to the writings of Gandhi, Reinhold Niebuhr, and Henry David Thoreau. Lewis also attended a Baptist church in Nashville pastored by the political activist Kelly Miller Smith who called for "a disciplined Negro Christian movement" and later became a founding member of the SCLC. Another influence on Lewis was Septima Clark who was spearheading training sessions in civil rights and literacy at the Highlander School in New Market, Tennessee.[41]

A student-led march on Nashville's city hall in 1960 was followed by sit-ins to desegregate public places. In 1961, Lewis joined the first wave of Freedom Riders, subjecting himself to bloody attacks in the campaign to end segregation in interstate bus service. His activism eventually landed him in the notoriously brutal prison known as Parchman Farm, in Mississippi. There he crossed paths with Stokely Carmichael who was making his first appearance in the southernmost theater of the movement.

Carmichael had been born in 1941 in Trinidad. His parents, at his mother's insistence, moved to New York City when he was five, but they left him and his siblings behind with relatives until Carmichael was eleven. When the children arrived in New York, his mother insisted on moving the family out of Harlem, where there was a sizable community of black West Indian immigrants, to what she saw as a better community in the Bronx. They were the only black family in the neighborhood.[42]

Rather than traveling across town to worship, his mother had the family join the local Methodist church where, as Mary King had emphasized, they were the only black people. This was a big shift for Carmichael. His early religious life in Trinidad had been busily ecumenical; his extended family had often attended Methodist, Presbyterian, and Anglican services, sometimes all in the same day. One continuity, however, was the strength of his father's commitment to his faith; he helped his son earn a Boy Scout badge for biblical knowledge by spending a year reading through the Bible with him. Carmichael called his father "one of the most deeply and sincerely religious men I had ever met before I encountered the Reverend Martin Luther King, Jr."[43]

In 1956, in the ebb of the Montgomery bus boycott, Carmichael entered the Bronx High School of Science under a program for gifted minority students. Through friends there, he was introduced to European political radicalism, Marxism, and Communism. It was the "religious question" that kept him from joining the Com-

munist party because, he explained, "like most Africans" he was religious and was shocked and offended by atheist ridicule of God.
Yet he endorsed an essentialist claim of African religiosity, something that Mays and others had fought hard to dislodge.[44]

Even when his own religious feelings lessened as he became
more open to what he calls a "scientific materialist orientation,"
Carmichael understood that "this religious waning was in *me*, not
in the African community. I never fell victim to that confusion."
Later, he explained in greater detail: "I instinctively understood
that if my struggle was to be among my people then any talk of
atheism and the rejection of God just wasn't gonna cut it. I just
knew that. My early political work in the rural South would con-
firm this. All our meetings were held in churches. They all began
with prayer. When they approved, people would say, 'Son, you doing the Lord's work.' . . . I did not want to be alienated from my
people because of Marxist atheism.[45]

Carmichael's intention to become a part of black political struggle motivated him to go to college at Howard University, which he
knew was a site of SNCC activity. Earlier that year, John Lewis and
other students had organized SNCC under the guidance of Ella
Baker, someone Carmichael would come to revere as a visionary.
At the end of his freshman year, he became a Freedom Rider, but
not on the buses which had become such a focus of violent white
resistance. Instead, his mission was to fly to New Orleans and ride
the train north to Mississippi. At the end of that journey, he was
arrested.[46]

He met Lewis at Parchman, where four hundred other protesters
were being held. One of the first things Carmichael noticed was
that the jail was full of religious people. He described meeting the
"seminarians" from Nashville, Lawson and Lewis, who "were serious about 'Christian love' and the redemptive power of 'the beloved community.'" But "as many preachers and religious people as

there were in that jail, there were real differences even among the faithful."[47]

When Lewis met Carmichael in the prison, he recalled years later, Carmichael struck him as a "tall, lanky, outspoken student from Howard University" who had no interest in nonviolence, Gandhi, or the Bible but who was "totally committed to our cause." Carmichael interpreted his first prison experience in masculinist terms, as "life altering, a rite of passage." Lewis' own political conversion, which came in 1960 during the Nashville sit-ins, was depicted in religious terms: "Now I knew. Now I had crossed over, I had stepped through the door into total, unquestioning commitment. This wasn't just about that moment of that day. This was about forever. It was like deliverance. I had, as they say in Christian circles when a person accepts Jesus Christ into his heart, come home. But this was not Jesus I had come home to. It was the purity and utter certainty of the nonviolent path." Later, writing specifically about the Freedom Rides and his imprisonment at Parchman, Lewis turned again to Christian examples. "I really felt then, and I still feel, that we in SNCC were a lot like members of the early Christian church, going out with virtually nothing but the clothes on our backs to bring the gospel of Freedom to the people." He credits SNCC's success to local women, wives and mothers in their forties and fifties, "resilient women," naming Hamer as his example.[48]

Carmichael had little faith in nonviolence or in the power of redemptive suffering. "I never saw my responsibility to be the moral and spiritual reclamation of some racist thug. I would settle for changing his behavior, period. Moral suasion, legal proscription, or even force of arms, whatever ultimately it took, that's what I'd be for." He allied himself with those who expressed deep disdain for the prevailing ethos in SNCC, including its embrace of the idealism of the "beloved community" and redemptive suffering.[49]

Not surprisingly, there are many discrepancies between the two men's accounts of how the abrupt change in SNCC leadership from Lewis to Carmichael occurred. Edelman remembers it as a coup d'état. But all agree that it represented a dramatic political shift within the organization, not just on long-standing issues of race and nationalism but on the basic question of the continued role of religion, religious leadership, and churches in the struggle for freedom.

After being replaced by Carmichael, Lewis returned to Fisk University where he had begun studying in 1961 after completing his ministerial training at American Baptist seminary. He felt the need for a broader liberal arts training and pursued a degree in philosophy. In a long paper on religion and the civil rights movement, he argued that the movement was a "religious phenomenon."

> It was church-based, church-sanctioned; most of its members and its activities flowed through and out of the black church, in small towns and rural communities as well as urban areas. The church, in a very real way, was the major gateway for the movement. It was the point of access in almost every community. By giving its blessing to movement organizers, the church leadership opened the door to its membership, who may not have known or understood at first what we were about but who had complete faith in what their church elders told them. No matter what it was, if it was coming out of their church, then the people were ready to climb aboard. If the church said it was all right, then it must be all right.[50]

Lewis' conclusions in that paper were consistent with his religious belief, his political views, and his argument that the meaning of "church" existed outside of rather than within its edifices. "That is what the church had come to mean to me. I felt the spirit, the hand of the Lord, the power of the Bible—all of those things—but only when they flowed through the church and out into the streets. . . . As long as God and His teachings were kept inside the walls of a sanctuary, as they were when I was young, the church meant next to nothing to me."[51]

In this, he and Carmichael would have been in agreement. Carmichael was acutely aware that religious motivation and churches were indispensable to the masses of people he had worked with in the movement and had helped to organize. This is apparent in the affection and respect he shows for Fannie Lou Hamer, especially her deep religious faith and the courage it gave her. The time he spent in the South with people like her both challenged and reinforced his ideas about the place of churches and religion in black political struggle. "Most of our meetings took place in small, rural churches. . . . In the summer of '64 in Mississippi alone, over thirty such churches—most of whose insurance had suddenly been canceled—were burned to the ground." The three SNCC workers killed in Mississippi were en route back to a church where members of the deacon board had been beaten; the church was burned to the ground because its board had agreed to host one of SNCC's freedom schools.[52]

Carmichael's experience led him to develop his own theory for reconciling notions about black religion with the religiously driven activism and courage he witnessed. "What I came to see was that our people's 'religiosity' was neither simply (as some opinion had it) passive escapism nor the tight-jawed and self-righteous sanctimony of self-proclaimed 'saints.' What I came to see very clearly was that with our people the religious impulse at its finest was something much more profound. Morally and socially effective, it incorporated a living vision of history, self, and struggle. A vision that was central to their survival, both spiritual and psychic." He configures that faith as "*African* Christianity" based on the "God of Abraham, Moses, and the prophets," but with no mention of Jesus. This was a God dispensing justice and righteous retribution, a God who "cast down the mighty . . . who raised up the lowly."[53]

In Mississippi, Carmichael realized that "these ideas were real, still living and informing the people's view of reality and themselves as much as they infused the language of their songs. So that, let us say, at a meeting in a lonely church . . . when we sang 'Guide my feets, Lord, while I run this race, for I don't want to run this race in vain' or 'Go down, Moses, way down in Egypt land, tell ol' Pharaoh, let my people go,' and 'Wade in the water chillun, God's gonna trouble the water,' it was prophecy being fulfilled and history being made."[54]

Carmichael found a key articulation of this theology in the power of black spirituals. Congregational singing made him feel that "we were at one with our ancestors," connected through the sounds to "those nameless Africans, enslaved in this strange land. . . . At these times when we would sing these songs, I'd always get an almost eerie feeling that, somehow by the power of that music, time was eclipsed." His encounter with the power of black sacred music yielded an interpretation that was different from Mary King's, but no less compelling.[55]

The reverence and the respect with which Carmichael described the religion of the rural people with whom he worked was withheld, however, from his discussions of the religious faith of his contemporaries, the younger Southern SNCC staffers like Lewis. He employed a double standard, ridiculing their beliefs and disputing the notion that the idea of a "beloved community" ever existed within SNCC. He dismissed the concept as a product of a "race-free, Christian, pacifist vision of lions lying down with lambs and swords beaten into plowshares, and grounded in Gandhian nonviolent activism."[56]

Carmichael claimed that the concept only "had currency among spiritual pacifists, the social gospel seminarians out of Nashville who had studied with the Reverend James Lawson" who, he did concede, had in fact written the concept of a "beloved community" into SNCC's founding document. Lewis' memoir, which was published before Carmichael's, had quoted directly from that document as being central to what SNCC was and what it would become: "We affirm the philosophical or religious ideal of nonviolence as the foundation of our purpose, the presupposition of our faith, and the manner of our action. . . . Judaic-Christian tradition seeks a social order of justice permeated by love."[57]

Two cross purposes are at work in these machinations in Carmichael's logic. On the one hand, he severs the concept of a "beloved community" from what he called "*African* Christianity." While a "beloved community" would include everyone, an African Christianity would not. He works hard to establish the distinction, dividing the religion of the rural people with whom the group worked from the beliefs of SNCC's members. This distinction was necessary because it was the notion of a "beloved community" that supported the inclusion of white allies inside the organization. Still, he never denied that it was the religiosity of black communities that sustained the movement.

Carmichael seems intent on defending himself against the charge that his lack of faith in nonviolence and the dismissal of whites from SNCC under his leadership helped destroy something he argued that group never was: an integrated, religiously based political organization. But in fact many of the founding SNCC members *were* religiously motivated men and women who articulated their vision for the organization in those terms.[58] This concern seems to be a driving motivation in his careful account of his relationship with Martin Luther King Jr. Despite his opposition to the strategy of nonviolence, Carmichael praises King for successfully cobbling together "a moral philosophy to justify resistance and the techniques to execute that struggle," blending Gandhian nonviolence, New England Transcendentalism, and African American religious culture. He takes care to portray his relationship with King as respectful and amicable. They spent time together on the long march through Mississippi completing the one begun by James Meredith before he was shot and wounded by a sniper in 1965.[59]

In the course of that march, soon after his election as SNCC's chair, Carmichael was catapulted into the national spotlight with his cry of "Black Power!" The Black Power speech itself was nothing new, and Carmichael had not even originated the term; what was different was that the national media were present because King was there. Carmichael said he detested the ensuing media coverage which he thought made him and King look like rival "high school cheerleaders." He repeatedly credited King for never repudiating him publicly or privately on Black Power. "The most he ever said was that the language was 'unfortunate,' being subject to misunderstanding by our white brothers and sisters."[60]

The underlying issue that Carmichael's slogan raised was a very old and resonant one: the persistent desire for independent black institutions that could serve as a base for community power. The dearth of those institutions had led many to look to black churches alone to fill that role. In the case of the civil rights movement, enough courageous ministers and congregations stepped forward to meet that need, although they remained a minority, though a sufficient one. Even on the important battlegrounds like Birmingham, activist preachers were a minority, as Andrew Young has pointed out. "Of the more than four hundred black churches in Birmingham, there were only fourteen that agreed to host the mass meetings that were our primary means of communicating with blacks in Birmingham." Indeed, "the Baptist preachers as a group voted to oppose Martin's coming." But for the commitment of that small "new breed of clergy," the movement's efforts in Birmingham would have been thwarted.[61]

Carmichael teased King that they both actually believed in the power and necessity of all-black institutions but were being treated differently. He started his banter with King by saying that when he was last at Ebenezer, King's church, he had not seen a single white face in the congregation, "not a one," he stressed. "'Well, Dr. King, here you head of a religious institution and a social organization, all black. Why, you the epitome of Black Power, not once but *twice* over. Yet the press, they looove you while they whuppin' my poor nappy head flat. Can you explain that?' He cracked up. 'Well, Stokely, it's simple. Maybe I just don't talk about it.'"[62]

Carmichael's Black Power position also represented a turning away from black religious institutions as the best or only site for community power and mobilization. It rejected the moderation, the conservatism, the nonviolence, and the interracial and ecumenical Christian ethos that many associated with that religious presence. Carmichael and his supporters also embraced a notion of black masculinity that rejected the passivism of a redemptive, Christian-based approach.

Young draws a contrast between the "Southern and spiritually strong John Lewis" and Carmichael, differences he attributes more to regional differences than to anything else. He argues that Lewis and other SNCC workers had come from a Southern religious tradition that enabled them to come to grips with the fear of death. "They were angered by the violence, but they knew the South too well to be surprised by it. Through faith, they would stand their ground and persevere, as blacks always had in the South." Young argues that Carmichael and his followers lacked this spiritual grounding and responded "out of their own fear and insecurity."[63]

Another issue that seemed to haunt Carmichael was the lingering controversy over his attitude toward the role of leadership for women in the movement. His book and Lewis' are written with sensitivity to the justified criticism that early civil rights history accounts had ignored or minimized the crucial role that black women played in the movement's successes. They both bend over backward to correct this and to credit individual black women leaders for their courage and commitment. They also make the larger point that the movement rested on the support and hard work of masses of black women across the South, especially through their churches.

In Carmichael's case, the notoriety of his comment that the only position for women in the movement was "prone" endured. The fact that Mary King's autobiography explicitly absolved him of any malicious intent had not deterred Lewis from repeating it in his memoir. Yet when Carmichael died at fifty-seven, his lengthy obituary in the *New York Times* did not mention the incident. During Carmichael's illness, Mary King, on her own initiative, had helped convince the *Times* obituary department that past reports about that incident should not be repeated when he died. This was a graceful gesture of friendship and lingering affection not just for Carmichael but for SNCC and the "beloved community" which King believed she had found in the civil rights movement and which Carmichael argued never existed.[64]

Their fellow SNCC member John Lewis believes that there is a "spirit of history" which serves as the basis for his faith and his political work. "The self, even a *sense* of self," he wrote, "must be totally removed in order to allow this spirit in. It is a process of giving over one's very being to whatever role history chooses for you."[65] Fannie Lou Hamer gave her life over to the spirit of that history, surviving a brutal beating and the triumph and defeats of the 1964 Democratic National Convention in Atlantic City, where she famously and plaintively asked, "Is this America?" Yet unlike her younger cohort of college student activists, Hamer's later opportunities in life were constrained by her race, her age, her gender, her limited education, and her fervent commitment to remain in her native Mississippi to fight injustice and poverty. When she died in 1977 at age sixty she was penniless, but was lauded at the Williams Chapel Missionary Baptist Church in Ruleville, Mississippi, where she had attended her first mass meeting. The history of her life, of her fellow activists named here, and of many unnamed others is linked to a movement of religious rebellion, peopled by a small but courageous minority, a remnant, as Burroughs used the term, who had faith in the power of a few to make changes that would affect us all.

7

Reconcilable Differences

DURING the civil rights movement, the perception emerged that black religion and politics were innately compatible and mutually reinforcing. The power of this idea eclipsed the history and memory of intraracial conflicts about the place of religion in political struggle. Yet those tensions were present before, during, and after the movement.

Indeed, the fact that black religion occupies a central place in the movement continues to provoke debates about the relationship between race, religion, and politics, and in unpredictable ways. There is no better evidence of this than the conflict that emerged in 2008 between Democratic presidential candidate Barack Obama and his longtime pastor, the Reverend Jeremiah Wright of Trinity United Church of Christ in Chicago. The public clash between the two men, media manipulations aside, demonstrates how the tensions between black religion and black politics have been exacerbated in the four decades since the civil rights movement ended. The specific differences between Obama and Wright are at once political and theological, but ultimately turn on their divergent interpretations of African American religious history. Both men are products of the very history they dispute.

IN 1969, James Forman, a former executive director of SNCC and a former officer of the Black Panther party, interrupted a Sunday morning service at Riverside Church in New York to issue a "Black Manifesto" demanding that American Christian churches and Jewish synagogues provide half a billion dollars in "reparations" to black communities to make amends for their complicity in past wrongs against black people. The manifesto elicited two surprising responses. The first is that a number of prominent white clergymen and largely white religious organizations endorsed Forman's demands, pledging substantial sums of money to organizations working to alleviate black poverty and suffering. These donations were made despite the fact that over 90 percent of the white lay members rejected the idea of reparations. The second surprise is that Forman had to be persuaded at the last minute to focus his demands only on white people, abandoning his original intent of also targeting black churches which he thought shared the blame for the sins of Western Christianity. Despite this concession, a diverse group of black religious and political leaders vehemently opposed Forman's tactics and his demands on white Christians and Jews.[1]

Forman's ideas, inflected with Marxism and an anticolonialist critique, remind us that debates about religion and politics in the immediate post–civil rights era engaged much more explicitly with black nationalism, black radicalism, and black internationalism, subjects always present but never as publicly prominent as in that period. In the same year that Forman issued his manifesto, the black theologian James Cone began articulating a distinctive "black theology," a conceptual move that Benjamin Mays had resisted in the 1930s in his work on blacks' ideas about God. Cone's work re-articulated a long-standing ethos of liberation in black religious thought, expressed across many centuries through spirituals and sermons and in the writings of a long line of black religious intellectuals. Cone's work had the practical political intent of helping black religious institutions to maintain their political vitality in the age of Black Power. In the same period, the ethicist Gayraud Wilmore, writing in 1973, made historical claims for the existence of a radical tradition in black Christianity, reaching back to arguments that Carter Woodson had made in the 1920s. He also argued that African Americans were "an incorrigibly religious people," a claim that E. Franklin Frazier and Benjamin Mays had opposed for its essentialism, but that Wilmore used to bolster religion's credibility at a time when black Christianity was under attack.[2]

In 1982, building on those ideas and a progressive approach to Marxism, Cornel West argued for a prophetic black Christianity with revolutionary potential. Later in that decade, black women theologians, among them Dolores Williams, Katie Cannon, and Emilie Townes, would challenge and supplement earlier works by constructing a "womanist theology" that veered away from the masculinist bias which permeated so much thought not only about God but about gender and power relations within churches. In these ways, black theologians and philosophers in the decades following the civil rights movement recast Christianity in ways that maintained its pertinence to the continued political struggles facing black men and women and their communities.[3]

The prominent place of religion within the civil rights movement also prompted social scientists to revive old debates about the relationship between charismatic leadership and organized political activism and about the kind of institutional apparatus needed for social movements to emerge and succeed. Relying on

the movement's successes, Aldon Morris conceptualized an enduring explanation of the role of religion in the movement's emergence and once again defended churches from charges that they
were mere "safety valves" and "nonorganization[s] fueled by emotionalism."[4]

The need to rethink long-standing paradigms also is demonstrated in the work of historians working in the immediate post–
civil rights era. Most important, works on slavery and enslaved
people adapted an emancipatory interpretation of black religion,
the most prominent example being Albert Raboteau's *Slave Religion*. Renewed interest in black religion also generated a plethora
of works by historians on the various black religious denominations.
But it would not be until the 1990s that Evelyn Higginbotham's
pathbreaking work on the central role of black women in Baptist
churches paved the way for other works on religion, race, and
gender.[5]

Interestingly, the burgeoning historical literature about the civil
rights movement, while acknowledging the obvious presence of religion, religious culture, and religiously motivated people, was slow
to interrogate the broader historical and political role of religion,
often simply accepting it as a "natural" part of black life. Some
studies sought to diminish religion's importance in favor of other
sites and motivations for mobilization at the grassroots and national levels. The simplistic dichotomies that restricted the earlier
generations of scholars profiled in this book are today being challenged and in some cases abandoned, but much work remains to
be done.[6]

ONE economic consequence of the movement's successes was the
creation of an expanded black middle class that now supports large, financially prosperous megachurches in major urban

and metropolitan centers. As varied as African American religion itself, many of these churches have harnessed resources sufficient to enact effective political and community interventions. This development created its own set of controversies. Some of these churches have been criticized for their politically conservative policies and religious allies, or for their dedication to a gospel of individual rather than communal prosperity.

These criticisms come at a time when many still expect black religion and religious institutions to deliver poor black communities out of the wilderness created by centuries of economic, political, and social isolation. This expectation is part of a larger dispute over whether responsibility for ending the dire economic consequences of persistent racial injustice rests with black community institutions or with the broader American commonwealth, or with both. Among the many black megachurches that have called for both is Chicago's Trinity United Church of Christ. The church and its pastor, Jeremiah Wright, first attracted Barack Obama's attention when he was a young community organizer, and did so precisely because of its social activism, its service to the urban poor and the unemployed. It was Wright's long-standing espousal of a brand of black liberationist theology that, when taken out of its private, racialized religious context, evoked the fear and scorn of a larger public.

For Obama, Trinity was one more stop in his search for community, for an anchoring place, and for the kind of redemptive political work he associated with the civil rights movement. When he was a child, his mother had offered him what he remembered as "the grainy black-and-white footage" of the civil rights movement: "a county jail bursting with children, their hands clasped together, singing freedom songs. Such images became a form of prayer for me, bolstering my spirits, channeling my emotions in a way that words never could." In these ways, his earliest ideas about the movement revolved around moments of collective redemption, symbolized for him when people of different colors and faiths "seemed to converge—the crowd in front of the Lincoln Memorial, the Freedom Rides, at the lunch counter." Years later, while a student at Columbia University, Obama attended a speech given by the SNCC veteran Kwame Toure (Stokely Carmichael) and was unnerved by the experience. Toure's "eyes glowed inward as he spoke, the eyes of a madman or a saint"; for Obama, seeing him "was like a bad dream," an embodiment of the way in which "the movement had died years ago, shattered into a thousand fragments."[7]

Obama was engaged in a deeply personal search for a "sense of wholeness" that did not rest on racial purity or "the bloodlines we'd inherited," and it was this quest that drove him, ironically, to the black religious world of Trinity and the Reverend Wright. There Obama heard stories of black "trials and triumphs," narratives that to him seemed "at once unique and universal." "Those stories—of survival, and freedom, and hope—became our story, my story; the blood that had spilled was our blood, the tears our tears; until this black church, on this bright day, seemed once more a vessel carrying the story of a people into future generations and into a larger world." To reject this experience, as his political critics demanded during his campaign, would have been to disrespect the religious inspiration and the black community that he had so fervently sought.[8]

For it was there, in Trinity's pews and under the sounds of Wright's preaching, that Obama found his way out of aloneness through a fresh "faith in other people" and a religious spirit that "carried within it, nascent, incomplete, the possibility of moving beyond our narrow dreams." Among the understandings that Obama attributed to that church was the idea "that religious commitment did not require me to suspend critical thinking, disengage from the battle for economic and social justice, or otherwise retreat from the world." For him, these revelations came "as a choice and not as an epiphany," yet he openly confessed that "kneeling beneath that cross on the South Side of Chicago, I felt God's spirit beckoning me. I submitted myself to His will, and dedicated myself to discovering His truth."[9]

Obama's ideas about race, religion, and politics, like much of what he believes, are driven by a sense of history, memory, and generational obligations. He has repeatedly invoked the story of Moses and Joshua, reminding his listeners and his readers, as had Martin Luther King Jr., that while Moses led his people to the Promised Land, it was Joshua and a sea of unified voices that completed the mission. Dubbing himself and his followers members of the "Joshua Generation," Obama has urged them to join forces and shout down the walls of Jericho in a unified and racially diverse campaign that reclaims the unfulfilled promises of the civil rights movement and its generation. And his appeal has resonated profoundly with those who made that history, those who remember it, and those seared by the same grainy black-and-white images that Obama's mother showed him and that I, nearly a decade older than he is, remember from my own childhood.[10]

Closer to the time when he actively aspired to national political office, Obama repeatedly presented his religious and political motivations as mutually reinforcing. Speaking in 2005 at an event honoring John Lewis, he commended the courage of the civil rights generation with inspiring him to take up public-service work and told the crowd that "we have songs left to sing and bridges left to cross." Later, when he announced his campaign for the Democratic presidential nomination, he stated that "it is time for our generation to answer that call." In a 2008 commemoration of Dr. King's birthday, Obama spoke as King had about the need for diversity and unity:

> In the struggle for peace and justice, we cannot walk alone.
> In the struggle for opportunity and equality, we cannot walk

alone. In the struggle to heal this nation and repair this world, we cannot walk alone. So I ask you to walk with me, and march with me, and join your voice with mine, and together we will sing the song that tears down the walls that divide us, and lift up an America that is truly "indivisible, with liberty, and justice for all."[11]

In all these ways, Obama's twenty-first-century ideas about race, religion, and politics remain firmly within the ideological, religious, and political traditions of Woodson, Du Bois, Bethune, Burroughs, Mays, and other black intellectuals and activists of the early twentieth century. Ideas about religious faith as a unifying and redemptive political force are as old as the Hebrew scriptures and as fresh as the writings and speeches of twentieth-century scholars and religious intellectuals before and during the civil rights era. Press reports have repeatedly characterized Obama's views as "post-black" and "post–civil rights," but his political and religious orientation might better be termed "neo-black" and "neo–civil rights." Just as the genre of music dubbed "neo-soul" has tried to reinvigorate and go beyond the forms that preceded it, Obama has enlivened and replicated the politics of the civil rights past he reveres, and has endeavored to transcend those politics with modern technologies.

Yet much of Obama's rhetoric of unification across regional, racial, ethnic, and class lines is reminiscent of that employed, although with far less subtlety, by the Reverend Jesse Jackson in his call for a "Rainbow Coalition" during his 1984 and 1988 presidential campaigns. Jackson, who did not hold elected office, was saddled with his own history of civil rights activism that was still too recent and too controversial to evoke popular veneration. His Democratic rival Al Gore used Jackson's oratorical eloquence to remind voters that they were electing someone not to be a preacher but to be a president.[12]

Like Obama, other black elected officials have sought the presidency, including the pioneering New York congresswoman Shirley Chisholm in 1972 and Senator Carol Moseley Braun of Illinois in 2004. All of these presidential runs by African Americans (including those of Alan Keyes and the Reverend Al Sharpton) were seen as symbolic or protest campaigns. That and the history of race in politics accounts partly for the way in which Obama's announcement of his candidacy was initially underestimated, including by his strongest rival, New York senator Hillary Clinton.[13]

Despite his best efforts, Obama cannot completely escape that history and the issue of race that his color and his physical appearance invoke. He has found that he cannot move beyond or transcend race, despite his eloquent employ of his biracialism and his transnational heritage. This became clear when Obama's opponents sought to use his affiliation with Wright and African American religion to "blacken" him. In his initial claim that to reject Wright and Trinity was to reject the "black community," Obama relied on the trope that the "black church" stands in for all that is honorable and good and acceptable about black life. By doing this, he perpetuated the false idea that one black church and one black minister reflected the enormous diversity of black believers and black churches and black ministers and black communities. But he knew that he could not afford to let the controversy separate him from the loyal black electorate on which his campaign depended. Ironically, when Obama did sever his ties with Trinity, he did so in reaction to remarks made at the church by a white Catholic priest who mocked Senator Clinton.

Obama's political career represents another facet of the gains from the civil rights movement, namely an enormous increase in the number and prominence of black elected officials. This development brings its own tensions, including conflicts over who best represents black communities and most effectively advances their interests. Just as significantly, the overwhelming and essential support that Obama has received from African American voters masks their own diversity by transcending their differences across region, religion, gender, and economic status. One constant, however, is that black women, who constitute a majority of the black electorate and black congregations, remain the largely unseen force in both arenas. These women, and black ministers, were among the very people Obama could not afford to offend in his initial public discussions of Wright and black religion.

Obama succeeded, at least temporarily, by employing a politics of black religion that deflected the politics of race threatening his presidential aspirations. Later, when he explicitly renounced and rejected Wright, he relegated his mentor to a bygone era marked by racial division and pain. Obama erected a generational divide between himself and Wright, but his disavowal disregarded the longer historical narrative from which Wright and Trinity had emerged.

Jeremiah Wright embodies many of the attributes of the highly educated, politically engaged clerical figure that was demanded by reformers such as Du Bois, Woodson, Mays, and Burroughs. He led a service-oriented church that was politically engaged and emotional in worship style; indeed, it was these aspects of the church and its pastor that originally appealed to Obama. Wright's sense of prophetic obligation also included a harsh critique of U.S. domestic and foreign policies that were inconsistent with Obama's electoral pursuits which rested on his faith in a universalist American democracy. Wright's commitments to black cultural nationalism and antimilitarism were antithetical to the patriotic political project that Obama worked so hard to construct as he pursued the ultimate American dream, growing up to be the president.

In a speech to the National Press Club in Washington, D.C., on April 28, 2008, Wright came to his own defense, explaining his sense of call and the mission of his church. Wright's address, which was largely ignored in the ensuing contentious encounter with the media, was a masterful account of black religious history stretching back to the 1600s, to slavery, and to Africa. In the same way that Obama had portrayed the "black community" and the "black church" as one, Wright equated the attacks on him with an attack on the "black church." They both were guilty of collapsing the diversity and distinctiveness among black churches for the sake of political argument. But Wright also cast his defense of the "black church" as part and parcel of a defense of the religion of Barbara Jordan, Fannie Lou Hamer, and his grandmother.[14]

In his historical recapitulation, Wright stood firmly with those who in the early twentieth century had argued for the existence of African cultural retentions in black religions. But he took this a step further by emphasizing the continued cultural exchanges between the religious practices of black people in the United States and those in Africa, the Caribbean, and South America. He recounted the history of the evolution of black and white churches in the United States, emphasizing that black independent churches were formed in the 1700s as a reaction against white parishioners' attempts to segregate or discriminate against black members.

Wright was careful to stress that those early black churches welcomed members regardless of race and that black churches have continued to do so, just like Trinity, whose members include whites, Hispanics, Asians, and black people from the Caribbean, South America, and Africa. In this way, he took on the familiar rhetorical question posed by Obama and others before him, including King and Mays: Why is eleven o'clock on Sunday morning still the most segregated hour in America? Wright answered it by relieving black churches of the responsibility, shifting the blame, as Mays had, to white Christians.[15]

At the same time, Wright paid homage to the United Church of Christ, the predominantly white denomination with which his church is affiliated. This denomination has its own history which stretches back to colonial-era Congregational churches in New England. As he explained, those white churches "came to the moral defense and paid for the legal defense of the Mende people aboard the slave ship *Amistad*, fought against slavery, played an active role in the Underground Railroad, and set up over 500 schools for the Africans who were freed from slavery in 1865." The denomination's commitments to ending racial injustices have endured, he stressed, citing its leadership in the fight "against apartheid in South Africa and racism in the United States of America." It was this model of political engagement that made the largely white denomination a good fit with Wright's church.[16]

Whatever their other disagreements, Obama and Wright both celebrated the fact that Trinity has always dedicated its considerable resources to improving the lives of the impoverished and the disadvantaged. The church is relatively new, founded in 1961 during the civil rights era, and led by Wright from 1972 to 2008. Its work exemplifies precisely the kind of church that many had demanded during a time when black communities had few resources. Thanks to recent economic gains, the members of the church commit their shared earnings to feed the homeless and the needy, own and operate housing complexes for the elderly, run childcare programs, and aid the unemployed. The congregation helps send young people to college and to seminary, contributes to the United Negro College Fund, and supports the historically black colleges affiliated with its denomination. It has pioneered a ministry that serves children, the elderly, prison inmates, and individuals recovering from drug and alcohol addiction. Like its larger denomination, it has welcomed, unlike most religious traditions, lesbians and gay men as members. At a time when many black congregations recoiled from the AIDS crisis, Trinity began providing services and ministries for people with AIDS and HIV infection.[17]

Wright told this story as part of his defense of the "black church."

But perhaps his most significant and most nuanced historical dispute was with those who tried to explain him, his ministry, and his church's work as a mere manifestation of "black theology." By linking him with the Black Power era, Obama portrayed Wright simultaneously as holding a "static" view of the possibility for racial reconciliation in the United States and as being out of touch with contemporary political reality. Wright refused to be categorized in this way while being careful not to disparage his fellow theologian and friend James Cone. Instead, Wright placed himself and his church's work in the much longer biblical and historical tradition of prophetic ministry and theology stretching back to the prophet Isaiah. According to his understanding of that tradition, the true Christian not only helps the poor and less able, but also works to change oppressive social orders by criticizing those who rule and hold power, whether in the state, the economy, or the military. Wright sees himself and his ministry as part of "God's desire for a radical change in a social order that has gone sour."[18]

When Wright said that he was a "preacher" and Obama a "politician," the statement was widely interpreted as an attack on Obama. In fairness, Wright was pointing to the obvious and very different ways that he and Obama have chosen to live out their shared religious convictions. Obama believes that through political leadership he can advance the perfectibility of American democracy, relying on his faith in the U.S. Constitution and the "band of patriots" who drafted it. Wright considers himself no less of a patriot, having served honorably as a Marine, but sees himself primarily as a prophetic minister, the role that Mays and others wanted an educated black ministry to assume. It was this role that Nannie Burroughs and Martin Luther King took on when they attacked the domestic and foreign policies of the federal government. So, too, Wright, when he pointed out that his church "took a stand against apartheid when the government of our country was supporting the racist regime of the African government in South Africa" and that "our congregation stood in solidarity with the peasants in El Salvador and Nicaragua, while our government, through Ollie North and the Iran-Contra scandal, was supporting the Contras, who were killing the peasants and the Miskito Indians in those two countries."[19]

In these and other ways, a preacher and a politician are destined for conflict even when both are African American Christians, and especially when one of them aspires to take the reins of the national state and its military power. "I do what pastors do," Wright said, and referring to Obama, "he does what politicians do." He was telling the truth and he was being consistent with his own personal and political history. "I said to Barack Obama, last year, 'If you get elected, I'm coming after you, because you'll be representing a government whose policies grind under people.'" That was likely no idle threat.[20]

The lesson of that controversy and of others detailed in this book is that the simplistic dichotomies that drive most discussions about race, religion, and politics still have traction because African American religion remains a subject of mystery, misunderstanding, and manipulation. There is one constant, however: black churches are still the strongest and most ubiquitous of black institutions. The intellectual heritage and history that has reckoned with that fact has roots that remain deep, entangled, and difficult to disaggregate. Black religion and politics remain inextricably and inescapably bound, but in ever new, intriguing, and compelling ways. The tension between the work of faith and the work of politics persists today, just as it did in the thoughts and deeds of the people who lived in centuries past.

Notes

Introduction

1. C. Eric Lincoln and Lawrence H. Mamiya, *The Black Church in the African American Experience* (Durham, N.C.: Duke University Press, 1990). Absalom Jones, *A Thanksgiving Sermon Preached January 1, 1808, in St. Thomas's, or the African Episcopal Church, Philadelphia: An Account of the Abolition of the African Slave Trade* (Philadelphia, 1808). Daniel A. Payne, *History of the African Methodist Church* (Nashville: AME Church, 1891; rpt. New York, 1968). Carol V. R. George, *Segregated Sabbaths: Richard Allen and the Emergence of Independent Black Churches, 1760–1840* (New York: Oxford University Press, 1973). For a discussion of later developments in black Methodism in Philadelphia, see Robert Gregg, *Sparks from the Anvil of Oppression: Philadelphia's African Methodists and Southern Migrants, 1890–1940* (Philadelphia: Temple University Press, 1993). William J. Walls, *The African Methodist Episcopal Zion Church: Reality of the Black Church* (Charlotte, N.C.: AME Zion Publishing House, 1974).

2. Albert J. Raboteau, *Slave Religion: The "Invisible Institution" in the Antebellum South* (New York: Oxford University Press, 1978). Idem, *A Fire in the Bones: Reflections on African-American Religious History* (Boston: Beacon Press, 1995), pp. 60–64. Lincoln and Mamiya, *The Black Church in*

the African American Experience, pp. 20–46. For histories of black churches in the South during this period, see James Melvin Washington, *Frustrated Fellowship: The Black Quest for Social Power* (Macon, Ga.: Mercer University Press, 1986); Clarence E. Walker, *A Rock in a Weary Land: The African Methodist Episcopal Church during the Civil War and Reconstruction* (Baton Rouge: Louisiana State University Press, 1982); William E. Montgomery, *Under Their Own Vine and Fig Tree: The African-American Church in the South, 1865–1900* (Baton Rouge: Louisiana State University Press, 1993). Annetta L. Gomez-Jefferson, *The Sage of Tawawa: Reverdy Cassius Ransom, 1861–1959* (Kent, Ohio: Kent State University Press, 2002).

3. Robert E. Hayden, "We Have Not Forgotten," in Hayden, *Heart-Shape in the Dust: Poems* (Detroit, Mich.: Falcon Press, 1940), p. 10. I first found the poem in John Blassingame, ed., *Slavery Testimony: Two Centuries of Letters, Speeches, Interviews, and Autobiographies* (Baton Rouge: Louisiana University Press, 1977), p. 601. In 1940, Hayden was at the beginning of what would be a long and distinguished career, culminating with his appointment in 1977 to a position later known as Poet Laureate for the Library of Congress. For more on Hayden, see Pontheolla T. Williams, *Robert C. Hayden: A Critical Analysis of His Poetry* (Urbana: University of Illinois Press, 1987). John Hatcher, *From the Auroral Darkness: The Life and Poetry of Robert Hayden* (Oxford: George Ronald, 1984). Laurence Goldstein and Robert Chrisman, *Robert Hayden: Essays on the Poetry* (Ann Arbor: University of Michigan Press, 2001). Fred M. Fetrow, *Robert Hayden* (Boston: Twayne, 1984).

4. On religion and migration, see Gregg, *Sparks from the Anvil of Oppression*. Kimberley Phillips, *AlabamaNorth: African-American Migrants, Community, and Working-Class Activism in Cleveland, 1915–45* (Urbana: University of Illinois, 1999). Milton Sernett, *Bound for the Promised Land: African American Religion and the Great Migration* (Durham, N.C.: Duke University Press, 1997).

5. Lincoln and Mamiya, *The Black Church in the African American Experience*, pp. 76–91. Hans Baer, *The Black Spiritualist Movement: A Religious Response to Racism* (Knoxville: University of Tennessee Press, 1984). Randall Burkett, *Garveyism as a Religious Movement* (Metuchen,

N.J.: Scarecrow Press and ATLA, 1978). Claude Andrew Clegg III, *An Original Man: The Life and Times of Elijah Muhammad* (New York: St. Martin's Press, 1997). C. Eric Lincoln, *The Black Muslims in America* (Boston: Beacon Press, 1961). Robert Weisbrot, *Father Divine and the Struggle for Racial Equality* (Champaign: University of Illinois Press, 1983).

6. While denominational structures do exist among black Baptists, expressed through national organizations called "conventions," they are marked by decentralization and by the near-total autonomy of local affiliates. Leroy Fitts, *A History of Black Baptists* (Nashville: Broadman, 1985). Moreover, many Baptist churches choose not to affiliate with either of the national conventions. There also are many Christian churches that are neither Baptist nor Methodist, including the growing numbers of Pentecostal or Holiness churches, such as the Church of God in Christ and other groups. See Cheryl J. Sanders, *Saints in Exile: The Holiness-Pentecostal Experience in African American Religion and Culture* (New York: Oxford University Press, 1996). Anthea D. Butler, *Women in the Church of God in Christ: Making a Sanctified World* (Chapel Hill: University of North Carolina Press, 2007). Even among Methodists, where hierarchies and the power to make clerical appointments are strong, local churches retain considerable independent authority.

7. George Washington Williams, *History of the Negro Race in America, 1619–1880: Negroes as Slaves, as Soldiers, and as Citizens* (New York: Arno Press, 1968; orig. pub. 1883), pp. 1–11. John Hope Franklin, *George Washington Williams: A Biography* (Durham, N.C.: Duke University Press, 1998). Mia Bay, *The White Image in the Black Mind: African American Ideas about White People, 1830–1925* (New York: Oxford University Press, 2000).

8. Hayden, "We Have Not Forgotten."

1. The Reformation of the "Negro Church"

1. W. E. B. Du Bois, ed., *The Negro Church* (Atlanta, Ga.: Atlanta University Press, 1903). Carter G. Woodson, *The History of the Negro Church* (Washington, D.C.: Associated Publishers, 1922). Benjamin Mays and Joseph William Nicholson, *The Negro's Church* (New York: Institute

of Social and Religious Research, 1933). Benjamin Mays, *The Negro's God as Reflected in His Literature* (Westport, Conn.: Greenwood Press, 1969; orig. pub. 1938).

2. For a discussion of Du Bois's ideas on African American religion and politics, see, Barbara Dianne Savage, "W. E. B. Du Bois and 'The Negro Church,'" *Annals of the American Academy of Political and Social Science*, 568 (March 2000): 235–249; and Herbert Aptheker, "W. E. B. Du Bois and Religion: A Brief Reassessment," *Journal of Religious Thought*, 39 (Spring–Summer 1982): 5–11. For more on Du Bois's religious upbringing and views, see David Levering Lewis, *W. E. B. Du Bois: Biography of a Race* (New York: Henry Holt, 1993); and Arnold Rampersad, *The Art and Imagination of W. E. B. Du Bois* (Cambridge, Mass.: Harvard University Press, 1976). See also David Levering Lewis, *W. E. B. Du Bois: The Fight for Equality and The American Century, 1919–1963* (New York: Holt, 2000), p. 307. Manning Marable, "The Black Faith of W. E. B. Du Bois: Sociocultural and Political Dimensions of Black Religion," *The Southern Quarterly: A Journal of the Arts in the South*, 23, no. 3 (Spring 1985): 15–33. Curtis Evans, "W. E. B. Du Bois: Interpreting Religion and the Problem of the Negro Church," *Journal of the American Academy of Religion*, 2, no. 75 (June 2007): 268–297. Edward J. Blum, *W. E. B. Du Bois: American Prophet* (Philadelphia: University of Pennsylvania, 2007).

3. Wilson Jeremiah Moses, *Black Messiahs and Uncle Toms: Social and Literary Manipulations of a Religious Myth*, rev. ed. (University Park, Pa.: Pennsylvania State University Press, 1992).

4. W. E. B. Du Bois, *The Philadelphia Negro* (Philadelphia: University of Pennsylvania Press, 1996; orig. pub. 1899), pp. 197, 201, 205–207, 234.

5. Ibid., pp. 196, 204, 311. For a critique of Du Bois's treatment of black women in *The Philadelphia Negro*, see Tera Hunter, "'The "Brotherly Love" for Which This City Is Proverbial Should Extend to All': The Everyday Lives of Working-Class Women in Philadelphia and Atlanta in the 1890s," in Michael B. Katz and Thomas J. Sugrue, eds., *W. E. B. Du Bois, Race, and the City: "The Philadelphia Negro" and Its Legacy* (Philadelphia: University of Pennsylvania Press, 1998), pp. 130–131, 144–145. Also Farah Jasmine Griffin, "Black Feminists and Du Bois: Respectability, Pro-

tection, and Beyond," *Annals of the American Academy of Political and Social Science*, 568 (March 2000): 28–40.

6. Du Bois, *The Negro Church*, p. 5.

7. Ibid., pp. 207–208. W. E. B. Du Bois, "The Damnation of Women," in Du Bois, *Darkwater: Voices from Within the Veil* (1920; rpt. New York: Washington Square Press, 2004), pp. 174, 179.

8. W. E. B. Du Bois, *The Souls of Black Folk* (Boston: Bedford Books, 1997; orig. pub. 1903), pp. 150–154.

9. Du Bois, *The Souls of Black Folk*, pp. 150–154. Idem, in *The Crisis*, 4, no. 1 (May 1912) and 11, no. 6 (April 1916): 302.

10. Kelly Miller, *Out of the House of Bondage* (New York: Arno Press, 1969; orig. pub. 1914), pp. 203–204, 214, 217.

11. Kelly Miller, from *An Appeal to Conscience: America's Code of Caste—A Disgrace to Democracy* (1918), excerpt reprinted in Herbert Aptheker, ed. *A Documentary History of The Negro People of the United States, 1910–1932* (Secaucus, N.J.: Citadel Press, 1969), pp. 233–235. Miller also considered similar issues in his book *Radicals and Conservatives, and Other Essays on the Negro in America* (New York: Schocken, 1968), first published in 1908 under the title *Race Adjustment*. See his essay there, "Religion as a Solvent of the Race Problem," pp. 147–165.

12. Deborah Gray White, *Too Heavy a Load: Black Women in Defense of Themselves, 1894–1994* (New York: Norton, 1999), pp. 73–74. Evelyn Brooks Higginbotham, *Righteous Discontent: The Woman's Movement in the Black Baptist Church, 1880–1920* (Cambridge, Mass.: Harvard University Press, 1993), pp. 120–149. For more general discussions of African American women and their challenges to black Christian theology, see Cheryl Gilkes, "'Go and Tell Mary and Martha': The Spirituals, Biblical Options for Women, and Cultural Tensions in the African American Religious Experience," *Social Compass*, 43, no. 4 (December 1996): 563–581; and idem "'Mother to the Motherless, Father to the Fatherless': Power, Gender, and Community in an Afrocentric Biblical Tradition," *Semeia*, 47 (1989): 57–85. See also Ida B. Wells, *Crusade for Justice: The Autobiography of Ida B. Wells*, ed. Alfreda Duster (Chicago: University of Chicago Press, 1970), pp. 297–304. Patricia A. Schechter, *Ida B. Wells-Barnett and*

American Reform, 1880–1930 (Chapel Hill: University of North Carolina Press, 2001). Emilie M. Townes, "Because God Gave Her Vision: The Religious Impulse of Ida B. Wells-Barnett," in Rosemary Skinner Keller, ed., *Spirituality and Social Responsibility: Vocational Vision of Women in the United Methodist Tradition* (Nashville: Abingdon Press, 1993), p. 162. For a longer discussion of the relationship between Wells's religious beliefs and her political activities, see Emilie M. Townes, *Womanist Justice, Womanist Hope* (Atlanta, Ga.: Scholars Press, 1993). Paula J. Giddings, *Ida: A Sword among Lions—Ida B. Wells and the Campaign against Lynching* (New York: Amistad, 2008), pp. 164–165. Mia Bay, *To Tell the Truth Freely: The Life of Ida B. Wells* (New York: Farrar, Straus and Giroux, forthcoming, 2009).

13. White, *Too Heavy a Load*, p. 72. For more on the "politics of respectability" as manifested in this critique, see Higginbotham, *Righteous Discontent*.

14. Higginbotham, *Righteous Discontent*, pp. 175–176.

15. Ibid., p. 175.

16. Ibid., pp. 172–174, 176.

17. Lorenzo J. Greene, *Selling Black History for Carter G. Woodson: A Diary, 1930–1933*, ed. Arvarh E. Strickland (Columbia: University of Missouri Press, 1996), pp. 1–2. August Meier and Elliott Rudwick, *Black History and the Historical Profession, 1915–1980* (Urbana: University of Illinois Press, 1986), pp. 1–2. Jacqueline Goggin, *Carter G. Woodson: A Life in Black History* (Baton Rouge: Louisiana State University Press, 1993), pp. xii, 18–22. For a general listing of Woodson's articles and essays, see Sister Anthony Scally, comp., *Carter G. Woodson: A Bio-Bibliography* (Westport, Conn.: Greenwood Press, 1985).

18. Meier and Rudwick, *Black History and the Historical Profession*, p. 2. Goggin, *Carter G. Woodson*, p. xii. Carter G. Woodson, *The Negro in Our History* (Washington, D.C.: Associated Publishers, 1922). John Hope Franklin, *From Slavery to Freedom* (New York: McGraw Hill, 1947). Idem, "The Place of Carter G. Woodson in American Historiography," *Negro History Bulletin*, 13, no. 8 (May 1950): 174–176.

19. Meier and Rudwick, *Black History and the Historical Profession*, p. 2. Goggin, *Carter G. Woodson*, p. xii. Woodson, *History of the Negro Church*.

20. Woodson, *History of the Negro Church*, pp. 249–250, 254, 257, 263.

21. Goggin, *Carter G. Woodson*, pp. 118–119, 85–86, 55. *Journal of Negro History*, 15, no. 1 (January 1930): 9–10; and 14, no. 1 (January 1929): 3. Meier and Rudwick, *Black History and the Historical Profession*, p. 36. Goggin, *Carter G. Woodson*, pp. 55. Greene, *Selling Black History for Carter G. Woodson*, pp. 3, 4, 9.

22. Woodson, *History of the Negro Church*, pp. 285, 303–304.

23. Ibid., pp. 273.

24. Ibid., pp. 304, 312.

25. Ibid., pp. 281–282.

26. Woodson, *The Negro in Our History*, pp. 593, 591, 592.

27. Ibid., pp. 593, 591, 592.

28. W. E. B. Du Bois, review of Woodson, *History of the Negro Church*, in *The Freeman*, October 4, 1922, pp. 92–93, reprinted in *Book Reviews by W. E. B. Du Bois*, ed. Herbert Aptheker (Millwood, N.Y.: KTO Press, 1977), pp. 67–68.

29. Ibid.

30. On Garvey, see Randall K. Burkett, *Garveyism as a Religious Movement: The Institutionalization of a Black Civil Religion* (Metuchen, N.J.: Scarecrow Press, 1978). Gayraud S. Wilmore, *Black Religion and Black Radicalism: An Interpretation of the Religious History of Afro-American People*, 2nd ed. (Maryknoll, N.Y.: Orbis Books, 1983), pp. 152, 174. Others have noted the extent to which black intellectuals and artists criticized black religion; see, for example, Mary Frances Berry and John Blassingame, *Long Memory: The Black Experience in America* (New York: Oxford University Press, 1982), p. 102.

31. Journalist George Schuyler made a similar observation about the black press's role in bringing to light abuses by church leaders, crediting the secular press for doing this at a time when the religious press would not. George Schuyler, "Black America Begins to Doubt," *American Mercury*, April 1932, pp. 423–430. For the thesis that the interwar period was a time of harshest attacks on black churches and the moment when black religion was "deradicalized," see Gayraud S. Wilmore, *Black Religion and Black Radicalism: An Interpretation of the Religious History of Afro-American People*, 2nd ed. (New York: Doubleday, 1983).

32. Burroughs, "Why People Go to the Dogs Instead of to Church," and "From a Woman's Point of View," 1929, both microfilm, Claude Barnett Papers.

33. Ibid.

34. Ibid. Burroughs, "Preachers Are Not Called To Do Everything," n.d., microfilm, Claude Barnett Papers.

35. "Jesus Was No Molly-Coddle, Nannie Burroughs Tells Forum," *Afro-American*, April 16, 1932, microfilm, Claude Barnett Papers.

36. A. James Gardner, "A Celebrated Speech by a Celebrated Woman," Nannie Helen Burroughs Papers, Manuscripts and Archives, Library of Congress.

37. Burroughs, "What Will Become of Us," *Washington Tribune*, February 15, 1934. "Nannie Burroughs Thrills Huge Shrine Auditorium Audience with Opening Address," September 15, 1937, Associated Negro Press release. Burroughs, "New Frontiers," n.d. All microfilm, Claude Barnett Papers.

38. W. E. B. Du Bois, "Will the Church Remove the Color Line?" *Christian Century*, December 9, 1931, pp. 1554–1556. Du Bois's piece moved several white readers to accuse him of unfairly judging the white Christian church, with one writer pointedly reminding him that his alma mater Fisk had been founded by Congregationalists. Carl A. Nissen (Manhattan, Kansas) and Dan F. Bradley (Cleveland), Letters to the Editor, both in *The Christian Century*, December 30, 1931. Du Bois's broad indictment of white Christianity was not new or unique. See, for example, Booker T. Washington and W. E. B. Du Bois, "The Negro in the South: His Economic Progress in Relation to His Moral and Religious Development," William Levi Bell Lectures for the Year 1907, Philadelphia Divinity School, Charles S. Blockson African American Collection, Temple University.

39. Du Bois, comment on "Segregation," an essay by Francis J. Grimke, both in *The Crisis*, June 1934, pp. 173–174. Du Bois, "Postscript," *The Crisis*, January 1934, p. 20. Du Bois, "Segregation—A Symposium," *The Crisis*, March 1934, pp. 79–82.

40. Du Bois, "Postscript," *The Crisis*, May 1934, p. 149. Idem, "Post-

script," *The Crisis*, April 1934, pp. 115–117. Idem, "Postscript," *The Crisis*, June 1934, pp. 182–184, in which he supports all-black fraternities as the kind of voluntary "segregation in which we glory." And finally, "Dr. Du Bois Resigns," *The Crisis*, August 1934, pp. 245–246.

41. Burroughs, "Nannie Burroughs Says the Doctor Is Tired, Fought a Good Fight, but Did Not Keep the Faith on the Segregation Issue," *The Afro-American*, April 28, 1934. Idem, "Unload Uncle Toms," *Los Angeles Weekly*, December 23, 1933. Idem, "Fighting Woman Educator Tells What Race Needs," *Pittsburgh Courier*, December 23, 1933. All microfilm, Schomburg Clipping File, "Burroughs," Schomburg Center for Research in Black Culture, New York Public Library.

42. Burroughs, "Parasites and Mendicants Are Our Handicaps: Salvation Lies in United Effort, Not in 'One-Man' Acts," *Philadelphia Tribune*, February 18, 1932. Idem, "I'd Wear a Fig-Leaf," *The Afro-American*, December 16, 1933. Idem, "What Will Become of Us," *Washington Tribune*, February 15, 1934. All microfilm, Schomburg Clipping File, "Burroughs," Schomburg Center for Research in Black Culture.

43. W. E. B. Du Bois, "The Co-Operative Negro Church," *Pittsburgh Courier*, June 19, 1937, in Herbert Aptheker, ed., *Newspaper Columns of W. E. B. Du Bois: Volume 1, 1883–1944* (White Plains, N.Y.: Kraus-Thomason, 1986), p. 212.

44. Carter Woodson's columns over the three months were as follows: "A United Negro Church," *New York Age*, August 15, 1931, p. 9; "Difficulties in Way of the United Church," *New York Age*, August 21, 1931, p. 9; "The Union of Churches Considered Utopian," *New York Age*, September 5, 1931, p. 9; "Radical Proposals with Respect to the United Negro Church," *New York Age*, September 12, 1931, p. 9; "Disunion of the Churches Accounts for the Negro Preacher in Politics," *New York Age*, September 19, 1931, p. 9; "Church Edifices Declared to be Property in Mortmain," *New York Age*, September 26, 1931, p. 9; "Theology a Factor in Disunion of Churches," *New York Age*, October 3, 1931, p. 9; "Superfluous Negro Preachers Prevent the Union of the Churches," *New York Age*, October 10, 1931, p. 9; and "Need for Union Emphasized in Recent Data on Churches," *New York Age*, October 17, 1931, p. 9.

45. Clarence E. Walker, A Rock in a Weary Land: The African Methodist Episcopal Church during the Civil War and Reconstruction (Baton Rouge: Louisiana State University Press, 1982). More recently, C. Eric Lincoln and Lawrence H. Mimiya, The Black Church in the African American Experience (Durham: Duke University Press, 1990). William E. Montgomery, Under Their Own Vine and Fig Tree: The African-American Church in the South, 1865–1900 (Baton Rouge: Louisiana State University Press, 1993); James T. Campbell, Songs of Zion: The African Methodist Episcopal Church in the United States and South Africa (Chapel Hill: University of North Carolina Press, 1998). Peter C. Murray, Methodists and the Crucible of Race, 1930–1975 (Columbia: University of Missouri Press, 2004), pp. 31–33, 35–39. Sydney Ahlstrom, A Religious History of the American People (New Haven: Yale University Press, 1972), p. 921.

46. Woodson, New York Age, September 12, 1931, and October 17, 1931. See also idem, New York Age, October 10, 1931.

47. Woodson, "A United Negro Church," New York Age, August 15, 1931. The idea of uniting all black churches behind a set of common social and political goals, but without dissolving their denominations, had been suggested by Howard University School of Religion Professor William Stuart Nelson in 1925. Nelson, "Close Ranks!" The Crisis, June 1925, pp. 71–72, in which he argued: "Imagine that for one day all the denominations of the race, all its professed Christians should pool their resources and their energies, unite upon a common plea for race redemption—then would we see our major problems and difficulties giving way before an irresistible force." His concerns were broader, however, since he believed that religious intolerance was but one of the factors hampering black unity; the other two were competitiveness among black fraternities and sororities, and divisions between youth and the elderly.

48. Goggin, Carter G. Woodson, p. 142. "The Death of the Founder," Negro History Bulletin, 13, no. 8 (May 1950): 170, 176. New York Age, August 15, 1931.

49. Tony Martin, "Carter G. Woodson and Marcus Garvey," Negro History Bulletin, 40, no. 6 (November–December 1977): 774–777. On Woodson's refusal to join anti-Garvey campaigns, see Goggin, Carter G.

Woodson, pp. 151–152. The commemorative essay is Woodson, "Marcus Garvey," *Journal of Negro History*, 25, no. 4 (October 1940): 590–592.

50. Goggin, *Carter G. Woodson*, pp. 169, 170–172.

51. Woodson, *New York Age*, October 29, 1931.

52. "Proceedings of Annual Meeting of the ASNLH, Held in New York City, November 8–12, 1931," *Journal of Negro History*, 17, no. 1 (January 1932): 5–7.

53. "Negro History Association Holds Successful Meeting in New York," *New York Age*, November 14, 1931.

54. Meier and Rudwick, *Black History and the Historical Profession*, pp. 36, 61.

55. Woodson, in *Pittsburgh Courier*, December 17, 1932. Idem, in *Journal of Negro History*, 3, no. 1 (October 1939): 9. That same issue also carried an article by Elise Derricotte titled "Our Women in the Modern World" in which she credited Christianity for advancing the progress of all women (ibid., p. 14). For an excellent analysis of Woodson's relationship with black women as coworkers and as historical subjects, see Pero Gaglo Dagbovie, "Black Women, Carter G. Woodson, and the Association for the Study of Negro Life and History, 1915–1950," *Journal of African American History*, 88, no. 1 (Winter 2003): 21–41. For a helpful discussion on gender and the rise of professional historians, see Bonnie G. Smith, *The Gender of History: Men, Women, and Historical Practice* (Cambridge, Mass.: Harvard University Press, 1998), pp. 14, 148, 150, 186.

56. Goggin, *Carter G. Woodson*, pp. 69–70. Meier and Rudwick, *Black History and the Historical Profession*, 78. For a copy of the study's report, see Charles H. Wesley, "The Negro Church in the United States," microfilm, Papers of Carter G. Woodson and the Association for the Study of Negro Life and History, 1915–1950. Despite Woodson's initial objections, he later published a small portion of Wesley's research in the *Journal of Negro History*. Wesley, "The Religious Attitudes of Negro Youth—A Preliminary Study of Opinion in an Urban and a Rural Community," *Journal of Negro History*, 21, no. 4 (October 1936): 376–393.

57. Benjamin Mays, *Born to Rebel: An Autobiography* (Athens, Ga.: University of Georgia, 1987; orig. pub. 1971), p. 131. Joseph William

Nicholson was a pastor in the Colored Methodist Episcopal Church (CME) and at the time was working on his doctorate at Northwestern University's School of Education. Nicholson's 1932 dissertation was an occupational study of black ministers that relied in part on some of the survey and interview materials for his work with Mays. Joseph William Nicholson, "An Occupational Study of the Christian Ministry among Negroes," dissertation, Northwestern University School of Education, August 1932. Pastor of the Jubilee Temple Methodist Episcopal Church in Chicago, Nicholson was a politically active minister who also served on the executive board of directors of the NAACP. Although Nicholson is listed as a coauthor of *The Negro's Church*, Mays, as the project's director, insisted that the authorship of each chapter be carefully specified. The introductory chapter was the only one written jointly, and the majority of the remaining chapters in the book were written by Mays alone, including the most salient and substantive ones. Of the chapters in *The Negro's Church*, Nicholson and Mays coauthored chapter 1, Nicholson wrote chapters 2, 6, 7, 8, 9, 14, and Mays wrote chapters 3, 4, 10, 11, 12, 13, 15, 16, 17.

58. Orville Vernon Burton, Foreword to Mays, *Born to Rebel*, pp. ix, xxii–xxvii.

59. Galen M. Fisher, *The Institute of Social and Religious Research, 1921–1934* (New York: Institute of Social and Religious Research, 1934), pp. 5–8, 14–16, 18, 53–59. Several prominent scholars were on the permanent staff of the institute, including H. Paul Douglass, Edmund de S. Brunner, and C. Luther Fry. During its existence, from 1921 to 1934, the institute sponsored and published more than eighty books and reports, most on the Protestant church in North America and on theological education. The most prominent book in the series was the classic 1928 study *Middletown*, in which the religious dimensions are woven into its broader community study. Two other institute publications focused specifically on race and religion: a volume on the education of black ministers and a study of race segregation by religious bodies. These were, respectively, W. A. Daniel, *The Education of Negro Ministers* (1925); and Trevor Bowen, *Divine White Right* (1934). See Mays, *The Negro's Church*, p. v.

60. Mays, *The Negro's Church*, pp. 9, 37. George Washington Williams, *History of the Negro Race in America, 1619–1880: Negroes as Slaves, as Soldiers, and as Citizens* (New York: Arno Press, 1968; orig. pub. 1883), p. 452. For more on Williams, see John Hope Franklin, *George Washington Williams: A Biography* (Durham, N.C.: Duke University Press, 1998).

61. Williams, *History of the Negro Race*, p. 515.

62. Mays, *The Negro Church*, pp. 10, 227.

63. Mays's associate Nicholson had focused on this issue as part of his dissertation, an occupational study of the black Christian ministry. Nicholson expressed fears about the spreading influence of the rural religious experience, concluding after a survey of more than 400 black ministers nationwide that nearly 90 percent of them had been born in Southern states. Nicholson, "An Occupational Study of the Christian Ministry among Negroes," dissertation, Northwestern University School of Education, August 1932.

64. Mays, *The Negro Church*, pp. 9–11, 14, 18–19.

65. Ibid., pp. 51, 92–93. See also Randal M. Jelks, "Benjamin Elijah Mays and the Creation of an Insurgent Negro Professional Clergy," *A.M.E. Church Review* (July–September 2002): 32–38.

66. Mays, *The Negro Church*, pp. 164–165.

67. Ibid., p. 101. C. Luther Fry, *The U.S. Looks at Its Churches* (New York: Institute of Social and Religious Research, 1930), p. 11.

68. U.S. Bureau of the Census, *Religious Bodies: 1906* (Washington, D.C.: Government Printing Office, 1910), pp. 28–31. Idem, *Census of Religious Bodies: 1926* (Washington, D.C.: Government Printing Office, 1928), pp. 18, 83–91, 137. Idem, *Religious Bodies: 1916* (Washington, D.C.: Government Printing Office, 1919), pp. 40–42. Idem, *Religious Bodies: 1936* (Washington, D.C.: Government Printing Office, 1941), pp. 32–35, 164–165.

69. Mays, *The Negro Church*, p. 101.

70. Ibid., p. 229.

71. Mays, *The Negro Church*, pp. 278, 286–287.

72. Robert L. Sunderland, "The Negro Church," *Journal of Religion*, 13, no. 2 (July 1933). Alain Locke, "Fewer, Better Churches," *Survey*

Graphic, July 1935. Frances A. Henson, "Proletarian Religion," *World Tomorrow*, August 31, 1933. W. E. Garrison, "Negro Churches," *Christian Century*, February 15, 1933. Robert P. Kreitler, "The Negro's Church," *The Churchman*, July 15, 1933. William Stuart Nelson, "The Negro's Church," *Religious Education Magazine*, January 1934, p. 330. Harold E. B. Speight, "The Negro's Church," *Christian Leader*, February 25, 1933. "Emotional Religion of Negro Seen Dying," *New York Times*, February 20, 1933. "Report Made on Two-Year Study of Church—Survey Cites Important Conclus'ons: Negro Church Is Self-Supporting and Controlled by Race—'Shouting on Wane,'" *Norfolk Journal and Guide*, February 15, 1933. "The Negro Church," *New York Age*, March 4, 1933. "Negro Emotionalism Passing," *Literary Digest*, March 4, 1933. All in Mays Papers, Manuscript Division, Moorland-Spingarn Research Center, Howard University.

73. Mays, *The Negro's God*, preface.

74. Ibid., p. 17.

75. Ibid., pp. 51–52

76. Ibid., p. 224. Nella Larsen, *Quicksand* (New York: Knopf, 1928).

77. Ibid., p. 26.

78. For this and other aspects of Larsen's life, see the definitive biography by Thadious M. Davis, *Nella Larsen, Novelist of the Harlem Renaissance: A Woman's Life Unveiled* (Baton Rouge: Louisiana State University, 1994), pp. 14, 280, 292.

79. Du Bois, in *The Crisis*, 35 (June 1928): 202, 211, reprinted in *Book Reviews by W. E. B. Du Bois*, ed. Herbert Aptheker (Millwood, N.Y.: KTO Press, 1977), pp. 113–114.

80. For an insightful and helpful analysis of Du Bois's notions of messianic faith as expressed in *Dark Princess*, see Marta Brunner, "'The Most Hopeless of Deaths . . . Is the Death of Faith': Messianic Faith in the Racial Politics of W. E. B. Du Bois," in *Re-Cognizing W. E. B. Du Bois in the Twenty-first Century*, ed. Chester Fontenot and Mary L. Keller (Macon, Ga.: Mercer University Press, 2004). Also see Homi K. Bhabha's introductory essay in W. E. B. Du Bois, *Dark Princess: A Romance* (New York: Oxford University Press, 2007).

81. Mays, *The Negro's God*, pp. 239–241, 244. On the claim of general disillusionment, Mays quotes at length from Walter Marshall Horton, *Theism and the Modern Mood* (New York: Harper and Brothers, 1930).

82. Woodson, book review, *Journal of Negro History*, 24, no. 1 (January 1939): 118–119.

83. Mays, *The Negro's God*, p. 253.

84. Ibid., p. 244.

85. Ibid.

2. Illusions of Black Religion

1. Winifred Raushenbush, *Robert E. Park: Biography of a Sociologist* (Durham, N.C.: Duke University Press, 1979), pp. 36–42, 101. Francille Wilson, *The Segregated Scholars: Black Social Scientists and the Development of Black Labor Studies, 1895–1950* (Charlottesville: University of Virginia Press, 2006), p. 145. John Bracey et al., eds., *The Black Sociologists: The First Half Century* (Belmont, Calif.: Wadsworth, 1971), pp. 5–8.

2. For a general overview of Johnson's life and career, see Patrick J. Gilpin and Marybeth Gasman, *Charles S. Johnson: Leadership Beyond the Veil in the Age of Jim Crow* (Albany: State University of New York Press, 2003). Anthony M. Platt, *E. Franklin Frazier Reconsidered* (New Brunswick, N.J.: Rutgers University Press, 1991). For an excellent discussion of masculinity and black sociologists in this era, see Marlon Ross, *Manning the Race: Reforming Black Men in the Jim Crow Era* (New York: New York University Press, 2004), pp. 9, 164–167, 175, 186.

3. Charles S. Johnson, *Shadow of the Plantation* (Chicago: University of Chicago Press, 1969; orig. pub. 1934).

4. Ibid., pp. 154, 152.

5. Ibid., pp. 151, 159–160, 178–179.

6. Allison Davis and John Dollard, *Children of Bondage* (Washington, D.C.: American Council on Education, 1941); Lloyd Warner, *Color and Human Nature: Negro Personality Development in a Northern City* (Washington, D.C.: American Council on Education, 1970; orig. pub. 1941); Charles S. Johnson, *Growing Up in the Black Belt: Negro Youth in the Rural*

South (New York: Schocken, 1967; orig. pub. 1941); E. Franklin Frazier, *Negro Youth at the Crossways: Their Personality Development in the Middle States* (New York: Schocken, 1967; orig. pub. 1940).

7. Johnson, *Growing Up in the Black Belt*, pp. 334–337, xxv.

8. Ibid., pp. 137–146.

9. Ibid., pp. 146–152. There were 125 questions in this test, but only 14 dealt with religion or the church.

10. Ibid., pp. 154–155, 157–164, 169.

11. Ibid., p. 169.

12. Frazier, *Negro Youth at the Crossways*, pp. 271–277.

13. The study relied on interviews conducted in Louisville with 28 boys and 33 girls, whose experiences were to serve as a check on the 95 boys and 112 girls studied in Washington. Although Frazier uses the terms "boys" and "girls" to describe the young people interviewed, they were not, with a few exceptions, preteens or children. The two interviewers in Louisville worked under the direction of Louis Parrish in the Sociology Department at the Louisville Municipal College for Negroes. The Washington interviews were conducted for Frazier by seven different interviewers, including the psychiatrist Harry Stack Sullivan who authored one of the two extended case studies in the book. Ibid., pp. xxxv, 200–234.

14. Ibid., p. 133.

15. Ibid., p. 115.

16. Ibid., pp. 115–117, 130–131.

17. Ibid., pp. 116, 131, 126. As for Frazier's claim that these young people thought God also was white, the interview excerpts lend little if any support for this conclusion, except perhaps in the very ambiguity of the question posed. "Is the Lord white?" or "What color is the Lord?" often elicited answers that could be referring to depictions of Christ and not to God at all, or sometimes to both. Ibid., p. 117. There are intriguing similarities between this line of questioning and that used in Marcus Garvey's 1921 "Universal Negro Catechism" as described in Mia Bay, *The White Image in the Black Mind* (New York: Oxford University Press, 2000), pp. 209–211.

18. Platt, *E. Franklin Frazier Reconsidered*, p. 18.

19. Research Projects, Negro Youth Study, E. Franklin Frazier Papers, Manuscript Division, Moorland Spingarn Collection, Howard University.

20. Ibid.

21. Ibid.

22. Robert E. Hemenway, *Zora Neale Hurston: A Literary Biography* (Urbana: University of Illinois Press, 1980; orig. pub. 1977). Valerie Boyd, *Wrapped in Rainbows: The Life of Zora Neale Hurston* (New York: Scribner, 2003). Carla Kaplan, ed., *Zora Neale Hurston: A Life in Letters* (New York: Doubleday, 2002).

23. Zora Neale Hurston, *The Sanctified Church* (Berkeley: Turtle Island, 1983), pp. 79, 81, 83, 85–90.

24. Ibid., pp. 91, 104–107.

25. Boyd, *Wrapped in Rainbows*, pp. 296, 254. Hurston, *The Sanctified Church*, pp. 49–68.

26. Boyd, *Wrapped in Rainbows*, pp. 281–282, 254, 284.

27. Ibid., pp. 282, 284.

28. Hortense Powdermaker, *Stranger and Friend: The Way of an Anthropologist* (New York: Norton, 1960). Brackette F. Williams and Drexel G. Woodson, "Hortense Powdermaker in the Deep South," Introduction to Hortense Powdermaker, *After Freedom: A Cultural Study in the Deep South* (Madison: University of Wisconsin Press, 1993; orig. pub. 1939), pp. ix–xl. For more on Powdermaker, see Gertrude Fraser, "Race, Class, and Difference in Hortense Powdermaker's *After Freedom: A Cultural Study in the Deep South,*" *Journal of Anthropological Research*, 47, no. 4, *The Legacy of Hortense Powdermaker* (Winter 1991): 403–416. Powdermaker's first book was *Life in Lesu: The Study of a Melanesian Society in New Ireland* (New York: Norton, 1933).

29. Powdermaker, *After Freedom*, pp. xviii–xix, xlix. Powdermaker, *Stranger and Friend*, pp. 144–146, 171.

30. Powdermaker, *Stranger and Friend*, pp. 171–173.

31. Ibid., pp. 171–176.

32. Powdermaker, *After Freedom*, pp. 245–246.

33. Ibid., pp. 247–248.

34. Ibid., p. 248.

35. Sudarshan Kapur, *Raising Up a Prophet: The African-American Encounter with Gandhi* (Boston: Beacon Press, 1992), pp. 3, 13, 17–21, 24, 28–32, 40, 48, 50. Dennis C. Dickerson, "Rooted in India: William Stuart Nelson and the Religious Origins of the Civil Rights Movement," *A.M.E. Church Review* (April–June 2007): 47–77.

36. Kapur, *Raising Up a Prophet*, pp. 34–35. E. Franklin Frazier, "The Negro and Non-Resistance," *The Crisis*, 27 (March 1924): 16–19.

37. Ibid., pp. 29, 44, 49.

38. Powdermaker, *After Freedom*, pp. 246–247.

39. Ibid., p. 273.

40. John Dollard, *Caste and Class in a Southern Town* (Garden City, N.Y.: Doubleday, 1957; orig. pub. 1937), pp. 242–244.

41. Charles S. Johnson, "A Study in Black and White: *After Freedom*," *The New Republic*, June 21, 1939. Carter G. Woodson, Review of *After Freedom*, in *Journal of Negro History*, 24, no. 2 (April 1939): 219–220. W. E. B. Du Bois, Review of *After Freedom*, in *Social Forces*, 18, no. 1 (October 1939): 137–139. Robert E. Park, Review of *After Freedom*, in *American Journal of Sociology*, 45, no. 4 (January 1940): 612–613. Horace Mann Bond, Review of *After Freedom*, in *Annals of the American Academy of Political and Social Science*, 205 (September 1939): 201–202. Melville J. Herskovits, "Cottonville and the Race Problem," Review of *After Freedom*, in *The Nation*, September 16, 1939, pp. 298–299.

42. Richard Wright, Introduction to St. Clair Drake and Horace R. Cayton, *Black Metropolis: A Study of Negro Life in a Northern City* (New York: Harcourt, Brace, 1945), pp. xxxi, xxxiv.

43. Horace R. Cayton, *Long Old Road* (Seattle: University of Washington Press, 1970; orig. pub. 1963). Drake would serve on the faculty at Roosevelt University from 1946 to 1968. From 1958 to 1961, he taught sociology at the University of Ghana while serving as an advisor to Kwame Nkrumah. He ended his academic career at Stanford University where in 1969 he established one of the first programs in African and Afro-American studies.

44. Drake and Cayton, *Black Metropolis*, p. 419.

45. Ibid., p. 381.

46. Ibid., pp. 422–424.

47. Ibid., pp. 418–424.

48. Ibid., pp. 427–428.

49. Ibid., pp. 617, 650, 620–623.

50. Ibid., pp. 683, 714.

51. Ibid., p. 632.

52. Ibid., pp. 612, 632.

53. Ibid., pp. 617, 650.

54. Gunnar Myrdal, *An American Dilemma: The Negro Problem and Modern Democracy* (New York: Harper, 1944).

55. Walter Jackson, *Gunnar Myrdal and America's Conscience: Social Engineering and Racial Liberalism, 1938–1987* (Chapel Hill: University of North Carolina Press, 1990), pp. 107, 223. David W. Southern, *Gunnar Myrdal and Black-White Relations: The Use and Abuse of "An American Dilemma," 1944–1969* (Baton Rouge: Louisiana State University Press, 1987).

56. Myrdal, *An American Dilemma*, pp. 863, 868, 866, 939.

57. Ibid., pp. 872–873.

58. Ibid., pp. 862–863, 877.

59. Ibid., p. 492.

60. Ibid., pp. 908, 923.

61. Ibid., pp. 923–924.

62. Drake and Cayton, *Black Metropolis*, pp. 398–401, 412.

63. Arthur Huff Fauset, *Black Gods of the Metropolis: Negro Religious Cults of the Urban North* (Philadelphia: University of Pennsylvania Press, 1944; rpt. 2001), p. v.

64. Fauset's early publications include *Folk-Lore from Nova Scotia* (New York: G. E. Strechert, 1931); "Negro Folk Tales from the South," *Journal of American Folk-Lore*, 40 (1927): 213–303; and "Tales and Riddles Collected in Philadelphia," *Journal of American Folk-Lore*, 41 (1928): 529–557. See also Arthur Huff Fauset, "American Negro Folk Literature," in Alain Locke, ed., *The New Negro* (New York: Atheneum, 1968; orig. pub. 1925), pp. 238–244. For more on Fauset's place in the field of anthropology, see Lee D. Baker, *From Savage to Negro: Anthropology and the Construction of Race, 1896–1954* (Berkeley: University of California Press,

1998). Frustrated by his own experience in the Philadelphia school system, Fauset helped to reorganize the local chapter of the American Federation of Teachers, later serving as one of its vice presidents. He also founded a local political organization that worked with the NAACP to help end the Philadelphia Transit Company's refusal to hire black employees. This information comes from an undated oral interview with Fauset: "A Retrospective as Told to Winnie Williams," Arthur Huff Fauset Collection, Special Collections Department, Van Pelt Library, University of Pennsylvania, Philadelphia (hereafter cited as "Fauset Collection"). Ira E. Harrison, "The Association of Black Anthropologists: A Brief History," *Anthropology Today*, 3, no. 1 (February 1987): 17–21.

65. Fauset, *Black Gods of the Metropolis*.

66. For example, Raymond Julius Jones's 1939 study of thirteen black religious cults focused almost exclusively on Apostolic, Pentecostal Assembly, and other Christian Holiness and Pentecostal churches in Washington, D.C. Jones and his work were the product of the Social Sciences Division at Howard University. See Raymond Julius Jones, *A Comparative Study of Religious Cult Behavior among Negroes, with Special Reference to Emotional Group Conditioning Factors* (Washington, D.C.: Howard University, 1939).

67. Fauset, *Black Gods of the Metropolis*, p. 76.

68. Melville Herskovits, *The Myth of the Negro Past* (New York: Harper, 1941), p. 207.

69. Fauset, *Black Gods of the Metropolis*, pp. 108–109.

70. A provocative intervention in this debate is Michael Gomez, *Exchanging Our Country Marks: The Transformation of African Identities in the Colonial and Antebellum South* (Chapel Hill: University of North Carolina Press, 1998).

71. The reviewers quoted are Everett C. Hughes, in *American Journal of Sociology*, 50, no. 2 (September 1944): 159–160; Eva B. Dykes, in *Journal of Negro History*, 29, no. 3 (July 1944): 381–383; and William O. Brown, in *American Sociological Review*, 10, no. 2 (April 1945): 332–333.

72. Fauset, *Black Gods of the Metropolis*, p. 109.

73. Fauset, "Father Divine—Sour Grapes?" *Philadelphia Tribune*, September 27, 1939, Fauset Collection.

74. Oliver C. Cox, *Caste, Class, and Race: A Study in Social Dynamics* (New York: Doubleday, 1948; rpt. 1970), p. 572, note 81.

75. Fauset, "God and Politics," *Philadelphia Tribune*, June 22, 1939, Fauset Collection.

76. Arthur Huff Fauset, "The Church Responds," *Philadelphia Tribune*, May 22, 1941, Fauset Collection.

77. E. Franklin Frazier, *Black Bourgeoisie* (New York: Free Press, 1957). Frazier's original lectures are not available at the University of Liverpool where they were delivered, but he seems to have made few changes other than obvious comments on contemporary events between the 1953 lectures and the version that was published more than ten years later.

78. E. Franklin Frazier, *The Negro Church in America* (New York: Schocken, 1974; orig. pub. 1963), pp. 7–8.

79. Ibid., pp. 9, 14, 19, 48–49.

80. Ibid., pp. 46–47.

81. Ibid., pp. 19, 56, 58, 60–71, 79.

82. Ibid., pp. 75.

83. Ibid., p. 90.

84. Du Bois, "Gandhi and the American Negroes," *Gandhi Marg* (Bombay, July 1957), reprinted in Du Bois, *Writings by W. E. B. Du Bois in Periodicals Edited by Others*, ed. Herbert Aptheker (Millwood, N.Y.: Kraus-Thomson Organization, 1982), pp. 286–288. Du Bois, "Crusader without Violence," *National Guardian*, November 9, 1959, a review of L. D. Reddick, *Crusader without Violence: A Biography of Martin Luther King, Jr.* (New York: Harper, 1959).

85. St. Clair Drake, Introduction to Johnson, *Growing Up in the Black Belt*, pp. xvii.

86. St. Clair Drake, Introduction to Frazier, *Negro Youth at the Crossways*, p. xvi.

87. Powdermaker, *Stranger and Friend*, pp. 199–200.

88. Ibid., pp. 200–201.

89. Gunnar Myrdal, *Against the Stream: Critical Essays on Economics* (New York: Pantheon, 1972), pp. 299–300. According to Walter Jackson, "Myrdal underestimated the church as a source of political leadership and he did not grasp the extent to which it gave coherence and meaning to the Afro-American community." Jackson, *Gunnar Myrdal and America's Conscience*, p. xx.

90. Drake and Cayton, *Black Metropolis: An Appendix* (New York: Harper and Row, 1962), pp. xlii, xliii, lix.

91. Fauset, *Black Gods of the Metropolis*, p. xi.

92. Ibid., p. v.

93. Hurston, *The Sanctified Church*, p. 91. Sigmund Freud, *The Future of an Illusion* (New York: Norton, 1961; orig. pub. 1927). Emile Durkheim, *The Elementary Forms of Religious Life*, trans. and introd. Karen Fields (New York: Free Press, 1995; orig. pub. 1912). Max Weber, *The Sociology of Religion* (Boston: Beacon Press, 1993; orig. pub. 1922). Karl Marx, *Marx on Religion*, ed. John Raines (Philadelphia: Temple University Press, 2002). Fritz Ringer, *Max Weber: An Intellectual Biography* (Chicago: University of Chicago Press, 2004).

Disputes about sociologists' failure to escape the racial confines of the discipline have raged within the profession. For examples, see James B. McKee, *Sociology and the Race Problem: The Failure of a Perspective* (Urbana: University of Illinois Press, 1993). For recent debates about the place of race in American sociology, see Craig Calhoun, ed., *Sociology in America: A History* (Chicago: University of Chicago Press, 2007)—especially, within that volume, Aldon D. Morris, "Sociology of Race and W. E. B. Du Bois: The Path Not Taken," pp. 503–534; and Howard Winant, "The Dark Side of the Force: One Hundred Years of the Sociology of Race," pp. 535–571. On anthropology's encounter with race, see Lee D. Baker, *From Savage to Negro: Anthropology and the Construction of Race, 1896–1954* (Berkeley: University of California Press, 1998). An excellent work of social science history is Theda Skocpol, Ariane Liazos, and Marshall Ganz, *What a Mighty Power We Can Be: African American Fraternal Groups and the Struggle for Racial Equality* (Princeton, N.J.: Princeton University Press, 2006).

94. Claude Clegg III, *An Original Man: The Life and Times of Elijah*

Muhammad (New York: St. Martin's, 1997). C. Eric Lincoln, *The Black Muslims in America* (Boston: Beacon Press, 1961). Edward E. Curtis IV, *Black Muslim Religion in the Nation of Islam* (Chapel Hill: University of North Carolina Press, 2006). Malcolm X, *The Autobiography of Malcolm X* (New York: Grove Press, 1965).

3. In Pursuit of Pentecost

1. "Dr. Mary Bethune Left Own Epitaph," *Daytona Beach Evening News*, July 18, 1955. "Dr. Bethune Sensed Death Months Ago; Planned Rites," *Pittsburgh Courier*, June 4, 1955.

2. Rackham Holt, *Mary McLeod Bethune: A Biography* (New York: Doubleday, 1964), p. 7. For comprehensive treatments of Bethune's life and her professional careers, see the excellent introductions to the microfilm collections of her writings and records prepared by Elaine M. Smith: "Introduction," Mary McLeod Bethune Papers: The Bethune Foundation Collection, Part 1: Writings, Diaries, Scrapbooks, Biographical Materials, and Files on the National Youth Administration and Women's Organizations, 1918–1955; "Introduction," Mary McLeod Bethune Papers: The Bethune Foundation Collection, Part 2: Correspondence Files, 1914–1955; "Introduction," Mary McLeod Bethune Papers: The Bethune Foundation Collection, Part 3: Subject Files, 1939–1955. The Bethune Foundation is located in Daytona Beach, Florida. See also Elaine M. Smith, "Mary McLeod Bethune's Last Will and Testament: A Legacy of Race Vindication," *Journal of Negro History*, 81, nos. 1–4 (Winter 1966): 105–122.

3. Joyce A. Hanson, *Mary McLeod Bethune and Black Women's Political Activism* (Columbia: University of Missouri Press, 2003), pp. 4, 25–27.

4. Holt, *Mary McLeod Bethune*, p. 1. Hanson, *Mary McLeod Bethune*, pp. 31–32, 36–41.

5. Hanson, *Mary McLeod Bethune*, pp. 36–43. For more on Bethune's early life and her motivations for service, see Audrey Thomas McCluskey and Elaine Smith, eds., *Mary McLeod Bethune: Building a Better World* (Bloomington: Indiana University Press, 1999).

6. Hanson, *Mary McLeod Bethune*, pp. 31–32, 36–41. Clarence G. Newsome, "Mary McLeod Bethune and the Methodist Episcopal Church North: In But Out," in Judith Weisenfeld and Richard Newman, eds., *This Far by Faith: Readings in African American Women's Religious Biography* (New York: Routledge, 1996), p. 127.

7. Hanson, *Mary McLeod Bethune*, pp. 46–49. Newsome, "Mary McLeod Bethune," p. 127–128.

8. Hanson, *Mary McLeod Bethune*, pp. 52–53.

9. Anthea Butler, *Women in the Church of God in Christ: Making a Sanctified World* (Chapel Hill: University of North Carolina, 2007), p. 110.

10. Ibid., pp. 76, 60, 64–65. Mary McLeod Bethune, "A Philosophy of Education for Negro Girls," n.d. [1935], microfilm, Mary McLeod Bethune Papers, 1923–1942, Amistad Research Center, New Orleans, Louisiana.

11. Hanson, *Mary McLeod Bethune*, p. 83. Newsome, "Mary McLeod Bethune," p. 129.

12. Hanson, *Mary McLeod Bethune*, p. 83. Holt, *Mary McLeod Bethune*, 85.

13. Hanson, *Mary McLeod Bethune*, pp. 76, 81–83.

14. Holt, *Mary McLeod Bethune*, p. 156. Newsome, "Mary McLeod Bethune," p. 129–130.

15. Peter C. Murray, *Methodists and the Crucible of Race, 1930–1975* (Columbia: University of Missouri Press, 2004), pp. 31–33, 35–39.

16. Ibid., pp. 40–43. Newsome, "Mary McLeod Bethune," pp. 132–133.

17. Bethune, "Christian Education and the Growth of a Race," n.d., microfilm, Bethune Papers, 1923–1942.

18. Bethune, "Letter to Harry Wright McPherson," November 26, 1938, in McCluskey and Smith, eds., *Mary McLeod Bethune: Building a Better World*, pp. 118–119. McPherson was a member of the board of trustees of Bethune-Cookman College.

19. Ibid.

20. Ibid., p. 6.

21. Bethune, "A Century of Progress of Negro Women," n.d., microfilm, Bethune Papers, 1923–1942.

22. Bethune, "The Progress of Negro Women," address to the Chicago Women's Federation, June 1933, reprinted as "The Sacrifices and Achievements of African-American Women," *Journal of Blacks in Higher Education* (Summer 2001): 35.

23. Bethune, "A Century of Progress of Negro Women," n.d., microfilm, Bethune Papers, 1923–1942.

24. Ibid. Letter to Bethune from A. Clayton Powell Sr., Abyssinian Baptist Church and Community House, New York, June 6, 1935, microfilm, Bethune Papers, 1923–1942.

25. Edward Lawson, "Straight from the Capital," Associated Negro Press, January 23, 1937, microfilm, Bethune Papers, 1923–1942.

26. McCluskey and Smith, eds., *Mary McLeod Bethune: Building a Better World*, p. 14.

27. Elmer Anderson Carter, "A Modern Matriarch," *Christian Advocate*, February 4, 1937, microfilm, Bethune Papers, 1923–1942.

28. Holt, *Mary McLeod Bethune*, pp. 205.

29. Bethune Remarks, Minutes, Founding Meeting of the NCNW, New York City, December 5, 1935. Papers NCNW, Bethune Museum, Archives, Washington, D.C.

30. Deborah Gray White, *Too Heavy a Load: Black Women in Defense of Themselves, 1894–1994* (New York: Norton, 1999), pp. 157–158. Butler, *Women in the Church of God in Christ*, p. xxx.

31. Bethune, "The Negro in Retrospect and Prospect," *Journal of Negro History*, 35, no. 1 (January 1950): 11. For a history of the controversy around the publication, see Kenneth R. Janken, *Rayford W. Logan and the Dilemma of the African-American Intellectual* (Amherst: University of Massachusetts Press, 1993).

32. Bethune, "Viewing the Facts Objectively," in Rayford Logan, ed., *What the Negro Wants* (Chapel Hill: University of North Carolina Press, 1944), pp. 248–258.

33. Ibid., pp. 251, 252, 255. "Petition to the Committee on Interracial

Relations of the Women's Missionary Council of the ME Church South," microfilm, Bethune Papers, 1923–1942.

34. Logan, *What the Negro Wants*, pp. 256, 258.

35. Bethune, "To the Officers and Members of the National Council of Negro Women," 13th Annual Convention, NCNW, October 1948; and "Farewell Address," NCNW, November 1949. Both in records of the NCNW, Series 2, Bethune Museum and Archives, Washington, D.C.

36. Ibid. Rebecca Stiles Taylor, "Women Present New Magazine: *Women United*," *Chicago Defender*, May 7, 1949. Bethune continued to advocate for an interfaith, interracial, international women's organization and, in 1952, organized a conference in Daytona Beach to urge just that. Bethune, "A Serious Call to Women of Valor," address, April 4, 1952; and Program, "1952 Women's Leadership Conference, Bethune-Cookman College, April 4–6, 1952. The idea of converting the NCNW into an organization for women without regard to race lived on even after Bethune's death. In 1957, an unsigned editorial in the *Chicago Defender* urged the group to "widen its scope so as to become international in outlook and interracial in composition" by dropping the word "Negro" from its name. The writer argued that "we cannot ask for democracy on the one hand and practice voluntary segregation on the other," or resist integration. Editorial, "The National Council of Negro Women," *Chicago Defender*, March 30, 1957.

37. Bethune, "Would Close Negro Schools for Democratic Education in the South," *Chicago Defender*, February 19, 1949.

38. Edwin Embree, quoted in Bethune, "Integration Is a Two-Way Street," *Chicago Defender*, April 8, 1950.

39. Bethune, "World-Wide Surge for Freedom Marks Last of Twentieth Century," *Chicago Defender*, July 11, 1953.

40. Ibid. See also Bethune, "A Great People Hears Its Conscience Speak; Realizes Segregation Not Decent," *Chicago Defender*, October 16, 1954. Idem, address, "Full Integration—America's Newest Challenge," Detroit, June 11, 1954. Microfilm, Bethune Papers, Part 3.

41. Bethune, "Warns against Violence or Hesitation at Integration," *Chicago Defender*, October 21, 1954.

42. Valerie Boyd, *Wrapped in Rainbows: The Life of Zora Neale Hurston* (New York: Scribner, 2003), pp. 423–425. Robert E. Hemenway, *Zora Neale Hurston: A Literary Biography* (Urbana: University of Illinois Press, 1980; orig. pub. 1977), p. 345, 336. Carla Kaplan, ed., *Zora Neale Hurston: A Life in Letters* (New York: Doubleday, 2002), pp. 591–592, 611–612, 738–740.

43. Ibid. Boyd, *Wrapped in Rainbows*, p. 425.

44. Bethune, "The Supreme Court Decision Imposes New Responsibility on Negro Press," *Chicago Defender*, July 17, 1954; and idem, "The Negro Press Accepts the Challenge of a New Period," *Chicago Defender*, July 10, 1954. For more on Bethune's relationship to the black press, see McCluskey, "Representing the Race: Mary McLeod Bethune and the Press in the Jim Crow Era," *Western Journal of Black Studies*, 23, no. 4 (Winter 1999): 236–245.

45. Bethune, "My Faith and My Job," Press release prepared for *Church Woman*, May 1954, microfilm, Bethune Papers, Part 1.

46. Bethune, Address, Red Cross Workers Training Session, American University, July 7, 1945, microfilm, Bethune Papers, Part 2.

47. Bethune, "Press Idea: Pentecost—Our Christian Heritage," microfilm, Bethune Papers, Part 1.

48. Holt, *Mary McLeod Bethune*, pp. 255–259.

49. Bethune, "Public Address, Montreal, Quebec," June 20, 1946, microfilm, Bethune Papers, Part 1. Idem, "Statement by Mary McLeod Bethune, Sesquicentennial Celebration of the A.M.E. Zion Church," Madison Square Garden, September 21, 1946. Both microfilm, Bethune Papers, Part 1.

50. Bethune, "Tribute to Mahatma Gandhi," Washington, D.C., February 11, 1948, microfilm Bethune Papers, Part 1.

51. Bethune, "The Negro in Retrospect and Prospect," *Journal of Negro History*, 35, no. 1 (January 1950): 14–15.

52. Ibid., p. 16.

53. Ibid., p. 13.

54. Holt, *Mary McLeod Bethune*, pp. 259–263. "Mrs. Bethune Highly Honored in Haiti," Negro Newspaper Publishers release, July 25, 1949, microfilm, Claude Barnett Papers, Series G.

55. Accounts of Buchman and MRA have been written largely either by devoted adherents or by vociferous critics, rarely with scholarly balance. Garth Lean, *Frank Buchman: A Life* (London: Constable, 1985). Peter Howard, *The World Rebuilt: The True Story of Frank Buchman and the Achievements of Moral Re-Armament* (New York: Duell, Sloan and Pearce, 1951). Tom Driberg, *The Mystery of Moral Re-Armament: A Study of Frank Buchman and His Movement* (London: Secker and Warburg, 1964). Paul Campbell, *Remaking Men* (New York: Arrowhead Books, 1954). Frank Buchman, *Remaking the World* (New York: R. M. McBride, 1949). Walter Clark, *The Oxford Group: Its History and Significance* (New York: Bookman Associates, 1951). More recent scholarship argues for the influence of MRA on the founders of Alcoholics Anonymous and Amnesty International. David R. Rudy and Arthur L. Grell, "Is Alcoholics Anonymous a Religious Organization? Meditations on Marginality," *Sociological Analysis*, 50, no. 1 (Spring 1989): 41–51. Tom Buchanan, "'The Truth Will Set You Free': The Making of Amnesty International," *Journal of Contemporary History*, 37, no. 4 (October 2002): 575–597. For an example of a white American attracted to MRA's claims of racial egalitarianism, see Tony Badger, "Southerners Who Refused to Sign the Southern Manifesto," *Historical Journal*, 42, no. 2 (June 1999): 517–534. Little if any scholarly attention has been paid to the MRA's aggressive outreach to African Americans.

56. Edward L. Queen II, Stephen Prothero, and Gardiner Shattuck Jr., eds., *The Encyclopedia of American Religious History* (New York: Facts on File, 1996), pp. 84–85.

57. Bethune, "Hope of Africa Not in Revolution, But a New Dimension Free From Hate," *Chicago Defender*, April 3, 1954. Idem, "Moral Re-Armament Movement Heavily Felt in Africa," *Chicago Defender*, April 24, 1954.

58. Vivian Mason, president of the National Council of Negro Women, to Bethune, August 3, 1954, microfilm, Bethune Papers, Part 2. Bethune, "Sees Moral Re-Armament as Means of World Salvation," *Chicago Defender*, August 7, 1954. Idem, "Tells Spiritual Basis for Good Human Relations," *Chicago Defender*, September 25, 1954.

59. "Dr. Bethune Finds Atmosphere for World Peace at Moral Re-Armament Assembly," *Afro-American,* July 31, 1954. "Mary M. Bethune Lauds MRA at Caux," *Pittsburgh Courier,* July 31, 1954. Other African Americans in attendance included educators Dr. J. M. Ellison, president of Virginia Union University, and Dr. Stephen Wright, president of West Virginia State College. Bethune, "Religious News of the World," transcript of radio interview with Dr. Glenn Murdock, WMFJ, Daytona Beach, Florida, August 13, 1954, pp. 1, 4, 7, microfilm, Bethune Papers, Part 3. For more on the MRA and the controversies concerning its work in Kenya during the time of the 1950s Mau Mau movements, see Caroline Elkins, "The Struggle for Mau Mau Rehabilitation in Late Colonial Kenya," *International Journal of African Historical Studies,* 33, no. 1 (2000): 25–57. Idem, *Imperial Reckoning: The Untold Story of Britain's Gulag in Kenya* (New York: Holt, 2006).

60. McCluskey and Smith, *Mary McLeod Bethune,* pp. 57, 51.

61. Bethune to Dean M. S. Maize, Florida A&M University, January 12, 1955. Bethune expressed similar sentiments in a letter to Edward P. Jackson, Columbus, Ohio, January 18, 1955. Both microfilm, Bethune Papers, Part 2.

62. Bethune to Barnett, September 26, 1954, microfilm, Barnett Papers, Series G. "Conversion and Skepticism," *Chicago Defender,* January 15, 1955.

63. Bethune, "Transcript of Remarks," Dellwood, Mt. Kisco, New York, July 30, 1954, Moral Re-Armament Papers, Library of Congress (hereafter referred to as "MRA Papers").

64. Bethune, Remarks, Mt. Kisco, New York, July 30, 1954, MRA Papers. Bethune to Ethel Mae Brown, Summerton, S.C., January 31, 1955. Microfilm, Bethune Papers, Part 2. Bethune, "Courageous Leadership Is Greatest Need of Our Time," *Chicago Defender,* October 30, 1954.

65. Bethune to Charles S. Johnson, January 24, 1955; and Charles S. Johnson to Bethune, April 12, 1955. Both microfilm, Bethune Papers, Part 2. Horace M. Bond to Dr. Frank Buchman, August 25, 1955; and Bond to the Nobel Committee, January 25, 1956; both in MRA Papers. Buchman had his eyes on a bigger prize; he expressed an interest in buying

Storer College in Harper's Ferry, West Virginia, a black college which had been established after the Civil War but which was a casualty of the decision to integrate higher education in that state after the *Brown* decision. Storer was later acquired by the federal government as part of the National Park Service site at Harpers Ferry. MRA Papers. For more on Storer, see Vivian Verdell Gordon, "A History of Storer College, Harpers Ferry, West Virginia," *Journal of Negro Education*, 30, no. 4 (Autumn 1961): 445–449.

66. "Tempest in the Hennery," *Chicago Defender*, October 15, 1955. "NACWC Award to Dr. Buchman," *Chicago Defender*, August 16, 1958. "Global Jaunts Climax 32nd NACWC Convention," *Chicago Defender*, September 17, 1960. In 1940, the Pullman Porters had hosted MRA lectures at one of its annual conventions. Buchman, "Moral Re-Armament in Our National Government," and William Rowell, "Moral Re-Armament in the Labor Movement," Program, "The Sixth Annual Convention of the Pullman Porters and Maids Protective Association," August 13–15, 1940, MRA Papers. For an excellent treatment of the religious thinking of A. Philip Randolph, the Pullman Porters' leader, see Cynthia Taylor, *A. Philip Randolph: The Religious Journey of an African American Labor Leader* (New York: New York University Press, 2006).

67. "Laud Meeting of Mrs. Bates, Faubus," *Chicago Defender*, January 2, 1960. "Credits MRA for Meet with Faubus," *Chicago Defender*, January 23, 1960. Vivian C. Mason to Ray Foote Purdy, Moral Re-Armament, March 27, 1956, MRA Papers. Irene Gaines, President, National Association of Colored Women's Clubs, to Mr. and Mrs. Alex Drysdale (regarding invitation to Frank Buchman), June 16, 1956, MRA Papers. Adrienne Lash Jones, *Jane Edna Hunter: A Case Study of Black Leadership, 1910–1950* (Brooklyn, N.Y.: Carlson Publishing, 1990): 143–144. Hunter also expressed her support for Moral Re-Armament in a letter to Bethune in which she referred to the movement as a "spiritual basis on which we must depend for future peace of the peoples of the world." Hunter to Bethune, April 3, 1952, microfilm, Bethune Papers, Part 1.

68. Bethune, "Don't Miss the Foot-Hold! Women and the Civil Rights Report, 1947," in McCluskey and Smith, *Mary McLeod Bethune*, p. 191.

Bethune was an honorary member of Hadassah, a Jewish women's service organization.

69. Bethune, "Spiritual Autobiography, 1946," in McCluskey and Smith, *Mary McLeod Bethune*, pp. 54–55. Bethune, "Writer Says Church Long Overdue in Taking Part in Discrimination Fight," *Chicago Defender*, December 12, 1953. Bethune struggled to find the right word to encompass such interfaith work, explaining that she used the word "church" in a universal sense as a stand-in for all groups who believed in the "divinity of the human spirit."

70. Howard Thurman to Bethune, October 9, 1947. Bethune to Howard Thurman, April 29, 1949. Bethune to Sue Thurman, December 7, 1950. Howard Thurman to Bethune, February 24, 1951. Bethune to Howard Thurman, March 2, 1951. Bethune to Dr. and Mrs. Thurman, April 30, 1951. Bethune to Sue Thurman, December 3, 1952. Bethune to Howard Thurman, April 20, 1953. Bethune to Dr. and Mrs. Thurman, February 17, 1954. Bethune to Howard Thurman, January 18, 1955. All microfilm, Bethune Papers, Part 2. Howard Thurman was the author of more than twenty books including *Jesus and the Disinherited* (New York: Abingdon-Cokesbury Press, 1949), and *With Head and Heart: The Autobiography of Howard Thurman* (New York: Harcourt Brace Jovanovich, 1979). For more on Thurman and his writings, see Dennis Dickerson, "African American Religious Intellectuals and the Theological Foundations of the Civil Rights Movement, 1930–1955," *Church History* (June 2005): 222–226. Walter Earl Fluker and Catherine Tumber, eds., *A Strange Freedom: The Best of Howard Thurman on Religious Experience and Public Life* (Boston: Beacon Press, 1998).

71. Bethune, "Religious Emphasis Week," address at Bethune-Cookman College, March 1955. Similar statements can be found elsewhere. Bethune, "How God Has Helped Me," *Adult Student*, n.d. Bethune, "Spiritual Re-Armament," address to the Narcissus Literary Club, March 20, 1955, microfilm, Bethune Papers, Part 1. Bethune to Howard Thurman, May 12, 1955, microfilm, Bethune Papers, Part 2 (referring to her desire to establish a Meditation Center at Bethune-Cookman).

72. Bethune, "Frank Buchman, Front Line Leader for World Peace,

Unity," *Chicago Defender*, April 30, 1955. Bethune had devoted two earlier columns that year to MRA: "Women Come Courageously to Rescue of Tensioned World," *Chicago Defender*, January 29, 1955; and "Brotherhood and Race Relations: The Great Duo of Human Rights," *Chicago Defender*, February 26, 1955.

73. Bethune, "The Basis of Human Purpose," n.d. Idem, "My Philosophy of Christianity," May 12, 1955. Idem, "What I Believe about Jesus Christ." Bethune, "Brotherhood and Race Relations: The Great Duo of Human Rights." All microfilm, Bethune Papers, Part 1.

74. Bethune to Charlotte Hawkins Brown, March 7, 1952. Bethune to Brown, February 12, 1955. Bethune, "Statement of Faith," n.d., microfilm, Bethune Papers, Part 2.

75. Bethune, "Statement of Faith."

76. Bethune, "Negro Needs the Equality of the Unrestricted Ballot," *Chicago Defender*, April 23, 1955. Newsome, "Mary McLeod Bethune and the Methodist Episcopal Church North," p. 137.

77. MRA Report, Bethune Memorial, Mackinac Island, Michigan, May 21, 1955. "'Moral Re-Armament' Words on Her Tomb," *New York Amsterdam News*, November 26, 1960. "Muriel Smith Heads the 31-Nation Cast in Atlanta's Moral Musical," *Chicago Defender*, February 12, 1958. "MRA Film Draws Stars, SRO Crowd," *New York World-Telegram and Sun*, n.d. Irene Thirer, "*Crowning Experience* at Warner," *New York Post*, October 24, 1960. Howard Thompson, "Screen: *Crowning Experience* Opens at Warner," *New York Times*, October 24, 1960. Rose Pelswick, "*The Crowning Experience* a Beautiful Film for Today's Ills," *Journal American*, n.d. The film ran for seven weeks at the Warner Theater on Broadway and the Fox Wilshire Theater in Hollywood; it was also shown in London, Australia, the Caribbean, Finland, France, West Germany, South Africa, Switzerland, India, Kenya, Liberia, Holland, Denmark, Ceylon, Canada, and Brazil. MRA Papers. "Hail Film Inspired by Dr. Bethune's Life," *Chicago Defender*, November 5, 1960. James W. Hardiman, ed., *The Crowning Experience Technicolor Book of the Film* (New York: Random House, 1960).

Bethune's son Albert in 1958 signed over to MRA all rights "to use the life story of Mary McLeod Bethune in any way that will serve their purpose of delivering the message to the millions all over the world." MRA later provided funds to support his travel and efforts to publicize the film. Buchman to Albert Bethune Jr., December 9, 1959, MRA Papers (explaining these legal arrangements and attaching a copy of the agreement that his father, Albert Sr., had signed).

MRA relied on plays, spectacles, and eventually film to advance its message. See Richard H. Palmer, "Moral Re-Armament Drama: Right Wing Theatre in America," *Theatre Journal*, 31, no. 2 (May 1979): 172–185. In the 1960s, MRA sponsored "Up with People," a traveling group of young singers who performed patriotic and inspirational music. MRA Papers.

78. "Mary McLeod Bethune, 1875–1955, Funeral Services." "Our Opinions: Mrs. Mary McLeod Bethune," *Chicago Defender*, May 28, 1955. "Mrs. Bethune's Death Marks Changing Negro Leadership," *Christian Century*, June 5, 1955. "Dr. Bethune Sensed Death Months Ago; Planned Rites," *Pittsburgh Courier*, June 4, 1955. Bethune Papers, Part 3. Microfilm, Schomburg Clipping File, "Bethune."

79. Bethune, Address, "We March Forward to Brotherhood," Brotherhood Program, University of Miami, February 14, 1950. Microfilm, Bethune Papers, Part 1.

4. The Advent to Civil Rights

1. Gordon Hancock to Nannie Burroughs, March 17, 1961, Burroughs Papers, Manuscripts and Archives, Library of Congress (hereafter cited as "Burroughs Papers"). For more on Hancock, see Raymond Gavins, *Perils and Prospects of Southern Leadership: Gordon Blaine Hancock, 1884–1970* (Durham, N.C.: Duke University Press, 1977).

2. Earl L. Harrison, *The Dream and the Dreamer* (Washington, D.C.: Nannie H. Burroughs Literature Foundation, 1956; rpt. 1972), p. 10.

3. For the definitive account of the founding and early development of the Woman's Convention and of Burroughs' role in it, see Evelyn Brooks Higginbotham, *Righteous Discontent: The Women's Movement in the*

Black Baptist Church, 1880–1920 (Cambridge, Mass.: Harvard University Press, 1993).

4. Sharon Harley, "Nannie Helen Burroughs: 'The Black Goddess of Liberty,'" *Journal of Negro History,* 81 (Winter–Autumn 1996): 62–71. Traki Taylor, "'Womanhood Glorified': Nannie Helen Burroughs and the National Training School for Women and Girls, Inc., 1909–1961," *Journal of Negro History,* 87 (Autumn 2002): 390–402. Opal Easter, *Nannie Helen Burroughs* (New York: Garland, 1995). Karen A. Johnson, *Uplifting the Women and the Race: The Lives, Educational Philosophies, and Social Activism of Anna Julia Cooper and Nannie Helen Burroughs* (New York: Garland, 2000).

5. "Venal Leaders Discredit Race by Offering Spurious Advice," *Philadelphia Tribune,* October 27, 1932. Anonymous, "Not Guilty," *Washington Tribune,* November 25, 1932. Nannie Burroughs, "Writer Asks How Dems Election Will Affect Negro," *Pittsburgh Courier,* December 3, 1932. "Leaders or Followers," *Pittsburgh Courier,* December 10, 1932. Burroughs Papers.

6. "Important Pieces of Work to Which We Should Give Our United Support," in *Twenty-Second Annual Report, Woman's Convention, Auxiliary to the National Baptist Convention,* Los Angeles, California, September 6–12, 1922, pp. 17, 20. "Men and Movements that Effect [sic] Race Life," in *Thirtieth Annual Report of the Woman's Convention Auxiliary, National Baptist Convention, Miss Nannie H. Burroughs, Corresponding Secretary,* Chicago, Illinois, August 14–25, 1930, pp. 14–15. Burroughs Papers.

7. "Work for Voters To Do," in *Twenty-Third Annual Report of the Executive Board and Corresponding Secretary of the Woman's Convention, Auxiliary to the National Baptist Convention,* Los Angeles, California, September 5–10, 1923, p. 27. "Negro Women in Politics," in *Twenty-Fourth Annual Report of the Executive Board and Corresponding Secretary of the Woman's Convention, Auxiliary to the National Baptist Convention,* Nashville, Tennessee, September 10–15, 1924, pp. 20–22. Burroughs Papers.

8. Burroughs, "Miss Burroughs Plans a 'New Deal' To Conserve Girlhood of the Race," *Pittsburgh Courier,* August 26, 1933.

9. Burroughs, "Says Manhood, Patriotism, Religion Going Out of Style among Negroes," *Pittsburgh Courier*, March 12, 1932.

10. Ibid.

11. *Thirtieth Annual Report of the Woman's Convention, Auxiliary National Baptist Convention, Miss Nannie H. Burroughs, Corresponding Secretary*, Chicago, Illinois, August 14–25, 1930, pp. 15–17; and "Unemployment," p. 17. Burroughs Papers.

12. *Annual Report of the Corresponding Secretary of the Woman's Convention Auxiliary to the National Baptist Convention*, Memphis, Tennessee, September 5–10, 1933, pp. 20–21, Burroughs Papers.

13. *Annual Report of Miss Nannie H. Burroughs, Corresponding Secretary of the Woman's Convention, Auxiliary to the National Baptist Convention*, Oklahoma City, Oklahoma, September 5–9, 1934, pp. 18–19. *Annual Report of the Corresponding Secretary of Woman's Convention, Auxiliary to the National Baptist Convention*, Memphis, Tennessee, September 5–10, 1933, pp. 20–21. Burroughs Papers.

14. *Annual Report of Miss Nannie H. Burroughs, Corresponding Secretary of the Woman's Convention, Auxiliary to the National Baptist Convention*, Oklahoma City, September 5–9, 1934, p. 20. *Annual Report of the Corresponding Secretary of Woman's Convention, Auxiliary to the National Baptist Convention*, Memphis, Tennessee, September 5–10, 1933, pp. 20–21. Burroughs Papers.

15. "National Training School for Women and Girls," *National Baptist Voice*, February 18, 1928, pp. 1, 4, 13, 16, typed transcript, in file labeled "American Baptist Seminary," Papers of the Southern Baptist Historical Library and Archives.

16. "Annual Address by Mrs. S. W. Layten, President, Woman's Convention, Auxiliary National Baptist Convention, Inc., St. Louis, Missouri, September 7–12, 1938," pp. 7–8, Una Lawrence Papers, Southern Baptist Historical Library and Archive, Nashville, Tennessee (hereafter cited as "Lawrence Papers").

17. For more on internal debates, see "Resolutions," signed by Mrs. Brown, Ga., Mrs. M. H. Flowers, Tenn., Mrs. Lewis, D.C., Mrs. Viola T.

Hill, Fla., and Mrs. H. M. Gibbs, Ala. (conceding that the parent body could take this action on its own behalf but not on behalf of the Woman's Convention and reiterating support for Burroughs and her thirty-seven years of service to the convention and the school), Lawrence Papers.

18. John Lewis, *Walking with the Wing: A Memoir of the Movement* (New York: Harcourt, Brace, 1998), p. 53. Harrison, *The Dream and the Dreamer.* The school is now known as American Baptist College. For more on its history, see www.abcnash.edu/history.html.

19. Noble Y. Beall, Missionary, "Real Dangers of the American Baptist Negroes," Lawrence Papers. Thanks to Nick Salvatore for bringing this report to my attention.

20. Ibid.

21. Una Roberts Lawrence to Nannie Burroughs, October 1934, Burroughs Papers. Their letters often attested to the rarity and difficulty of interracial Christian work among women in this period. Their primary joint project was the publication of *The Worker,* a magazine for women who were active within churches. It contained instructional materials for Sunday schools and missionary societies, and was intended for both black and white. At one point, Lawrence complained to Burroughs that there was too much emphasis on race issues in a magazine intended for white women. Burroughs politely but very firmly disagreed. "I shall always try to be patient and tolerant, but on the other hand," she replied, "I shall have to speak the truth in kindness." Lawrence to Burroughs, June 19, 1935, and Burroughs to Lawrence, n.d., Burroughs Papers. For more on the relationships between black and white Baptists in the South, see Paul Harvey, *Redeeming the South: Religious Cultures and Racial Identities among Southern Baptists, 1865–1925* (Chapel Hill: University of North Carolina Press, 1997).

22. Nannie Burroughs to Una Lawrence, September 22, 1937, Lawrence Papers.

23. Ibid. Also Burroughs to Lawrence, June 10, 1936, Lawrence Papers.

24. Burroughs, "Press Release and Statement," National Baptist Convention, St. Louis, Missouri, September 8, 1938, Lawrence Papers.

25. Ibid.

26. Reverend W. H. Jernagin to Una Lawrence, July 23, 1938, Lawrence Papers.

27. Ibid.

28. William Pickens, "Pickens Says She's Bigger than 'A Baptist Member,'" *Pittsburgh Courier*, October 22, 1938, NAACP Papers, Library of Congress (hereafter cited as "NAACP Papers").

29. Russell Conwell Barbour, "N.A.A.C.P. Leader Insults Baptist Leaders: Three Million Baptists Resent Such Policy; Will Have Nothing To Do with Organization," *National Baptist Voice*, November 12, 1938, Burroughs Papers.

30. Walter White to Rev. J. C. Austin, December 3, 1938, with copies to Mordecai Johnson, William Haynes, J. Raymond Henderson, NAACP Papers.

31. See Burroughs to Walter White, December 9, 1938, NAACP Papers.

32. Lawrence to Burroughs, March 13, 1947, Lawrence Papers.

33. Nannie Burroughs to Rev. Russell C. Barbour, September 28, 1942, Burroughs Papers.

34. Nannie Burroughs to Rev. Noble Y. Beall, August 20, 1940, Burroughs Papers.

35. *Annual Report of Miss Nannie H. Burroughs, Corresponding Secretary of the Woman's Convention, Auxiliary to the National Baptist Convention*, Memphis, Tennessee, September 10, 1942, p. 15, Burroughs Papers.

36. *Annual Report of Miss Nannie H. Burroughs, Corresponding Secretary of the Woman's Convention, Auxiliary to the National Baptist Convention*, Birmingham, Alabama, September 4–8, 1940, pp. 14, 19. *Annual Report of Miss Nannie H. Burroughs, Corresponding Secretary of the Woman's Convention, Auxiliary to the National Baptist Convention*, Cleveland, Ohio, September 10–14, 1941, p. 16. *Annual Report of Miss Nannie H. Burroughs, Corresponding Secretary of the Woman's Convention, Auxiliary to the National Baptist Convention*, Memphis Tennessee, September 10, 1942, pp. 22–23. Burroughs Papers.

37. *Annual Report of Miss Nannie H. Burroughs, Corresponding Secre-*

tary of the Woman's Convention, Auxiliary to the National Baptist Convention, Memphis, Tennessee, September 10, 1942, pp. 22–23. *Annual Report of Miss Nannie Burroughs, Corresponding Secretary of the Woman's Convention, Auxiliary to the National Baptist Convention,* Cleveland, Ohio, September 10–14, 1941, pp. 16–17. Burroughs Papers.

38. *Annual Report of Miss Nannie H. Burroughs, Corresponding Secretary of the Woman's Convention Auxiliary to the National Baptist Convention,* Memphis, Tennessee, September 10, 1942, p. 17. Burroughs Papers.

39. *Annual Report of Miss Nannie H. Burroughs, Corresponding Secretary of the Woman's Convention, Auxiliary to the National Baptist Convention,* Memphis, Tennessee, September 10, 1942, pp. 16–17. *Annual Report of Miss Nannie H. Burroughs, Corresponding Secretary of the Woman's Convention, Auxiliary to the National Baptist Convention,* Atlanta, Georgia, September 4, 1946, p. 12. Burroughs Papers.

40. *Annual Address by Dr. Nannie H. Burroughs, President, Woman's Convention, Auxiliary National Baptist Convention, Inc.,* Los Angeles, California, September 8, 1949, pp. 6, 7, 15, 16, 17, Burroughs Papers.

41. *The Fifth Message of Miss Nannie H. Burroughs to the Woman's Convention to the National Baptist Convention USA, Inc.,* September 1953, pp. 26–27, Burroughs Papers.

42. *The Second Message of Miss Nannie H. Burroughs to the Woman's Convention to the National Baptist Convention USA, Inc.,* Philadelphia, Pennsylvania, September 7, 1950, pp. 11, 19, Burroughs Papers.

43. Thurgood Marshall to Burroughs, November 30, 1953, Burroughs Papers.

44. Marshall to Burroughs, August 27, 1954, Burroughs Papers.

45. Burroughs to Marshall, September 29, 1954, and Burroughs to Marshall, September 21, 1954, Burroughs Papers.

46. *The Sixth Message of Miss Nannie H. Burroughs to the Woman's Convention to the National Baptist Convention USA, Inc.,* September 9, 1954, pp. 22–23, Burroughs Papers.

47. Alberta King to Burroughs, April 24, 1944, and April 19, 1950, Burroughs Papers.

48. Nannie Burroughs to David V. Jemison, October 1, 1951, October

25, 1961, and December 31, 1951. Alberta King to Burroughs, October 31, 1951, and December 29, 1953. Burroughs Papers.

49. Alberta King to Burroughs, October 31, 1951, April 19, 1950, October 31, 1951, December 17, 1951, and March 2, 1952. Burroughs Papers.

50. Alberta King to Burroughs, August 21, 1954, and Burroughs to Martin Luther King Jr., September 21, 1954. Burroughs Papers. The outline of King's speech can be found in Martin Luther King Jr. Papers Project at Stanford University, www.stanford.edu/group/King.

51. *The Seventh Annual Message of Miss Nannie H. Burroughs to the Woman's Convention to the National Baptist Convention U.S.A., Inc.,* Memphis, Tennessee, September 8, 1955, p. 11, Burroughs Papers.

52. Ibid., pp. 12, 25.

53. Ibid., p. 14.

54. Alberta King to Burroughs, February 9, 1956, and Burroughs to Martin Luther King Sr., February 4, 1956. Burroughs Papers.

55. *The Eighth Annual Message of Miss Nannie H. Burroughs to the Woman's Convention to the National Baptist Convention U.S.A., Inc.,* Denver, Colorado, September 6, 1956, pp. 31–32. Idem, "Here Are My Predictions for 1957." Burroughs Papers.

56. Ibid.

57. Martin Luther King Jr. to Burroughs, February 7, 1956, and September 18, 1956. Burroughs Papers.

58. Telegram from Martin Luther King Jr. to Burroughs, November 12, 1956, and letter from Alberta King to Burroughs, November 20, 1956. Burroughs Papers.

59. Burroughs, "Twelve Things Whites Must Stop Doing," Burroughs Papers.

60. *The Tenth Annual Message of Miss Nannie H. Burroughs to the Woman's Convention to the National Baptist Convention U.S.A., Inc.,* Chicago, October 11, 1958, p. 8, Burroughs Papers.

61. Ibid., pp. 16, 26.

62. Ibid., p. 27.

63. *The Eleventh Annual Message of Miss Nannie H. Burroughs, Presi-*

dent of the Woman's Convention, U.S.A., Inc., San Francisco, California, September 9, 1959, p. 26, Burroughs Papers.

64. Mary McLeod Bethune, "Cite Progress in Washington as Example of Accomplishment," *Chicago Defender,* November 21, 1953.

65. Burroughs, "Three Basic Causes of the Present Race Crisis in America," September 9, 1959, Burroughs Papers.

66. Barbara Ransby, *Ella Baker and the Black Freedom Movement: A Radical Democratic Vision* (Chapel Hill: University of North Carolina Press, 2003), pp. 15, 17, 35, 45, 58, 59, 63.

67. Ibid., pp. 184, 185, 188, 193.

68. Burroughs, "We Must Fight Back, but . . . with What and How?" *Pittsburgh Courier,* May 30, 1959.

69. Burroughs to the Reverend Joseph Jackson, April 16, 1953, Burroughs Papers.

70. Wallace Best, "'The Right Achieved and the Wrong Way Conquered': J. H. Jackson, Martin Luther King, Jr., and the Conflict over Civil Rights," *Religion and American Culture: A Journal of Interpretation,* 16, no. 2 (2006): 201–202.

71. Alberta King to Burroughs, November 20, 1956, and August 19, 1957. Burroughs Papers.

72. Best, "The Right Achieved," pp. 201–205.

73. Ibid., p. 204.

74. Ibid. See www.nationalbaptist.com and www.pnbc.org.

75. "Nation Pays Tribute to Miss Burroughs," *Baltimore Afro-American,* May 27, 1961. "Dr. Burroughs Rites Set for Washington," *Pittsburgh Courier,* May 27, 1961, where she was referred to as "perhaps the most influential Negro churchwoman in the United States." Burroughs' death generated special attention to her work on behalf of black women. Robbie Robinson, "Hundreds Pay Respects to Dr. Burroughs," *Pittsburgh Courier,* June 3, 1961, which called her the "last of the great female pioneers" and cited her for her determination to free "her sisters" from "ignorance, dirt, immorality, slovenliness, and domination by men."

76. Martin Luther King Jr., "A Knock at Midnight," Associated Negro Press, May 8, 1963. A version of this sermon was first developed by

King in 1955 but was elaborated into a chapter by the same name in his book *Strength To Love* (New York: Harper and Row, 1963), pp. 56–66. Clayborne Carson, *The Autobiography of Martin Luther King, Jr.* (New York: Warner Books, 1998). Thomas F. Jackson, *From Civil Rights to Human Rights: Martin Luther King, Jr., and the Struggle for Economic Justice* (Philadelphia: University of Pennsylvania Press, 2007).

77. Mays, "Will We Do As Well?" *Pittsburgh Courier*, June 10, 1961.

78. Harrison, *The Dream and the Dreamer*, p. 44.

5. Southern Black Liberal Protestantism

1. Benjamin Mays, *Born to Rebel: An Autobiography* (Athens: University of Georgia Press, 1971), p. 264.

2. Religion is an understudied but very promising route for examining global orientations among African Americans including conceptions and constructions of diaspora. See, for example, R. Marie Griffith and Barbara Dianne Savage, eds., *Women and Religion in the African Diaspora: Knowledge, Power, and Performance* (Baltimore: Johns Hopkins University Press, 2006). James T. Campbell, *Songs of Zion: The African Methodist Episcopal Church in the United States and South* (New York: Oxford University Press, 1995). Scholars have given considerable attention to the global outlook of African American intellectuals and activists in the twentieth century, especially its embrace of Africa and anticolonialism. Robin D. G. Kelley, "'But a Local Phase of a World Problem': Black History's Global Vision, 1883–1950," *Journal of American History*, 86 (December 1999): 1045–1077. Brenda Gayle Plummer, *Rising Wind: Black Americans and U.S. Foreign Affairs, 1935–1960* (Chapel Hill: University of North Carolina Press, 1996). James H. Merriweather, *Proudly We Can Be Africans: Black Americans and Africa, 1935–1965* (Chapel Hill: University of North Carolina, 2002). Melani McAlister, *Epic Encounters: Culture, Media, and United States' Interests in the Middle East, 1945–2000* (Berkeley: University of California Press, 2001). Carol Anderson, *Eyes Off the Prize: The United Nations and the African American Struggle for Human Rights, 1944–1955* (New York: Cambridge University Press, 2003).

3. Mays, *Born to Rebel*, pp. 157–162, 165–167. Idem, "The Church Surveys World Problems," *The Crisis*, 44, no. 10 (October 1937): 299, 317. Idem, "World Churchmen Score Prejudice," *The Crisis*, 44, no. 11 (November 1937): 341.

4. Benjamin Mays, "The Color Line around the World," *Journal of Negro Education*, 6, no. 2 (April 1937): 134–143. Sudarshan Kapur, *Raising Up a Prophet: The African-American Encounter with Gandhi* (Boston: Beacon Press, 1992), pp. 3–8, 13, 26–27. On the theological and political significance that traveling to India has for African American religious intellectuals, see Dennis Dickerson, "African American Religious Intellectuals and the Theological Foundations of the Civil Rights Movement, 1930–55," *Church History*, 74, no. 2 (June 2005): 217–235.

5. Kapur, *Raising Up a Prophet*, pp. 81–82, 87–93, 95–97. Mays, *Born to Rebel*, pp. 155–156.

6. Mays, "The Eyes of the World Are upon America," *Missions*, 35, no. 2 (February 1944): 74–79.

7. Mays, "The Church Surveys World Problems," pp. 299, 316, 317. Idem, "World Churchmen Score Prejudice," p. 341.

8. Mays, "Amsterdam on the Church and Race Relations," *Religion in Life: A Christian Quarterly*, 9, no. 1 (Winter 1940): 102.

9. Mays, "The Church Surveys World Problems," p. 316.

10. Mays, "The American Negro and the Christian Religion," *Journal of Negro Education*, 8, no. 3 (July 1939): 532, 533.

11. Mays, "Christian Youth and Race," *The Crisis*, 46, no. 12 (December 1939): 365, 370. Idem, "The American Negro and the Christian Religion," p. 537.

12. Mays, "The American Negro and the Christian Religion," pp. 537–538.

13. See Commission on the Church and Minority Peoples, "Minutes," September 16, 1943. Accounts of individual meetings include: "Consultations on the Church and Minority Peoples," St. Paul, Minnesota, March 10, 1944. "Conference on the Church and Minority Peoples," Seattle, Washington, March 14, 1944. "Consultations on the Church and Minority Peoples," Los Angeles, California, March 20, 1944. See also "Min-

utes," April 21, 1944, and May 8–10, 1945. All in National Council of Churches Records, Presbyterian Historical Society, Philadelphia.

14. The quotations are from Commission on the Church and Minority Peoples, "Minutes," September 16, 1943, and "Consultations on the Church and Minority Peoples," Los Angeles, California, March 20, 1944. National Council of Churches Records, Presbyterian Historical Society, Philadelphia.

15. "Memorandum on Community Tensions: The Church and Race," Special Meeting, Federal Council of Churches of Christ in America, March 5–7, 1946, Columbus, Ohio, pp. 6–7. "The Church and Race Relations," official statement approved by the Federal Council of Churches of Christ in America at a special meeting, Columbus, Ohio. George Edmund Haynes, "Along the Interracial Front: 'Pull Down Barriers! Vote Three National Bodies,'" press release, Department of Race Relations, Federal Council of Churches, March 29, 1946. All of the preceding can be found in National Council of Churches Records, Presbyterian Historical Society, Philadelphia.

16. Mays, *Born to Rebel*, p. 32.

17. Ibid. Sadie Gray Mays, "Child Welfare Legislation in Georgia," M.A. thesis, University of Chicago, December 1931.

18. Sadie Gray Mays, "Hallelujah, I Am Not White!" n.d., Mays Papers, Manuscript Division, Moorland-Spingarn Research Center, Howard University (hereafter cited as "Mays Papers").

19. Ibid.

20. Ibid.

21. Emma C. W. Gray, "The Grays of Gray, Georgia," *Negro History Bulletin*, 15, no. 9 (June 1952): 179–184, 199. Mays, *Born to Rebel*, pp. 32–33.

22. Sadie Gray to President R. S. Wilkinson, State College, June 23, 1926, and June 28, 1926. Wilkinson to Gray, September 13, 1926. Benjamin Mays to Wilkinson, August 29, 1926, and September 11, 1926. Mays to Thomas McLeod, Governor of South Carolina, September 30, 1926. Mays Papers.

23. "Mrs. S. G. Mays Quits Social School Post," *Atlanta World*, July

29, 1934. Sadie G. Mays to Editor, *Washington Tribune*, September 24, 1936. Sadie Mays to Mary McLeod Bethune, November 9, 1939. Sadie Mays, "Three Years and Eight Months: A Story of the Development of the National Youth Administration's Program for Negroes in the District of Columbia and Suggestions for Its Future Progress," June 30, 1940. Sadie Mays to Claude Jones, Superintendent, National Training School for Boys, March 12, 1938. Claude Jones to Sadie Mays, March 14, 1938. All in Mays Papers.

24. Obituary for Sadie Mays, Funeral program, October 10, 1969, Mays Papers.

25. Sadie Mays, "Hallelujah, I Am Not White!" n.d., Mays Papers.

26. Sadie Mays, quoted in "Ninth Annual Institute on Socio-Religious Affairs, Paine College, Augusta, Georgia, February 13–14, 1943," Mays Papers.

27. Benjamin Mays, quoted ibid.

28. Mays, "Fifty Years of Progress in the Negro Church: Tremendous Gains since 1900—Full Integration in All Churches Seen in 50 Years," *Pittsburgh Courier*, April 8, 1950, Mays Papers.

29. Ibid.

30. Mays, "The Christian in Race Relations," Henry B. Wright Lectures, Yale University Divinity School, April 16, 1952, p. 3.

31. Ibid., p. 4.

32. W. A. Visser 't Hooft, World Council of Churches, to Benjamin Mays, December 16, 1953, Mays Papers.

33. Mays, "The Church amidst Ethnic and Racial Tensions," address to the Second Assembly of the World Council of Churches, August 21, 1954, Mays Papers.

34. Ibid.

35. Mays, *Born to Rebel*, pp. 260–261.

36. Ibid., p. 261.

37. Mays, "The Quicker We Clear Up the Racial Mess in U.S.A., the Better It Will Be for the World," *Pittsburgh Courier*, March 7, 1953. Idem, "In Order to Save Its Own Soul, the Church Must End All Forms of Segregation in Worship," *Pittsburgh Courier*, February 28, 1953.

38. Mays, "Challenge to the Churches Issued by U.S. Supreme Court Decision," *Pittsburgh Courier*, July 10, 1954. Idem, "Will Churches Meet the Challenge Offered Them by the High Court?" *Pittsburgh Courier*, July 24, 1954. Idem, "We Serve Other Gods," *Pittsburgh Courier*, February 26, 1955. Idem, "The Church Will Be Challenged at Evanston," *Christianity and Crisis*, 14, no. 14, August 9, 1954, p. 108.

39. Mays, "Women's Division of United Negro College Fund," address, April 11, 1950. Idem, address at United Negro College Fund dinner, Philadelphia, May 7, 1952, Mays Papers.

40. Mays, "He Doesn't Believe Negro Institutions Will Perish in an Integrated Society," *Pittsburgh Courier*, July 17, 1954. Idem, "College for Negroes in a Segregated Society," address, February 20, 1955. Idem, "The Past, Present, and Future of the Thirty-One Colleges That Make Up the United Negro College Fund," address, April 5, 1956. Idem, "Address delivered before the Inter-Alumni Council," Detroit, June 18, 1957. Idem, "Why Support the United Negro College Fund," address, Buffalo, May 7, 1958. Idem, "United Negro College Fund Address," Cleveland, April 22, 1959. All in Mays Papers.

41. Mays, "Why Do We Come?" address on behalf of United Negro College Fund Capital Fund Drive, October 1962. Also idem, "The Future Role of the Private Negro College," address at Morehouse College, April 28, 1961. Both in Mays Papers.

42. Mays, "The Second Hurdle," *Pittsburgh Courier*, April 24, 1965, Mays Papers.

43. Mays, "Who Will Preach to Negroes in 1980?" *Pittsburgh Courier*, April 23, 1955.

44. Mays, "The Negro in Christian Ministry," address in Greenwich, Connecticut, March 6, 1959, pp. 11–12, Mays Papers.

45. On the role of women in the National Baptist Convention, see the pioneering work by Evelyn Brooks Higginbotham, *Righteous Discontent: The Women's Movement in the Black Baptist Church, 1880–1920* (Cambridge, Mass.: Harvard University Press, 1993). On black women and the varieties of their religious activism, see Judith Weisenfeld, *African American Women and Christian Activism, New York's Black YWCA, 1905–1945*

(Cambridge, Mass.: Harvard University Press, 1997). Also Judith Weisenfeld and Richard Newman, eds., *This Far by Faith: Readings in African American Religious Biography* (New York: Routledge, 1996). For astute analysis of gender relations in churches with female preachers, see Wallace Best, "'The Spirit of the Holy Ghost is a Male Spirit': African American Preaching Women and the Paradoxes of Gender," in Griffith and Savage, eds., *Women and Religion in the African Diaspora*, 101–127; and Wallace Best, *Passionately Human, No Less Divine: Religion and Culture in Black Chicago, 1915–1952* (Princeton: Princeton University Press, 2005).

46. Mays, *Born to Rebel*, 234–240. On religious women as activists, see Cheryl Townsend Gilkes, "Exploring the Religious Connection: Black Women, Community Workers, Religious Agency, and the Force of Faith," in Griffith and Savage, eds., *Women and Religion in the African Diaspora*, 179–198.

47. Mays, "My View: The National Conference on Religion and Race," *Pittsburgh Courier*, February 2, 1963.

48. Anna Arnold Hedgeman, *The Trumpet Sounds: A Memoir of Negro Leadership* (New York: Holt, Rinehart, 1964), pp. 175–177. Mark Chapman, *Christianity on Trial: African American Religious Thought before and after Black Power* (Maryknoll, N.Y.: Orbis Books, 1996), 139–141. For more on the Conference on Religion and Race, see Mathew H. Altmann, *Race: Challenges to Religion, Original Essays, and an Appeal to the Conscience* (Chicago: Regnery, 1963).

49. "Negro Clergy and Laymen Active in All Phases of Historic Conference on Race and Religion," press release, Associated Negro Press, January 23, 1963. Anna Arnold Hedgeman Interview, pp. 179–181, Black Women's Oral History Project Interviews, Schlesinger Library, Radcliffe College, Harvard University. Interview with Anna Arnold Hedgeman, July 25, 1967, and August 28–29, 1968, Civil Rights Documentation Project, Moorland-Spingarn Research Center, Howard University.

50. Mays, quoted in Freddie Colson, "Mays as Mentor to King," in Lawrence Edward Carter, ed., *Walking Integrity: Benjamin Elijah Mays, Mentor to Martin Luther King Jr.* (Macon, Ga.: Mercer University Press, 1998), p. 209.

51. Mays, "Let the Pastors Declare Themselves," *Pittsburgh Courier,* June 1, 1963. Idem, "The Church Should Have a Policy," *Pittsburgh Courier,* June 8, 1963. Idem, "And God Was Embarrassed," *Pittsburgh Courier,* May 18, 1963. Idem, "And They Call It Christian," *Pittsburgh Courier,* November 23, 1963. Idem, "Southern Ministers Get Another Chance," *Pittsburgh Courier,* March 7, 1964. Idem, "The Churches Will Follow," *The Christian Century,* 71, no. 17 (April 22, 1964): 514. Idem, "Will the Churches Be the Last?" *Pittsburgh Courier,* January 9, 1965. Idem, "Why the Churches Will Be the Last," *Pittsburgh Courier,* September 18, 1965. All in Mays Papers.

52. Ibid.

53. Mays, "Prisoner in Harkness Hall," *Pittsburgh Courier,* May 3, 1969. Idem, "Where Are the Answers?" *Chicago Defender,* December 14, 1968. Idem, "Black Dorms No Solution," *Pittsburgh Courier,* March 22, 1969. Idem, "Black Students—Helping? Hurting?" *Pittsburgh Courier,* May 17, 1969. Idem, "Killing Black Colleges," *Pittsburgh Courier,* June 13, 1970. Mays Papers.

54. Mays, "White Power vs. Black Power," address, n.d., Mays Papers.

55. Mays, "Job Discrimination against Women Wrong," *Pittsburgh Courier,* March 10, 1962, Mays Papers.

56. Mays, "It's Up to Women to Get Equal Amendment Okay," *Pittsburgh Courier,* March 24, 1973, Mays Papers.

57. Benjamin Mays, "Men-Women Parity," *Pittsburgh Courier,* July 31, 1976, Mays Papers.

58. Mays, "A Tribute to Woman and a Tribute to Motherhood," address at North Carolina A&T College, May 10, 1964, Mays Papers.

59. Ibid. See also his warning against fear of educated women, concluding that "women are being educated and they still want to be the mothers of the human race." Mays, "Three Classes of People," address at Southern Baptist Convention, Chicago, Illinois, May 12, 1950. Both in Mays Papers.

60. Mays, "A Tribute to Woman and a Tribute to Motherhood."

61. Ibid.

62. Mays, "Joanne Little's Case," *Pittsburgh Courier,* September 13, 1975.

63. Mays, "Let Us Not Integrate or Segregate Ourselves Out of Exis-

tence," address at Grambling College, Grambling, Louisiana, November 13, 1968. Idem, "Integration Not All Gain," *Pittsburgh Courier*, July 5, 1969. Both in Mays Papers.

64. On Mays's election to the Atlanta school board, see Mays, "Man in a New Job," *Pittsburgh Courier*, January 24, 1970.

65. Mays, "Integration Not All Gain."

66. Mays, "We All Slept," *Pittsburgh Courier*, October 13, 1973.

67. Mays, "The Black Man's Environment and His Minority Status: A Challenge to the Black Church," address to Black Ecumenical Commission, Boston, July 30, 1971, Mays Papers.

68. Ibid.

69. Ibid.

70. Mays, "The Church and the Development of Black Leadership in America," address to Conference on Blacks and Religion, University of Tennessee, Knoxville, February 20, 1978, Mays Papers.

71. Mays, "Where Are the Answers?" *Chicago Defender*, December 14, 1968.

72. Mays, "The Urgent Need of Reconciliation in Today's World: A Challenge to the Church," *Criterion*, 11, no. 3 (Spring 1972): 11–12. Idem, "The Church: New Challenges for Survival," *Tuesday Magazine*, 9, no. 2 (February 1974): 15, Mays Papers. *Tuesday Magazine* was a monthly magazine carried as an insert in major national newspapers, with a combined circulation of 2.3 million.

73. Mays, "The Church: New Challenges for Survival," p. 13. Idem, "Church Integrated?" *Pittsburgh Courier*, December 11, 1976.

74. Mays, "Progress and Prospects in American Race Relations," *Journal of Ecumenical Studies*, 16, no. 1 (winter 1979): 128, 132.

75. Ibid.

6. A Religious Rebellion

1. Chana Kai Lee, *For Freedom's Sake: The Life of Fannie Lou Hamer* (Urbana: University of Illinois, 2000), pp. 18–19. For another account of Hamer's life, see Kay Mills, *This Little Light of Mine: The Life of Fannie Lou Hamer* (New York: Dutton, 1993).

2. Ibid., p. 25.

3. Ibid., pp. 31–38.

4. Ibid., p. 43.

5. Charles Payne, I've Got the Light of Freedom: The Organizing Tradition and the Mississippi Freedom Struggle (Berkeley: University of California Press, 1995), p. 309.

6. On the revival metaphor, see David L. Chappell, A Stone of Hope: Prophetic Religion and the Death of Jim Crow (Chapel Hill: University of North Carolina Press, 2004).

7. Marian Wright Edelman, Lanterns: A Memoir of Mentors (Boston: Beacon Press, 1999), pp. xiii, 4, xiv.

8. Ibid., pp. 4, 5, 6, 125.

9. Ibid., pp. 38, 45, 56, 46.

10. Ibid., pp. 54, 55, 59, 50.

11. Ibid., pp. 50, 52–53.

12. Ibid., pp. 53, 64.

13. Ibid., pp. 55, 63, 65.

14. Ibid., pp. 67, 68, 69, 72, 73, 76.

15. Ibid., pp. 81, 88.

16. Ibid., pp. 101, 104.

17. Ibid., p. 110.

18. Ibid., pp. 116, 119, 122.

19. Ibid., p. 132. For a historical treatment of black women's preaching and sermons, see Bettye Collier-Thomas, Daughters of Thunder: Black Women Preachers and Their Sermons, 1850–1979 (San Francisco: Jossey-Bass, 1998).

20. Mary King, Freedom Song: A Personal Story of the 1960s Civil Rights Movement (New York: Quill/Morrow, 1987), pp. 59–60.

21. Ibid., pp. 2, 275.

22. Ibid., pp. 5, 276–278.

23. Ibid., p. 24.

24. Ibid., pp. 273, 274.

25. Debra L. Schultz, ed., Going South: Jewish Women in the Civil Rights Movement (New York: NYU Press, 2001), pp. 18, xv, 92, 107–109, 83. Schultz's book is based in part on interviews with fifteen Jewish women

interviewed between October 1993 and December 1994. The women had been in the South at some point during the period 1960 to 1967. Many of them gathered as part of the thirtieth-anniversary reunion of the Mississippi Freedom Summer Project held in June 24, 1994.

26. Ibid., p. 195.

27. Elizabeth Sutherland, ed., *Letters from Mississippi* (New York: McGraw-Hill, 1965), pp. 12, 16–17, 29. The book generated its own controversy because it neglected attention to the local activists and students. A new edition of the book includes the poetry of young Mississippi students who participated in the Freedom schools. Elizabeth Sutherland Martinez, *Letters from Mississippi* (Brookline, Mass.: Zephyr Press, 2007). All page citations are to the original edition.

28. Ibid., pp. 52, 44.

29. Ibid., pp. 48, 193, 152, 135.

30. King, *Freedom Song*, pp. 27–28.

31. Ibid., p. 501.

32. Ibid., pp. 464, 470 (quoting Andrew Young).

33. Ibid., p. 7.

34. Elizabeth Jacobs, "Revisiting the Second Wave: In Conversation with Mary King," *Meridians: Feminism, Race, Transnationalism,* 7, no. 2 (2007): 102, 106, 107–108.

35. King, *Freedom Song*, pp. 182, 183, 186.

36. John Lewis with Michael d'Orso, *Walking with the Wind: A Memoir of the Movement* (New York: Simon and Schuster, 1998), p. 21.

37. Ibid., pp. 7, 11, 21, 22.

38. Ibid., pp. 45–46.

39. Ibid., pp. 46–47.

40. Howell Raines, *My Soul Is Rested: Movement Days in the Deep South* (New York: Penguin, 1983), p. 97. Lewis, *Walking with the Wind,* pp. 53, 64.

41. For more on Nashville and its place in the civil rights movement, see David Halberstam, *The Children* (New York: Random House, 1998). Raines, *My Soul Is Rested,* p. 98.

42. Stokely Carmichael (Kwame Toure), *Ready for Revolution: The Life*

and Struggles of Stokely Carmichael (New York: Scribner, 2003), pp. 80, 21, 51.

43. Ibid., pp. 75, 76, 30, 21.

44. Ibid., pp. 91–94.

45. Ibid., pp. 91, 93, 94.

46. Ibid., pp. 141–142.

47. Ibid., pp. 196, 206.

48. Lewis, *Walking with the Wind*, pp. 171, 101, 188, 189. Carmichael, *Ready for Revolution*, pp. 194, 198.

49. Carmichael, *Ready for Revolution*, pp. 168, 169, 172, 217.

50. Lewis, *Walking with the Wind*, p. 400.

51. Ibid.

52. Carmichael, *Ready for Revolution*, pp. 289, 371.

53. Ibid., pp. 289, 290, 291.

54. Ibid., p. 291.

55. Ibid.

56. Ibid., pp. 306–307.

57. Ibid., p. 307. Lewis, *Walking with the Wind*, p. 19.

58. Carmichael, *Ready for Revolution*, p. 308.

59. Ibid., p. 176.

60. Ibid., pp. 507, 509, 513, 514.

61. Andrew Young, *An Easy Burden: The Civil Rights Movement and the Transformation of America* (New York: HarperCollins, 1996), p. 209.

62. Carmichael, *Ready for Revolution*, p. 514.

63. Young, *An Easy Burden*, pp. 398, 399–400.

64. Carmichael, *Ready for Revolution*, pp. 434, 435.

65. Lewis, *Walking with the Wind*, p. 64.

7. Reconcilable Differences

1. Jerry K. Frye, "The 'Black Manifesto' and the Tactic of Objectification," *Journal of Black Studies*, 5, no. 1 (September 1974), pp. 65–76. R. S. Lecky and H. E. Wright, eds., *Black Manifesto: Religion, Racism, and Reparations* (New York: Sheed and Ward, 1969). James R. Wood, "Legiti-

mate Control and 'Organizational Transcendence,'" *Social Forces*, 54, no. 1 (September 1975): 199–211.

2. Gayraud S. Wilmore, *Black Religion and Black Radicalism: An Interpretation of the Religious History of Afro-American People* (New York: Orbis, 1983; orig. pub. 1973), p. 172. James Cone, *Black Theology and Black Power* (New York: Seabury, 1969). Idem, *A Black Theology of Liberation* (Philadelphia: Lippincott, 1970). Charles H. Long, *Significations: Signs, Symbols, and Images in the Interpretation of Religion* (Philadelphia: Fortress Press, 1986). Dwight Hopkins, *Black Theology USA and South Africa: Politics, Culture, and Liberation* (Maryknoll, N.Y.: Orbis Books, 1989). Idem, *Down, Up and Over: Slave Religion and Black Theology* (Minneapolis: Fortress Books, 2000). Robert Franklin, *Another Day's Journey: Black Churches Confronting the American Crisis* (Minneapolis: Fortress Books, 1997).

3. Cornel West, *Prophesy Deliverance! An Afro-American Revolutionary Christianity* (Philadelphia: Westminster, 1982). Idem, *Race Matters* (Boston: Beacon Press, 1993). Cornel West and Eddie S. Glaude, eds., *African American Religious Thought: An Anthology* (Louisville, Ky.: Westminster John Knox Press, 2003). Eddie S. Glaude, *Exodus! Religion, Race, and Nation in Early Nineteenth-Century Black America* (Chicago: University of Chicago Press, 2000). Katie Cannon, *Black Womanist Ethics* (Atlanta: Scholars Press, 1988). Idem, *Katie's Canon: Womanism and the Soul of the Black Community* (New York: Continuum, 1996s). Delores S. Williams, *Sisters in the Wilderness: The Challenge of Womanist God-Talk* (Maryknoll, N.Y.: Orbis Books, 1993). Emilie Townes, *Womanist Justice, Womanist Hope* (Atlanta: Scholars Press, 1993). Idem, *Troubling in My Soul: Womanist Perspectives on Evil and Suffering* (Maryknoll, N.Y.: Orbis Books, 1993). Jacquelyn Grant, *White Women's Christ and Black Women's Jesus: Feminist Christology and Womanist Response* (Atlanta: Scholars Press, 1989). Jacquelyn Grant, ed., *Perspectives on Womanist Theology* (Atlanta: ITC Press, 1995). Kelly Brown Douglass, *Sexuality and the Black Church: A Womanist Perspective* (Maryknoll, N.Y.: Orbis Books, 1999). Cheryl Gilkes, *If It Wasn't for the Women: Black Women's Experience and Womanist Culture in Church and Community* (Maryknoll, N.Y.: Orbis Books, 2000).

4. Aldon D. Morris, *The Origins of the Civil Rights Movement: Black Communities Organizing for Change* (New York: Free Press, 1984), p. 7. Frederick C. Harris, *Something Within: Religion in African-American Political Activism* (New York: Oxford University Press, 1999). Cathy J. Cohen, *The Boundaries of Blackness: AIDS and the Breakdown of Black Politics* (Chicago: University of Chicago Press, 1999). Michael Dawson, *Black Visions: The Roots of Contemporary African-American Political Ideologies* (Chicago: University of Chicago Press, 2001).

5. Albert Raboteau, *Slave Religion: The "Invisible Institution" in the Antebellum South* (New York: Oxford University Press, 1978). Eugene Genovese, *Roll, Jordan, Roll: The World the Slaves Made* (New York: Oxford University Press, 1974). Lawrence Levine, *Black Culture and Black Consciousness* (New York: Oxford University Press, 1978). Carol V. R. George, *Segregated Sabbaths: Richard Allen and the Emergence of Independent Black Churches, 1760–1840* (New York: Oxford University Press, 1973). James Melvin Washington, *Frustrated Fellowship: The Black Quest for Social Power* (Macon, Ga.: Mercer University Press, 1986). Clarence E. Walker, *A Rock in a Weary Land: The African Methodist Episcopal Church during the Civil War and Reconstruction* (Baton Rouge: Louisiana State University Press, 1982). More recently, C. Eric Lincoln and Lawrence H. Mamiya, *The Black Church in the African American Experience* (Durham: Duke University Press, 1990). William E. Montgomery, *Under Their Own Vine and Fig Tree: The African-American Church in the South, 1865–1900* (Baton Rouge: Louisiana State University Press, 1993). James T. Campbell, *Songs of Zion: The African Methodist Episcopal Church in the United States and South Africa* (Chapel Hill: University of North Carolina Press, 1998). Evelyn Higginbotham, *Righteous Discontent: The Women's Movement in the Black Baptist Church* (Cambridge, Mass.: Harvard University Press, 1993). Cheryl J. Sanders, *Saints in Exile: The Holiness-Pentecostal Experience in African American Religion and Culture* (New York: Oxford University Press, 1996). Glenda Elizabeth Gilmore, *Gender and Jim Crow: Women and the Politics of White Supremacy in North Carolina, 1896–1920.* (Chapel Hill: University of North Carolina Press, 1996). Judith Weisenfeld, *African American Women and Christian Activism: New York's Black YWCA, 1905–*

1945 (Cambridge, Mass.: Harvard University Press, 1997). Ralph E. Luker, *The Social Gospel in Black and White: American Racial Reform, 1885–1912* (Chapel Hill: University of North Carolina Press, 1991). Charles Marsh, *God's Long Summer: Stories of Faith and Civil Rights* (Princeton, N.J.: Princeton University Press, 1997). Nick Salvatore, *Singing in a Strange Land: C. L. Franklin, the Black Church, and the Transformation of America* (New York: Little, Brown, 2005). Houston Roberson, *Fighting the Good Fight: The Story of the Dexter Avenue King Memorial Baptist Church, 1865–1977* (New York: Routledge, 2005). Curtis J. Evans, *The Burden of Black Religion: Representing, Vindicating, and Uplifting the Race* (New York: Oxford University Press, 2008).

6. Charles Payne, *I've Got the Light of Freedom: The Organizing Tradition and the Mississippi Freedom Struggle* (Berkeley: University of California Press, 1995). The literature on Martin Luther King Jr. is voluminous and still growing. Among books that pay special attention to his religious beliefs and writings, see Michael Eric Dyson, *I May Not Get There with You: The True Martin Luther King, Jr.* (New York: Free Press, 2000). David Garrow, *Bearing the Cross: Martin Luther King, Jr., and the Southern Christian Leadership Conference* (New York: William Morrow, 1986). Taylor Branch, *Parting the Waters: America in the King Years, 1954–1963* (New York: Simon and Schuster, 1988). Idem, *Pillar of Fire: America in the King Years, 1963–65* (New York: Simon and Schuster, 1998). Idem, *At Canaan's Edge: America in the King Years, 1965–68* (New York: Simon and Schuster, 2006). Charles Marsh, *God's Long Summer: Stories of Faith and Civil Rights* (Princeton, N.J.: Princeton University Press, 1997). Vincent Harding, *Martin Luther King: The Inconvenient Hero* (Maryknoll, N.Y.: Orbis Books, 1996). For a provocative interpretation of religion in the era of civil rights, see David L. Chappell, *A Stone of Hope: Prophetic Religion and the Death of Jim Crow* (Chapel Hill: University of North Carolina Press, 2004). Lawrence S. Little, *Disciples of Liberty: The African Methodist Episcopal Church in the Age of Imperialism* (Knoxville: University of Tennessee Press, 2000). Anthea Butler, *Making a Sanctified World: Women in the Church of God in Christ* (Chapel Hill: University of North Carolina Press, 2006). Wallace Best, *Passionately Human, No Less Divine: Religion*

and Culture in Black Chicago, 1915–1952 (Princeton, N.J.: Princeton University Press, 2005). Marla Frederick, *Between Sundays: Black Women and Everyday Struggles of Faith* (Berkeley: University of California Press, 2003). Judith Weisenfeld, *Hollywood Be Thy Name: African American Religion in American Film, 1929–1949* (Berkeley: University of California Press, 2007). Diane Batts Morrow, *Persons of Color and Religious at the Same Time: The Oblate Sisters of Providence, 1828–1860* (Chapel Hill: University of North Carolina Press, 2002). Carolyn Moxley Rouse, *Engaged Surrender: African American Women and Islam* (Berkeley: University of California Press, 2004). Martha S. Jones, *All Bound Up Together: The Woman Question in African American Public Culture, 1830–1900* (Chapel Hill: University of North Carolina Press, 2007). New scholarship also had turned to the study of African-derived religions in the Americas and to the religious practices of contemporary Africans. For examples, see Rachel Harding, *A Refuge in Thunder: Candomblé and Alternative Spaces of Blackness* (Bloomington: Indiana University Press, 2000). Paul C. Johnson, *Secrets, Gossip and Gods: The Transformation of Carib Religion* (New York: Oxford University Press, 2002). Yvonne Chireau, *Black Magic: Religion and the African American Conjuring Tradition* (Berkeley: University of California Press, 2003). Isabel Mukonyora, *Wandering a Gendered Wilderness: Suffering and Healing in an African Initiated Church* (New York: Peter Lang, 2007). Diedre Helen Crumbley, *Spirit, Structure and Flesh: Gender Practices in Three African Instituted Churches* (Madison: University of Wisconsin Press, 2008).

7. Barack Obama, *Dreams from My Father: A Story of Race and Inheritance* (New York: Random House, 1995; rpt. 2004), pp. 134–135, 163, 140.

8. Ibid., p. 294. Obama used some of the same phrasing in "We the People," an address at the Constitution Center, Philadelphia, March 18, 2008. The texts of many of Obama's speeches are available at www.barackobama.com.

9. Obama, *Dreams from My Father*, pp. 294, 429. Idem, *The Audacity of Hope: Thoughts on Reclaiming the American Dream* (New York: Three Rivers Press, 2006), p. 209.

10. Barack Obama, "A Politics of Conscience," address at the United Church of Christ Synod, Hartford, Connecticut, June 23, 2007. For other references to the Joshua Generation, see Barack Obama, "Howard University Convocation," address delivered at Howard University, Washington, D.C., September 28, 2007.

11. Barack Obama, "John Lewis's 65th Birthday Gala," address delivered on February 21, 2005. Idem, "Announcement for President," address delivered in Springfield, Illinois, February 10, 2007. Idem, "The Great Need of the Hour," address delivered in Atlanta, Georgia, January 20, 2008. All at www.barackobama.com.

12. Adolph Reed, *The Jesse Jackson Phenomenon: The Crisis of Purpose in Afro-American Politics* (New Haven: Yale University Press, 1986). Marshall Frady, *Jesse Jackson: The Life and Pilgrimage of Jesse Jackson* (New York: Random House, 1996).

13. Shirley Chisholm, *Unbought and Unbossed* (Boston: Houghton Mifflin, 1970). Idem, *The Good Fight* (New York: Harper and Row, 1973).

14. Reverend Jeremiah Wright, Address to the National Press Club, Washington, D.C., April 28, 2008. The text can be found at www.chicagotribune.com.

15. Ibid.

16. Ibid.

17. Ibid.

18. Ibid.

19. Ibid.

20. Ibid.

Acknowledgments

WHEN my mother read the acknowledgments for my first book, she said to me, "You had a lot of people helping you." As usual, she was right and what was true then is also the case now. Books are very solitary productions, but without the support of others they would never make it into print.

Even in this digital age, historians still depend primarily on archives and archivists who do the often unheralded work of protecting and processing records and documents. I owe special gratitude to Joellen El Bashir and her colleagues at Howard University's Moorland Spingarn Research Center for their expertise and patient good humor over the years as I plowed through their rich collections of materials, in particular those on Benjamin Mays and E. Franklin Frazier. Washington, D.C., is also home to the Library of Congress and the Mary McLeod Bethune Museum and Archives, both of which have holdings essential to this work. Important research was conducted at these archives as well: the Southern Baptist Historical Library and Archives and the African Methodist Episcopal Church Archives, both in Nashville; the

Schlesinger Library, Radcliffe Institute, Harvard University; the Charles L. Blockson Afro-American Collection at Temple University and the Presbyterian Historical Society Archives, both in Philadelphia.

Generous funding from several institutions made my research, travel, and writing possible. The University of Pennsylvania, through its Research Foundation Awards and the Penn Women Trustees' Council Summer Faculty Research Fellowships, has provided a supportive home base for this work. Fellowships at the Schomburg Center for the Study of Black Culture at the New York Public Library and the Center for the Study of Religion at Princeton University came during the early stages of this work. I was able to hasten this project's completion during a year's fellowship at Harvard's Radcliffe Institute for Advanced Study, thanks to its splendid libraries and a very fun group of interdisciplinary fellows and staff members. A number of people were especially supportive of me at crucial moments and enabled me to do my best work: Mary Frances Berry, Joe Farrell, Sheldon Hackney, Sam Preston, and Tukufu Zuberi, all Penn colleagues, and Drew Gilpin Faust, William Graham, Evelyn Higginbotham, and Henry Louis Gates Jr., all at Harvard. The family of two Penn alumni, the late Bernard and Geraldine R. Segal, have supported this work by their endowment of the professorship which I now hold and which is dedicated to the study of human rights, civil liberties, and race relations.

This book also has benefited from my participation in several collaborative projects. Most intensive was my service as codirector, at the invitation of R. Marie Griffith at Princeton, in a three-year Ford Foundation–funded project on Women and Religion in the African Diaspora in which thirteen scholars worked to produce a conference and a volume on that subject. Also timely and helpful was my participation in the Pew Foundation–funded Project on the Public Influences of African-American Churches, at the Leadership Institute at Morehouse College; the International Conference on African Americans and the Bible, at Union Theological Seminary; and the Conference on the Study of African American Problems in Honor of W. E. B. Du Bois, sponsored by the Center for Africana Studies at the University of Pennsylvania.

Every scholar needs readers, critics, and listeners. I extend very special thanks to those friends and colleagues who took time away from their own important work to read and comment on the manuscript as it took shape. Kathleen M. Brown and R. Marie Griffith were my earliest and most frequent readers. Both helped me immeasurably with their cogent criticisms, as did Dennis Dickerson, Martha S. Jones, and Judith Weisenfeld who read a penultimate draft. A number of other colleagues and friends read portions of this project and I am grateful to all of them: Kathy Peiss and Farah Jasmine Griffin, along with Peter Agree, Mia Bay, Herman Beavers, Camille Charles, Thadious Davis, Gary Gerstle, John Jackson, Ayako Kano, Amy Kaplan, Bruce Kuklick, Anne Norton, Grey Osterud, Guthrie Ramsey, Nick Salvatore, Kenneth Shropshire, Laura Sorscher, Deborah Thomas, Deborah Gray White, and Tukufu Zuberi. Joyce Seltzer at Harvard University Press fearlessly took on this project in its end stages and has helped to make this a better book.

I am grateful to the following institutions where I presented my work and received helpful comments: Columbia University, Emory University, Harvard University, Vanderbilt University, Yale University, the University of Chicago, the University of Rochester, and the University of Maryland. My ideas were honed at meetings sponsored by the American Historical Association, the American Studies Association, the Association for the Study of African American Life and History, the Organization of American Historians, the Social Science History Association, and the Southern Intellectual History Circle. I also benefited from the work of a

number of students who served as research assistants, including Taj
Frazier, Kim Gallon, Peter Hobbs, Ellen Scott, Kathleen Smith,
Brandi Thompson, Elizabeth Todd, and Nicole Myers Turner.

Friends who patiently kept asking "So how's the book?" gave
me much-needed encouragement. They include Deborah Broadnax,
Anne Campbell, Cecelia DeMarco, Joanna Banks, Eve Wilkins,
Amy and Lane and Tyler Davenport, Lynn Brown, Sharon Haney,
Vivian Bythewood, Shawn Copeland, Karen Wilkerson, Neville
Strumpf, Jeanne Stanley, and Julia Sawabini. Mrs. Wilhelmena
Griffin has helped me to laugh through good times and bad. Laura
Sorscher and her daughters Madison and Schuyler Alig lovingly
welcomed me into their lives, reminding me to take time to play.

As always, my family and friends in Virginia are my greatest inspiration. Our numbers have thinned due to the loss of many dear
relatives and friends, but my mother, Mrs. Mildred S. Fields,
teaches us by example how to grieve and how to move forward. I
owe special gratitude to my sister, Alice Annette Fields, whose
generosity and faithfulness allowed me the peace of mind needed
to do this work. To both my mother and my sister, and to my
brother, sister-in-law, nieces, and favorite nephew (Glenn, Felita,
Nikki, Courtney, and Sean Fields), I can only say thanks for all
your love and support. The many who have passed on continue to
live in our hearts and memories.

Index